Shemoneh Esrei
Exploring the Fundamentals of Faith through the *Amida* Prayer

I0807327

MAGGID

Yeshivat Har Etzion ישיבת הר עציון

Rabbi Ezra Bick

שיח ישעי

Shemoneh Esrei

Exploring the Fundamentals of Faith Through the Amida Prayer

TRANSLATED BY

Jonny Brull

Yeshivat Har Etzion
Maggid Books

Shemoneh Esrei
Exploring the Fundamentals of Faith through the Amida Prayer

First English Edition, 2022

Maggid Books
An imprint of Koren Publishers Jerusalem Ltd.

POB 8531, New Milford, CT 06776-8531, USA
& POB 4044, Jerusalem 9104001, Israel
www.korenpub.com

The publication of this book was made possible through the generous support of *The Jewish Book Trust*.

ISBN 978-1-59264-743-9, *paperback*

Printed and bound in the United States

מוֹדִים אֲנַחְנוּ לָךְ

Dedicated in loving memory of

Tom Weisz z"l

משה מאיר בן אברהם הכהן ורבקה רחל

A man of integrity and humility
with a relentless pursuit of the wisdom of Torah.
A son of Holocaust survivors, he built a family of Torah
with his children, grandchildren, and great grandchildren.
He continues to be a source of inspiration
and strength to all who knew him.

תַּלְמִידֵי חֲכָמִים אֵין לָהֶם מְנוּחָה אֲפִילוּ לָעוֹלָם הַבָּא

Shelli Weisz and family

Contents

Introduction

The *Amida* prayer, the "*Shemoneh Esrei*" (Eighteen Blessings), recited three times a day, six days a week, is the central expression of prayer of God-fearing Jews from their earliest childhood. The Sages declared that the text of the prayer was composed by the Men of the Great Assembly – "One hundred and twenty elders, and among them several prophets, instituted eighteen blessings in order" (*Megilla* 17b). This statement establishes that the prayer text is the creation of rabbis and sages – among them several prophets – from the time of the foundation of the Second Temple. At a later period, Shimon HaPakuli arranged eighteen blessings before Rabban Gamliel in Yavneh, and the Gemara explains (*Megilla* 18a) that they had been forgotten and then were reestablished. This formulation emphasizes the importance of the precise text of the prayer. Two congresses of the religious leadership took place in order to compose the prayer – one at the foundation of the Second Temple, and another after its destruction. The explanation for the phenomenon "they were forgotten and then reestablished" is rooted in the destruction of the Temple – not just as a result of the shock that could have led to forgetfulness, but in reaction to the deep change that took place in the dynamic of the relationship between the worshipper and his God. The Men of the Great Assembly, the Rabbinic leadership of the returning exiles from Babylonia, composed a prayer which accompanied the Temple service that was being renewed in their days. Hundreds of years later, at the time of the destruction, the entire relationship between the worshipper of God and the King of Israel was in jeopardy, and undoubtedly went through a significant revolution. *They forgot them* – the heart found it difficult to find the words, they were retained in neither memory nor consciousness, until Rabban Gamliel came and instituted the text anew, opened the gates of prayer before the Jew who now stands alone and bereft, outside of the Temple, without priest and devoid of altar, and yet compelled to fulfill the human need and the Divine commandment to serve his Creator.

The essays included in this book are based upon talks delivered over the course of approximately twenty years to groups of students at Yeshivat Har Etzion, my intellectual home. The decision to attempt to analyze the text of the *Amida* in depth was based upon the assumption that the wisdom of the Sages is embedded within the text, and that within the *Shemoneh Esrei* we can find the fundamentals of faith and divine service. There is an accepted principle in our hands from the Ashkenazic *Rishonim* that it is not only the general themes of the *Shemoneh Esrei* that are a source of wisdom, but that every word and letter, as well as the number of words in every blessing, conceal within them deep meaning and thought (see *Tur O.C.* 113, citing the "*Doreshei Reshumot* who are the *chasidim* of Ashkenaz" regarding the number of words in each blessing). The basis of the lessons was not the desire to analyze the topic of the obligation of prayer, but rather the desire to study a Rabbinic source on the topics of faith and divine service. Specifically, this is a source more authoritative than the entire Aggadic literature, being a halakhic text that was instituted to be recited by the entire nation, and, in addition, a source in which central institutions of Rabbinic authority invested maximal depth of thought, thereby laying the foundations of practical halakhic life. The basic approach was *to learn*, just as yeshiva students learn other Rabbinic sources, and through analysis and perseverance to achieve deep insights. The *siddur* – at least the section of the *Shemoneh Esrei* – is a fundamental work of the Sages, and it is incumbent upon us to delve into it just as we delve into Talmudic discussions across the Gemara.

In order to achieve a deep understanding of the prayer, I relied on several sources. First of all, as is obvious to anyone who examines the *siddur,* the text of the *Amida* is based on Biblical verses. The Sages used the words of the prophets openly and deliberately in their composition of the *Shemoneh Esrei.* It may well be that this phenomenon emanates from the Sages' desire to refrain from self-formulation as much as possible. My master and teacher Rabbi Joseph B. Soloveitchik *zt"l* emphasized to us the logical and moral deterrent which stands before every person who comes to pray – how can man know what is fitting to utter before his Maker and what permission he has at all to appeal in his own words to the King of kings?! The Sages took the words of the prophets as a source and license to formulate prayer, and this alone shows how precise and deliberate the formulation is. Therefore, when we come to analyze a blessing, we must check the Biblical source, see in what context the words were said, what their meaning is in their original context, and why the Sages borrowed that source for the text of the blessing. It is important to remember that the Biblical context was well known by the Sages and the verses were fluent in their mouths, and one should assume that they also relied on the fact that it is familiar to worshippers and constitutes the cultural and philosophical background of their use of the language.

Second, there are often explicit Rabbinic sources which shed light on some of the blessings. There are references to some of the blessings, and there are commentaries which decipher for us the Sages' approach to the different ideas that are reflected in the blessings.

Third, in contrast to the vast literature compiled by the *Rishonim* into Biblical and Talmudic commentaries, nothing comparable extends to commentary on prayer. Despite this, there are a handful of fundamental books. First and foremost is the book *Peirush HaTefillot* by R. Yehuda b. R. Yakar, Ramban's teacher, which is packed with insights, allusions, sources, and ideas regarding the text of prayer. This book, which is not sufficiently well known, deserves a place of honor in the library of anyone who wishes to understand the text of prayer. Alongside continual use of this book, I have tried to look at all the other explanations given for the simple understanding of the language of prayer, to the best of my ability.

The topic of prayer – its laws, its meaning, understanding its text, and explaining the experience implanted therein – was a major and special occupation of my master and teacher, *HaGaon HaChasid* Rabbi

Joseph B. Soloveitchik. On many occasions the Rav also used the prayer text or liturgical poems as a source for delving into fundamental ideas in Judaism, and he related to prayer as a Torah source in every respect. There is no doubt that it is from him that I learned to relate to the prayer text as a source for study and analysis. It is difficult for me to say precisely what in the coming pages draws directly from his teachings, but it is clear that his influence is present on every page.

Understanding prayer is not just the result of textual analysis. The experience of one who prays, especially in the *Shemoneh Esrei* which is the daily prayer and to a large extent the religious environment of our entire spiritual life, constitutes a cradle from which intellectual understanding blossoms. I merited to pray most of my life, day by day, next to giants of prayer, giants of the generation in prayer, including my master and teacher Rabbi Joseph B. Soloveitchik, my master and teacher Rabbi Aharon Lichtenstein *zt"l*, and my teacher Rabbi Yehuda Amital *zt"l*, whose voice I often hear in my own prayers to this very day. Especially in my father's family, prayer was an essential foundation of service of God. My grandfather Rabbi Chaim Yechiel Michel Bick *zt"l*, whose commitment to proper prayer was reflected in the fact that he prayed his entire life from a first edition *Beit El Siddur* which he inherited from his ancestor Rav Yaakov Emden *zt"l*, was known, aside from his greatness in Torah, as a one-of-a-kind *chazan* from his youth in the community of Medzibuzh. I only merited to pray a little by his side, but the soul of his approach to prayer continued in the house of my father, who was also a *chazan* on special occasions, especially on the High Holy Days. Alongside the tradition of the Oral Law in halakha, there is also a tradition of the Oral Law in prayer, and it is specifically this that is preserved as tradition today and has largely not been committed to writing. I merited to receive from my father and teacher, Yeshayahu Bick *z"l*, much of this tradition, in both its material content, and more so, I hope, in its soul. I know that it deeply influences the contents of this book.

My father passed away on the fifth day of Chanukka 5770. On his final day, he neither spoke nor ate. When I took him to light the Chanukka candles and I lit them for him – this being the only time that he did not light himself – he barely responded, until I began reciting *Tehillim* 30, *Mizmor shir chanukkat haBayit leDavid*, which is recited after lighting and which we sang in the tune that we received from my grandfather Rabbi Chaim. Suddenly, my father opened his eyes, and together with me he sang the entire chapter, until "*That my whole being shall sing to You and not be silent; HaShem, my God, I shall thank You forever.*" Then he was silent, and continued no more.

This book is my *siach*, my discourse, and "*siach* is nought other than prayer," but it is to a large extent the discourse of my father as well.

> You turned my lament into my dance, You undid my sackcloth and girded me with joy. HaShem, my God, I shall thank You forever.

Ezra Bick
Adar Rishon 5782

Acknowledgments

This book would not have been possible without the active participation of several generations of attentive, inquisitive, and argumentative students, whose contributions, though immeasurable, are present on every page.

Jonny Brull not only translated and reviewed the entire book, but also was singularly responsible for convincing me to initiate the translation project. I would also like to thank R. Pinchas Cohen, who while engaging with the content has also constantly encouraged me to publish the translation.

Yeshivat Har Etzion and Maggid Books were singularly helpful in getting out this book in a timely and professional manner. My gratitude to Yoel Weiss, Executive Vice President of the Etzion Foundation, and Matthew Miller, Publisher of Koren Jerusalem. At Maggid Books, special thanks to Nechama Unterman for her careful editing, to Editorial Director Rabbi Reuven Ziegler and Managing Editor Caryn Meltz, as well as to Aryeh Grossman, Ita Olesker, and Tani Bayer.

Chapter 1

Semikhat Geula LiTfilla: Adjoining Redemption to Prayer

This volume will examine the text of the *Amida* prayer, namely, the "*Shemoneh Esrei*" – the Eighteen Blessings. Our objectives are, firstly, to analyze the language of the blessings in order to understand them in depth and, secondly, to uncover the ideas implicit within the blessings and to identify some of the basic principles of Judaism and Jewish thought that the Sages embedded in the *Shemoneh Esrei*. The formulation of the *Shemoneh Esrei* will assist us not only as the content of our petition to God, but also as a primary text for study and as a source for the principles and beliefs of the Sages vis-à-vis the relationship between God and man.

This is not an exposition on the subject of prayer itself, its essence, significance, or place within Jewish life. There is much to investigate and expound upon regarding the commandment of prayer and the prayer experience; this, however, is not our aim. Thus, it would be only right to begin straight away with examining the language of the *siddur*. However, it is not possible to begin without a short introduction which defines the type of prayer that is reflected in the *Amida*. This understanding will serve as a guide in our future efforts to fully grasp the meaning of each and every blessing. For this purpose, as well as in order not to diverge more than is necessary from the textual framework, I wish to begin by examining the text that appears *before* the *Amida*, and its connection to prayer. We shall examine the halakha that requires *semikhat geula litfilla*, to adjoin redemption to prayer, which recommends that there be no interruption between the blessing of *Geula* (redemption, the blessing which follows *Keriat Shema*) – "*Barukh Gaal Yisrael* (Blessed is He who has redeemed Israel)" – and the *Shemoneh Esrei*.

1. *TEFILLA* = *AMIDA*

Firstly, note the interesting phenomenon that is demonstrated in the formulation of the halakha of *semikhat geula litfilla*. The Sages state that "*yismokh geula litfilla*" – one must adjoin redemption to prayer. The term "*geula*," redemption, refers to the blessing of *Gaal Yisrael*. "*Tefilla*," prayer, in this statement refers to the *Amida*. This is a fine example of a common phenomenon in Talmudic literature. The simple term "*tefilla*" by itself, connotes the *Amida* prayer, consisting of nineteen blessings on a weekday and seven blessings on a Shabbat and festivals. In other words, the *Amida* is the prayer par excellence, the archetypal *tefilla*. In the eyes of the Sages, the other passages that constitute part of what we call the prayer service are prefaces, additions, and in fact sometimes have no intrinsic connection to prayer itself. "*Tefilla*," as a basic and autonomous concept, refers to the *Amida*. When the Sages sought to formulate the text that would comprise the essential concept of prayer (which, according to Rambam, in contrast to the position of *Tosafot*, is a Biblical precept), they chose the formulation of this very prayer. Hence, our study of the text of the *Amida* is, in actuality, a study of the essence of prayer itself.

2. *GEULA* AND *TEFILLA*: REDEMPTION AND PRAYER

In the *Shulchan Arukh* (*O.C.* 66:8) it is ruled that "*tzarikh lismokh geula litfilla*," one must adjoin redemption to prayer. The implication of this halakha is that it is forbidden to interrupt between the blessing of *Geula* and the start of the *Amida*. It is not just an extraneous interruption, such as speaking with a friend, that is forbidden at this juncture; even responding to other parts of the service is prohibited. For example, if one were praying and at the exact moment when he finished the blessing of *Geula* he heard the *chazan* begin reciting *Kedusha* or Kaddish, it is forbidden for him to respond. The halakhic authorities disagree regarding whether one is even able to answer "*Amen*" to the blessing of *Geula* itself recited by the *chazan*, and from here arises the practice to finish the blessing together with the *chazan*, in order to avoid the need to respond "*Amen*" to his blessing.

In the Gemara, this adjoining is not formulated as an obligation, but as a recommendation. "R. Yochanan said: Who is destined for the World to Come? One who adjoins *geula* to *tefilla*" (*Berakhot* 4b).[1] In a similar vein, the Gemara states: "R. Yose b. Elyakim declared in the name of the Holy Congregation of Jerusalem: One who adjoins *geula* to *tefilla* is immune to injury the entire day" (ibid. 9b).[2] The style of this recommendation, accompanied by the generous promise of a guaranteed reward in the World to Come, baffled the commentators.

Rabbeinu Yona HeChasid of Gerona questioned:

> It must be explained: Is merely adjoining *geula* to *tefilla* really deemed so rewarding that it guarantees one a place in the World to Come?

He answers as follows:

> The reason one merits such a great reward is because when God redeemed us and took us out of Egypt, it was so that we should serve Him, as is written, "For they are My servants whom I have taken out of the Land of Egypt." In the blessing of *Gaal Yisrael*, we mention the kindness that the Creator performed for us. And *tefilla* is "*avoda*," service, as it is said (*Bava Kamma* 92b): "And you shall serve HaShem your God (*Shemot* 23:25) – this refers to *tefilla*." Therefore, when one mentions the Exodus from Egypt and

1. In the Gemara this sentence concludes "to the *tefilla* of Arvit," and the intention is to apply this rule *even* to the *Amida* of Arvit, and even more so to Shacharit.
2. *Tosafot* there claim that this statement refers specifically to one who adjoins *geula* to *tefilla* and prays *vatikin*, i.e., at sunrise.

> immediately prays, he demonstrates that, just as a slave is bound to his master, he too recognizes the goodness and redemption in which the Creator redeemed him, and that he is His slave and serves Him. And since he recognizes that he is His slave as a result of the fact that He redeemed him, and thus he fulfills His will and commandments, it follows that he will merit the World to Come as a result. (Talmidei R. Yona, *Berakhot* 2b in *Rif*)

R. Yona's explanation of the importance of *semikhat geula litfilla* is based on the definition of prayer as "*avoda*," service. According to the Sages, prayer is *avoda shebalev*, service of the heart.[3] Rambam bases his position that prayer is a Biblical precept on the Sages' defining it as service. It seems that this equation, *tefilla* = *avoda*, is widely accepted and is understood to be a parallel between prayer (service of the heart) and the sacrifices, namely, the Temple service. Now in English, prayer is often called service, but I am not sure that we understand the implication of the term. R. Yona's words bring us to the inner meaning of the concept of service. *Avoda*, service, is a form of *avdut*, servitude, as a slave serves and obeys his master. According to R. Yona, the mitzva to serve God emanates from the fact that God redeemed us from slavery in Egypt and by doing so literally "acquired" us to be His slaves. The notion that redemption from slavery in Egypt subjugates us to the Redeemer is an interesting idea in and of itself, although that is not our topic at present. R. Yona concludes – and his entire explanation as to why one merits the World to Come for *semikhat geula litfilla* is based on this conclusion – that the central expression of being a slave to one's master is by way of performing his master's will and his commands. The essence of slavery is obedience and the acceptance of authority. The fulfillment of mitzvot that emanates from internalizing a relationship of slavery with respect to God is what brings one to merit the most desirable of rewards, a place in the World to Come. One who adjoins redemption to prayer, that is to say one who accepts upon himself God's authority due to his

3. "And so it says, 'And to serve Him with all your heart' (*Devarim* 11:13) – what is this service of the heart? You must say that it is prayer" (*Mekhilta DeRashbi* 23:25). In the same vein, see *Yerushalmi Berakhot* 4:6 and *Sifrei Devarim Eikev piska* 41.

recognition of the fact that the redemption from Egypt constitutes an acquisition of him by God, merits the World to Come. This is because, by doing so, he commits himself as a performer of the mitzvot of the Torah both now and hereafter.

But precisely this understanding of prayer as service poses a problem. Where in prayer, and particularly in the *Shemoneh Esrei,* do we see an acceptance of authority and obedience? On the contrary: the main body of the *Shemoneh Esrei* consists of requests for our needs and not our subjugation to the needs of the Master. Its content seems to be diametrically opposed to the idea developed by R. Yona. We do not serve the Master but instead request – in a subtle manner, of course – that He serve us! This being the case, why is it labeled "*avoda,*" service, in the sense of performing His will and obeying His commandments, like a slave does for his master? The recital of *Shema,* which is defined by the Sages as *kabbalat ol malkhut shamayim,* the acceptance of the yoke of heavenly kingship, would seem a more fitting choice as the primary medium for *avoda,* rather than the *Amida.*

3. *AVDUT* AND *AVODA*: SERVITUDE AND SERVICE

The answer lies, I think, in understanding the true nature of the servitude. A slave obeys his master's will and receives instruction from him regarding how to behave. But this is just an expression of a far deeper and more significant point. A slave obeys his master because he has no goals of his own, just as he has no property of his own. He has no future of his own, nor does he have his own aspirations based on a sense of purpose that is unique to him. The aims and goals of his life are those of his master. Everything that he has comes from his master. In a word, the slave is totally *dependent* on his master, from whom he receives not just instruction and sustenance, but also meaning, significance, direction, and purpose. The slave has nothing of his own. The ultimate meaning of slavery is total dependence that provides everything and leaves nothing over for the autonomy of the slave.

There is, however, one crucial difference between the slavery in Egypt, i.e., human bondage, and servitude to God. The Egyptian master has his own needs, and the slave is required to provide them. The master has selfish goals, and it is incumbent upon the slave to serve those goals. But the Master of creation has no selfish needs, and consequently does not require His servants to provide for Him. On the contrary: total dependency on God does not command the *nullification* of man's own goals; rather it *provides* true goals for man. What the human master demands from his slave is to provide him with his own needs, thus *emptying* the slave of all meaning. What the Divine Master demands from man is the benefit of man, his perfection and welfare, and consequently Divine servitude completes and perfects man by *giving* him meaning. Granted, the slave/man is obligated to something external rather than to himself; however, this is precisely what awards man valuable inner meaning, as the Master/God does not intend for submission to Him to deprive man of his true destiny.

The servant of God derives his goals and ends from Him, just as any other slave does from his master. The slave sees in his Master – and in Him alone – the source of all his happiness. Given that the Master of the Jewish slave is the ultimate Good who wants only the best for His creations, with no demands of His own, this dependency awards man self-worth. Such a dependency allows man to acquire for himself a value set above all other values – that which is dubbed "*tzelem Elokim*," the image of God: to resemble God and to develop into becoming like Him, so to speak. The "free," uncommitted man is in the image of man. The man who serves God is in the image of God, which is his ultimate end and his true destiny.

How is prayer, the request for one's needs, a service of God? He who prays and supplicates declares that there is no other source of happiness or worth other than God. Just like the regular slave, he depends entirely on his Master and turns only to Him to fulfill his needs. There is no other source for direction in his life other than from his Master, God. *Ein lanu ela Avinu shebashamayim*, "We have no one other than our Father in heaven" – this is the fundamental essence of prayer. Through prayer we make ourselves dependent on God, and this dependency is the essentiality of servitude and service. Is there anywhere else to where man can turn to satisfy his thirst for significance, for the means to survive? He who prays as a slave before his Master answers in the negative: *Ki eineinu lekha teluyot*, "For our eyes look to You, and You alone."

The Sages established that *ein tefilla ela tachanunim*: the central defining element of prayer is supplication. At the heart of the daily *Amida* is a list of requests. Other blessings too, such as the *Amida* on Shabbat, are formulated as requests; even the blessing of thanks (*Modim*) in its closing line concludes with a request – *Vekhol hachayim yodukha sela*, "May all the living give thanks to You." Some religions shifted the main focus of the man-God conversation to one of praise or song, deeming it a more fitting service for the mortal man standing before the King of kings. Judaism, however, did not agree to such a change. Prayer is not essentially praise; rather it is the service of God, and service is expressed through dependency. Man, a physical being with needs and constraints, is obligated to identify the root of his happiness and the source for filling his limitations. If he imagines that he is able to provide his own needs unaided, he will stand independent, a "free" man, without dependency or servitude. The truth, however, is that what we lack can be satisfied by God alone. Recognition of this fact – *that* is real prayer and supplication, a genuine declaration of servitude to God, and is true service of the heart.

The service of the angels is to sing songs of praise; the service of man is to submit and subjugate himself. We serve by stating: Without You I am nothing, dust and ashes, therefore I turn to You...for everything: wisdom, forgiveness, health, redemption, sustenance, justice, reward, both national and personal needs – everything that the Sages included in the *Shemoneh Esrei*. And where did we learn to view God in such a way, not just as a convenient supply house but as the Master of everything and the source of our lives? R. Yona answers: From the Exodus from Egypt, when God redeemed us from being slaves to exploitative man and brought us into His service, to a servitude that grants us the freedom of accepting His values and His munificence for ourselves.

In summation, the content of the *Amida* is primarily requests. The inner meaning and implication of this activity is servitude, placing ourselves before God as totally dependent on Him. Our requests are a fulfillment of the service of God, for by turning to Him for our needs we are stating that there is none other than Him from whom we can obtain anything, and that everything in our life comes from Him alone. Given this, it is understood that the regularity of prayer and its recital thrice daily is not in order to remind God of our needs, but is in order to fulfill our service of Him, and to define our entire life as dependent on Him, at every given moment, as the basic definition of our existence.

4. *BITACHON*: TRUST

R. Yona offers a second explanation for the importance of *semikhat geula litfilla*. This answer is necessarily different than the first, but one can immediately perceive that underlying it is the same idea regarding looking to God as the only source which can satisfy our needs. He writes:

> Alternatively, when one mentions the redemption from Egypt and prays immediately afterward, he shows that he trusts in God for his prayer, since he requests his needs from Him. For one who does not trust Him will not request anything from Him. And this idea is found in [*Midrash*] *Shemot Rabba* on *Parashat Bo*, where it is written that when Israel saw the miracles and the wonders which God did for them, overcoming the laws of nature, they trusted in Him, as is written, "And Israel saw the great hand which God wielded against Egypt; and the people feared God, and they believed in God" (*Shemot* 14:31). So now, when one mentions that redemption where our forefathers trusted in God and He saved them, and then he immediately prays, it is clear that he also trusts in God to answer him, just as He answered Israel when they trusted in Him. That is why one mentions that redemption (*geula*) and prays immediately. And trust (*bitachon*) is the foundation of fear of God and faith in Him, so he will thereby merit the World to Come. (Ibid.)

R. Yona offers two suggestions as to what underlies the *Shemoneh Esrei*. The first explanation revolves around the concept of service (*avoda*), and the second around trust (*bitachon*). As we have seen regarding service, the two ideas are closely related, for both trust and service are based on one's appealing to God as the source of everything.

The distinction between R. Yona's two explanations does not affect our topic, given that they both view prayer as an expression of one's dependency on God. The difference between them does not relate to the definition of prayer, but rather to explaining the connection between prayer – prayer adjoined to redemption – and meriting the World to Come. The former explains that dependency leads to obedience, which is expressed in fulfilling the mitzvot, this of course being the key to the World to Come. The latter identifies the attribute of trust that is rooted in dependency, and trust "is the foundation of fear of God and faith in Him, so he will thereby merit the World to Come." The difference between the explanations, therefore, is that according to the former the key to the World to Come lies in action, i.e., performance of the mitzvot, whereas according to the latter it lies in attributes of the heart – "fear and faith." The former views prayer as a first step in committing to a future of action, while the latter sees him who prays as having a faithful persona in the present, this persona befitting him to merit the World to Come. Of course, this distinction is fundamental across the entire range of religious thought, but it does not affect our discussion of prayer as service.

Chapter 2

Opening One's Lips

The basic unit of the *Amida* is the "*berakha*," blessing. The *Shemoneh Esrei* – literally "Eighteen" – is so named because it originally comprised eighteen blessings. Halakha mandates that a blessing open with "*Barukh*" (Blessed), which is indeed the case with the first blessing of the *Amida*, which opens with the words, "*Barukh Ata HaShem Elokeinu veElokei avoteinu*," "Blessed are You, HaShem, our God and the God of our fathers." Given that the structure of a blessing is fundamental to the composition of the *Amida*, our analysis will naturally address, for the most part, these structures. This being so, it would seem logical to define "*Barukh*" as the starting point of the *Amida*, the word with which the first blessing begins. However, before this word lies a verse, a phrase that is not part of any blessing, and we shall begin our analysis by examining this one anomaly and its significance.

1. *HASHEM SEFATAI TIFTACH*

Before the first blessing of the *Shemoneh Esrei*, there appears in the *siddur* a verse taken from *Tehillim* (51:17): "*HaShem sefatai tiftach ufi yaggid tehilatekha*," "God, open my lips, and my mouth shall utter Your praise." Nowadays, at the start of Mincha and *Musaf* in Ashkenazic practice appears an additional verse: "*Ki shem HaShem ekra havu godel leElokeinu*," "When I call out HaShem's name, ascribe greatness to our

God" (*Devarim* 32:3). In halakhic literature other verses are mentioned, such as: "*Shome'a tefilla adekha kol basar yavo'u*," "Hearer of prayer, all flesh will come to You" (*Tehillim* 65:3), and, in Sephardic practice: "*Sof davar hakol nishma*," "At the end of the day, everything is heard" (*Kohelet* 12:13), or "*Tikkon tefillati ketoret lefanekha*," "May You establish my prayer like incense before You" (*Tehillim* 141:2). There is, however, a difference between the verse "*HaShem sefatai tiftach*" and the other verses. This difference is clearly reflected in the way that the halakhic authorities forbade the recitation of any verse at Shacharit and Arvit other than "*HaShem sefatai tiftach*." And why did they do so? As we saw in the previous chapter, it is necessary to connect the blessing of *Gaal Yisrael* to the *Amida*, to adjoin *geula* to *tefilla*. We must therefore avoid any interruption between the blessing of *Geula* and the *Shemoneh Esrei*. This halakha applies only to those prayers where *Geula* is recited. Given that the mitzva of *Shema* applies "when you lie down and when you rise up," namely in the morning and the evening, so too does *Geula*, one of the blessings of *Keriat Shema*, apply at Shacharit and Arvit alone. It is for this reason that there is no issue adding anything that one wishes before the *Amida* of Mincha. However, at Shacharit and Arvit it is forbidden to make an interruption. Therefore, even though at Mincha or *Musaf* it is permissible to add verses such as "*Ki shem HaShem ekra*" and "*Shome'a tefilla*," at Shacharit and Arvit these verses constitute an interruption between *geula* and *tefilla* and therefore may not be added.

However, as mentioned, "*HaShem sefatai tiftach*" is indeed said even at Shacharit and Arvit. This seemingly contradicts the rule of *semikhat geula litfilla*, adjoining redemption to prayer. The Gemara addresses this problem:

> How can one connect *geula* to *tefilla* at Shacharit? Did not R. Yochanan say: Before [the *Shemoneh Esrei*] one says "*HaShem sefatai tiftach*," and afterward he should say "*Yihyu leratzon imrei fi*" ("May the words of my mouth and the thoughts of my heart be accepted before You, O God, my Rock and Redeemer")? The answer is that since the Sages required one to say "*HaShem sefatai tiftach*," it is as if it is part of one long *tefilla* [i.e., *geula* is

> indeed connected to *tefilla*, which begins from "*HaShem sefatai tiftach*"]. (*Berakhot* 4b)

One should not see this verse as an embellishment to the *Amida*, a mere introduction, that is not truly part of prayer itself; if this were the case, it would not be possible to recite it at Shacharit as it would constitute an interruption between *geula* and *tefilla*. The Gemara explains that this verse is an enactment of the Sages and is therefore considered an integral part of the *Amida* itself, despite the fact that it is not part of a blessing. Despite the definition of prayer as a composition of blessings, the addition of this verse before the blessings constitutes "one long *tefilla*." The problem of *semikhat geula litfilla* is thus solved, as the blessing of redemption is indeed connected and joined to the real beginning of prayer, namely the verse "*HaShem sefatai tiftach*." This conclusion requires us to ascertain the significance of reciting this verse and the reason that the Sages felt a need to institute its recital and to join it to the *Amida* itself. What is so important about this verse and why is it necessary?[1]

2. THE RIGHT TO PRAY

"God, open my lips, and my mouth shall utter Your praise."

In my opinion, this is not a request of God to aid us to pray. I do not mean to claim that one does not require the assistance of God in order to speak; however, one needs help in moving one's lips no more than in moving one's hands and legs. Even breathing requires the assistance of God, who is Master of everything. Such a need would not justify prefacing prayer with this verse. My claim is that this is not a request for assistance, but rather a request for permission.

---

1. Based on this gemara, my teacher Rabbi Joseph B. Soloveitchik required that the *chazan* begin his repetition of the *Amida* with this verse. Were this verse considered a mere introduction recited *before* the *Amida*, it would have been possible to rely on its recital before the silent *Amida* for the *chazan*'s repetition too. However, since it is not an introduction to, but an integral part of prayer, the *chazan* who repeats the entire *Amida* is obligated to recite – aloud – this verse too before beginning with "*Barukh*" (see *Shulchan Arukh* 111:2 and *Magen Avraham* ad loc. 4).

Man, facing God, recognizes that he is unworthy to utter the praises of God, that the very thought of God's praise, God's majesty, God's kingship, on his lips is inappropriate. Who am I and how dare I presume to bear the glory of God's majesty on my poor, sinful lips? Or – if we rephrase this idea within the context of the previous chapter, where we explained that prayer is the service and servitude of the King – who am I to be counted among the servants of the King? Servitude is seen by us, of course, as lowly and humiliating, but regarding the servants of God this is not so. To be called an *eved HaShem,* a servant of God, is an honor and a privilege, and this honor must be granted by God. The problem here is not the physical ability to move one's lips and give praise, but rather the permission to assume a position of cosmic significance, to count ourselves among the servants of the King of kings, Master of the universe. In order to join the ranks of the servants of the King, one must be *accepted.* Man, standing before his Creator, is mute, his lips sealed, until the King raises His golden scepter and points to him, and only then may he open his lips in order to utter the praises of God.

"God, open my lips" – give me the right, O God, to speak before You, to utter Your praises, to count myself among those who serve You, for if not, I remain silent and mute.

With this we return to the paradox I described in the previous chapter. To serve God is to receive from Him the contents of the *tzelem Elokim,* the image of God. Nullifying ourselves before Him means to be affirmed and empowered. By serving God, we do not fade away, lose dignity and a sense of self, but on the contrary: we become truly human, in the sense that to be human is to be in the image of God. So too is the case with prayer, which is service of the heart. To serve God through prayer is to be empowered and to receive a status of *eved HaShem,* servant of God – to be a *tzelem Elokim.* Before I utter a single word, before I formulate even one request, my very standing before Him as a servant constitutes a huge request for the most important of values, to be a servant of God and thus a man of worth, to be ready to receive significance, meaning, mitzvot, everything; for everything comes from Him and there exists no other source. The Sages chose the words of King David in order to express this request, that precedes all private requests and specific prayers. O God, open my lips – and only then dare I utter Your praise.

3. THE ABILITY TO PRAY

What is the meaning of the words "Open my lips"? Opening the lips is, of course, a metaphor for speech; however, we must understand what lies behind this metaphor and ascertain its significance. It seems that hidden within the metaphor lies the basic meaning of the concept of "*tzelem Elokim*."

By saying "God, open my lips, and my mouth shall utter Your praise," we seem to imply that the praises are waiting inside of us, bottled up, unable to pass the sealed portals of our lips. There is no need to formulate and compose long, complex prayers; there is only a need to open the locked gates and, consequently, the words will spill out, "My mouth shall utter Your praise." This implies that there is an enormous gap between my inner depths and my outer expression. In the deepest recesses of the heart, of which even my own consciousness may be unaware, resides an entire world of connection to God, lie values of holiness and purity, and a direct link with the Infinite. However, the moment I try to express all of this, something feeble and superficial emerges instead, devoid of all glory and grandeur. Only the power of God can help me bridge this gap and unleash the inner fullness of my soul's expression.

Why does such a gap exist? The concept of "*tzelem Elokim*," the image of God in which man was created, refers to man's potential. Man is created in His image, meaning that there is no plan, description, or model for man that defines and limits him, other than God. Everything is created according to a plan that details its characteristics and abilities. A dog, for example, is created according to the blueprint called "dog," within which are listed the abilities and characteristics of a dog. Man is created in the model that is called "God." In actuality, in the external expression of *tzelem Elokim*, a person at any given moment is no more than the finite, limited state that he has attained. The camera freezes man's state at that particular moment. But man is not really defined as finite or limited; man was not created in the image of man, according to a blueprint of what a man should be. By definition, man was created from the outset in the image of God, free of restriction that could limit his abilities. The word of creation was that man should be "*thus!*" – in accordance with the blueprint and model, no less than God.

The definition of man is not what he is, but what he can be, what he should be, the infinite striving to transcend any restriction of value in his ascent to the infinite. Therefore, the inner meaning of man, that which we term his "*tzelem Elokim*," is expressed in his striving to transcend himself, to elevate himself to a higher state. As a result of this, there exists a constant gap between man's inner meaning – the potential to reach God – and the external, objective reality. Man's inner potential is "imprisoned" within him, hidden and buried deep down. Limited in the external reality, man is unable to utter God's praises. Not only is he unfit, but he is incapable, and does not even come close to the level required in order to comprehend God and His praises. If, however, man's lips are opened, one can find those words inside which are hidden deep within his *tzelem Elokim*. Man calls out before God: What do I want, but that You should open my lips, open their locks, and my mouth shall utter Your praise that is stored within me.

If one does not pray, or prays to himself, he can at most be equal to himself, flesh and blood, dust and ashes. He can express in words only that which he can express in action. If, however, one prays to God, entering into the service of the King of kings and subjugating oneself to Him, thereby recognizing Him as the source of all value and meaning in his life, he can become something of infinite value. Such a person grows steadily closer to ultimate worth and expresses his true, inner personality as a reflection of what is truly hidden within him: a *tzelem Elokim*.

4. THE WAY TO PRAY

There is another point that must be raised regarding the assistance that we ask of God in order to pray. Aside from the right to stand and serve, and the ability to stand in such a way that my prayers and praises should be meaningful, there is also the problem of how to formulate the prayer, the question of knowing how to pray correctly.

There are two types of prayer. One is spontaneous, bursting forth from the depths of the heart, true and honest, elemental and unsophisticated. When man is in trouble or danger, his prayer does not reflect his service of God, but his immediate, experiential needs. There is no formal service or standardized *tefilla*, but a "*ze'aka*," a *cry*. *Tefilla* takes place in the palace of the King; *ze'aka* bursts forth and ascends from inside the cave, from the straits of distress.

> *Maskil* to David, when he was in the cave: a prayer.
> My voice to God I cry (*ez'ak*), my voice to God I beg.
> I shall spill before Him my words, my trouble before Him I shall tell.
> When my spirit surrounds me, and You know my path,
> On the way which I go, they have hidden a trap for me.
> Look right and see, I have no friend, I have lost all escape, there is none to look out for me.
> I cried (*zaakti*) to You, O God,
> I said: You are my refuge, my portion in the land of the living.
> (*Tehillim* 142)

Man, within the cave, seeks not the royal palace in which to serve the King, but a refuge in which to hide from the enemy. From the midnight of the soul, man cries out to God to save him. This requires no preparation, no formalities, no keeping to royal protocol. One need not be wise or scholarly to formulate such a prayer. In fact, one should not "formulate" such a prayer at all. There are no requirements of set times or special locations, no need for a *minyan* of ten, no obligation to keep to precise dictates of introductory praise or concluding thanks. The legitimacy of *ze'aka*, a cry, is in the heart of the *zo'ek*, the individual who cries out.

But daily prayer, service of the heart, is fundamentally different. Service of the King does not burst forth from a burning house, but is incorporated into the King's court, as part of one's servitude and service. The reason why the Sages composed the *Shemoneh Esrei*, according to Rambam (*Hilkhot Tefilla* 1:4), is that the common man, stumbling over his words, was unable to formulate an appropriate prayer whereby to express himself properly. In serving the King there are rules of procedure – what comes first and what last, how to stand and when to bow, at which time and in which location. The legitimacy of prayer lies in its being the service of God, and this service must be performed in an appropriate manner, one that befits the King of kings. In the King's house there is behavioral protocol, and every visitor must "play by the rules." For a prayer such as this, the Sages deliberated over every word, searching for the Biblical sanction and support for their formulation, in order to produce the perfect prayer. As such, prayer is an ordered work, a "*siddur*."

It is not simple to know how to pray in this manner. How do I know what to say? Shall I address God as "merciful" or as "gracious"? As "merciful Father" or as "mighty King"? Which of my needs are important enough to be mentioned first, which should come last, and which should not be mentioned at all? For the most part, the Sages based their formulation of prayer on the masters of prophecy, on verses in the Tanakh. In other words, the Sages relied upon a Divine source in order to know what to say before Him. It is for this reason too that we first say: "God, open my lips, and my mouth shall utter Your praise."

In our further study of the formulation of the *Shemoneh Esrei* we will examine the sources for each blessing. We shall see that the Sages carefully combined Biblical phrases into a seamless whole. One of the fundamental methods which we shall use in order to understand the blessings is to examine the sources used within them, in order to shed light upon the *Amida* from the Tanakh. The assumption that prayer reflects not merely that which befits the suffering of the soul and man's most pressing needs, but also that which is appropriate to recite before God, obligates us to first request that He open our lips so that our mouth may indeed utter His praises, those which befit *Him*, and not merely those that suit us.

Chapter 3

Avot: Fathers

בָּרוּךְ אַתָּה יהוה, אֱלֹהֵינוּ וֵאלֹהֵי אֲבוֹתֵינוּ
אֱלֹהֵי אַבְרָהָם, אֱלֹהֵי יִצְחָק, וֵאלֹהֵי יַעֲקֹב
הָאֵל הַגָּדוֹל הַגִּבּוֹר וְהַנּוֹרָא, אֵל עֶלְיוֹן
גּוֹמֵל חֲסָדִים טוֹבִים, וְקוֹנֵה הַכֹּל
וְזוֹכֵר חַסְדֵי אָבוֹת
וּמֵבִיא גוֹאֵל לִבְנֵי בְנֵיהֶם לְמַעַן שְׁמוֹ בְּאַהֲבָה.
מֶלֶךְ עוֹזֵר וּמוֹשִׁיעַ וּמָגֵן.
בָּרוּךְ אַתָּה יהוה, מָגֵן אַבְרָהָם.

Blessed are You, Lord our God and God of our fathers,
God of Avraham, God of Yitzchak, and God of Yaakov;
The great, mighty and awesome God, God Most High,
who bestows great acts of kindness and creates all,
who remembers the kindness of the fathers
and brings a redeemer to their children's children
for His name's sake, with love.
King, Helper, Savior, Shield:
Blessed are You, Lord, Shield of Avraham.

The Sages named the first blessing of the *Amida* "*Birkat Avot*," the blessing of the fathers. The forefathers, Avraham, Yitzchak, and Yaakov, are mentioned twice in this blessing: once at the beginning, as part of the name of God – "The God of our fathers: God of Avraham, God of Yitzchak, and God of Yaakov" – and once toward the end – "Who remembers the kindness of the fathers." Even more significant is the mention of Avraham's name in the "*chatima*," the closing words, of the blessing. The *chatima* summarizes the primary theme of each blessing. The first blessing closes with "*Barukh…Magen Avraham*," "Blessed… Shield of Avraham."

But this does not explain why the blessing is called the blessing of the forefathers. Is the subject of the blessing the forefathers? Of course not – the subject of the blessing is God! The fact that the Sages chose to refer to God, among other ways, as "God of our fathers" does not constitute a good enough reason to name the blessing after the forefathers. The mentioning of the forefathers in the blessing does not define the essence of the blessing.

This question is not only restricted to the name which the Sages gave to the blessing. Even without this name we should nonetheless be astounded by the *chatima* of the blessing. Why would the Sages choose to end the blessing with the name of Avraham Avinu? The *chatima* must include the theme of the blessing. In what sense can we determine that the theme of the blessing is connected to God's being specifically the Shield of Avraham? In light of the name of the blessing, it seems that concluding with Avraham's name reflects a more general idea: generally speaking, the blessing is the blessing of the fathers, but more specifically it is the blessing of Avraham. This idea requires clarification.

The Midrash, referring to the promise given by God to Avraham when commanding him to set out on his journey from his homeland to the Land of Israel, explains the inclusion of the fathers in the first blessing as follows:

> R. Shimon b. Lakish said: "I shall make you a great nation" (*Bereshit* 12:2) – this is what we say, "The God of Avraham." "I shall bless you" – this is what we say, "The God of Yitzchak." "I shall make your name great" – this is what we say, "The God of Yaakov." You might think to conclude with all three. Therefore, it is written, "You shall be a blessing" – we conclude with you,

> [Avraham,] and say, "Shield of Avraham," and do not conclude with all of them. (*Bemidbar Rabba* 11:2)[1]

The Midrash clearly does not answer our question, but rather strengthens the very premise of it. The connection between the blessing and the forefathers is not incidental but essential and has been promised since the very origin of the Jewish people. The Midrash seems to be claiming that within God's promise to Avraham, "I shall make you a great nation," there is embedded from the very outset a promise that he, his son, and his grandson will be memorialized in the first blessing of the *Shemoneh Esrei*. Indeed, our question is not solved but intensified!

Let us begin with the very concept of "*av*," a forefather. Only three people are granted the title of forefather. Avraham is a forefather of the Jewish people. This concept is not to be taken in the biological sense alone, for were this the case then the existence of three forefathers would be incomprehensible. If "forefather" meant "the first," then his son Yitzchak would have to be the first son, rather than the second forefather. It is obvious that the concept of forefathers does not refer to biology, but to exemplarity. The very concept of the Jewish people rests upon three paradigms, three influences, three founders. There are three models of personality which merge to form the Jewish people. Each forefather expresses a different personality, and each of them offered a different contribution to the archetype of the Jew.

When we declare at the start of the *Amida* that we are praying to the God of our fathers (and not simply to God), we position our relationship with God within the framework that the fathers established. We, the children and heirs of the fathers, turn to God, to Him whom the fathers served in their lifetime. What is the basis for our connection to God? The fact that we continue in the ways of the fathers. They uncovered the path to God, and they taught us how to pray.

In fact, the Sages state that the forefathers literally taught us how to pray. According to R. Yose b. R. Chanina, the forefathers established the daily prayers.

---

1. See Rashi, *Bereshit* 12:2.

> R. Yose b. R. Chanina said: The prayers were instituted by the forefathers. R. Yehoshua b. Levi said: The prayers were instituted in place of the daily sacrifices.... A *baraita* teaches in accordance with R. Yose b. R. Chanina: Avraham instituted the morning service (Shacharit), as is written, "And Avraham arose early in the morning to the place where he had stood" (*Bereshit* 19:27), and "standing" means "praying," as is written, "And Pinchas stood and prayed" (*Tehillim* 106:30). Yitzchak instituted the afternoon service (Mincha), as is written, "And Yitzchak went out to speak (*lasuach*) in the field toward evening" (*Bereshit* 24:63), and "speaking" (*sicha*) means "praying," as is written, "A prayer of the poor man when he wraps himself, and before God he pours out his speech (*sicho*)" (*Tehillim* 102:1). Yaakov instituted the evening service (Arvit), as is written, "And he encountered (*vayifga*) the place and slept there" (*Bereshit* 28:11), and "encounter" (*pegia*) means "praying," as is written, "And you, do not pray for this nation and raise not for them a cry or a prayer, and do not touch (*tifga*) me" (*Yirmeyahu* 7:16). (*Berakhot* 26b)

The Gemara states that each forefather established a different prayer.[2] It is important to note the difference between this statement and the general declaration by the Sages that the forefathers observed all of the mitzvot in the Torah. Here, the Sages do not say that the forefathers prayed, but that they *instituted* prayer. The meaning here is the opposite of the general declaration. The declaration that the forefathers kept the mitzvot of Sinai means that they entered themselves into the historic future Jewish covenant. The mitzvot which obligate us from Sinai were kept by

2. The opinions in the Gemara appear to oppose one another – either the prayers were instituted by the forefathers, or the prayers are in place of the daily sacrifices. Rambam accepts the opinion that the daily prayers were instituted in place of the daily sacrifices. Nonetheless, he also writes that the forefathers instituted the prayers. He seemingly understands that there is no contradiction between the two opinions. Even if, from a halakhic standpoint, there is a connection between each prayer and a sacrifice or parallel Temple service, which is reflected in some of the laws of prayer, the *source* of prayer is fundamentally rooted in the forefathers' personal service of God.

them. But, in the case of prayer, the relationship is the opposite. They did not pray because Jews are obligated to pray; rather we are obligated to pray because they prayed. The mitzva of Shabbat is the reason that the forefathers observed Shabbat. The fact that the forefathers prayed is the reason for the mitzva of prayer.

This being the case, it follows that there is a difference between prayer and the other mitzvot vis-à-vis its origin. In more extreme terms: prayer does not emanate from the halakhic Jewish experience, but from the initial relationship between man and God. Prayer is not a halakhic Jewish action, at least not at its root, but rather a religious elementary experience, an experience based on the religious personality and his relationship with God. The forefathers are not halakhically Jewish in the usual sense of the word, but they nonetheless prayed.

In fact, we stress this point in our prayers when we declare that we are praying to the God of Avraham, Yitzchak, and Yaakov. We pray to the God of the fathers, to the God whom they discovered and to whom they prayed, and they bequeathed their prayer to us. At Sinai, as we know, God presented Himself as the one who took the Jewish people out of Egypt, rather than as Creator of the world. However, in prayer we do not address Him who took us out of Egypt, but specifically the Creator of everything, the God of the fathers. Just as the Exodus from Egypt constitutes the basis for the covenant between the Jew and God, creation is the foundation of the connection between man and God. We continue the prayer of the fathers and, therefore, we must pray in the same manner, as individuals who discover God from within self-experience.

This notion, that prayer is first and foremost a human experience rather than a Jewish one, which addresses the Creator of everything rather than the Forger of the covenant and our Redeemer from Egypt, is emphasized in the formulation of the blessing. The language of prayer is, for the most part, based upon Biblical verses. At the heart of the blessing of the fathers appear the names "*E-l Elyon gomel chasadim tovim vekoneh hakol,*" "God the Most High, who repays great acts of kindness, and has made everything." "E-l Elyon" is a name of God that is unique to this blessing. Nowhere else do we address God with this name. Even in Tanakh it is rarely found, and it seems to me that its very usage sounds foreign to the Jewish ear. The name "E-l Elyon," the most high God, has a universal resonance rather than a Jewish one. A few minutes of reflection discloses who originated the usage of this name. When Avraham returns victorious from battle against the four kings, he meets Malki-Tzedek the king of Shalem, who brings forth bread and wine, and blesses Avraham:

> Blessed be Avram to God the Most High (E-l Elyon), who has made heaven and earth. And blessed be God the Most High (E-l Elyon), who has delivered your enemies into your hand. (*Bereshit* 14:19–20)

Immediately afterward, Avraham adopts the usage of this name when speaking to the king of Sedom: "I lift up my hand to HaShem, the Most High (E-l Elyon), who has made heaven and earth" (ibid. 22). It should be noted that the phrase in the continuation of our blessing, "*vekoneh hakkol*," "who has made everything," is a variation of the continuation of the Malki-Tzedekite term for God, "*Koneh shamayim vaaretz*," "Maker of heaven and earth." Even the *chatima* of the blessing, "Shield (*Magen*) of Avraham," is reminiscent of the phrase "Who has delivered (*miggen*) your enemies into your hand." Hence, the central part of the blessing is taken from the language of a gentile, and the God mentioned in the blessing is E-l Elyon, the God of Malki-Tzedek.

According to the Sages, Malki-Tzedek was Shem the son of Noach, who represents the righteous gentile. Everything that I have said until now, about the forefathers in general and about Avraham specifically, is even more true regarding Shem the son of Noach. The prayer, at least in its initial sense, is based on the relationship between Shem the son of Noach and his God. Avraham, father of the Jewish religion, adopts the name used by Malki-Tzedek (with the addition of the Tetragrammaton). When we address the God of our fathers, the God of the Jews, it becomes apparent that the God of our fathers is "*E-l Elyon koneh shamayim vaaretz*," "God the Most High, Maker of heaven and earth," the God whom the righteous gentile addresses. Malki-Tzedek, priest of E-l Elyon, is one of the founding fathers of Jewish prayer, and this reality appears in the blessing of the fathers. The purpose of the first blessing is to present to us who it is that we are praying to – and it is E-l Elyon, God of the fathers, the shared God of Avraham and Malki-Tzedek.

However, the idea that prayer gives expression to universal man does not turn prayer into something general, expressing only the widest common denominator. On the contrary, given that prayer is based on man's *tzelem Elokim,* this itself contains the assertion that each and every one of us is an entire world, a unique individual. This point is stressed immediately at the start of the blessing. "Our God and the God of our fathers: God of Avraham, God of Yitzchak, and God of Yaakov": our God who is the God of our fathers, whom we inherited from our fathers – and He is the God of Avraham, as well as the God of Yitzchak, and also the God of Yaakov. What is the reason for explicating the fathers? Is there a need to remind us that our fathers are Avraham, Yitzchak, and Yaakov? But more than this, notice the triple repetition. Not "God of Avraham, Yitzchak, and Yaakov," but rather "God of Avraham, God of Yitzchak, and God of Yaakov." The blessing virtually declares that the God of Avraham is different from the God of Yitzchak, who is different from the God of Yaakov. Not due to multiplicity, Heaven forbid – He is both our God and the God of our fathers. Rather, each forefather had a different relationship with God, for the exact same reason that each forefather established a different prayer. As we have stressed, there are three fathers, not one father and two sons. Each forefather is an element, an archetype, unique. On the one hand, we pray to the God of our fathers, and are merely the children-heirs who follow in their footsteps. But what are their footsteps, precisely, and what is their path? It is that each of them blazed his own path, each of them had his own unique relationship with God. Somewhat paradoxically, we imitate the unique individuality of our fathers. They were the fathers, and we are the children. But what does it mean to be the child of these fathers? It means to follow their example of individuality. If each forefather has a God, if there is the God of Avraham, the God of Yitzchak, and the God of Yaakov, then to some extent there is also the God of Rachel, the God of Moshe, and the God of Shraga. Each of us steps onto the wide paved avenue and uncovers the unique path that is fitting for him, and for him alone.

In summary: The aim of the first blessing is to introduce to the worshipper the God unto whom he is praying. The theme of the blessing is: to whom are we praying? The Sages formulated their answer to this question in the context of the fathers, namely that the God to whom I pray is the God of the fathers. Hence, they direct our prayers to be rooted in a multigenerational heritage on the one hand, and, on the other hand, to be personal, initial, and original; on the one hand, a structured precept, and, on the other hand, a precept to be individualistic. The established Jewish prayer is the prayer of the fathers as individuals, who walked where no man had walked before, lacking both map and road signage. Furthermore, the prayer of the fathers shares its root with the prayer of the non-Jew, and the God of the prayer is not the Deliverer from Egypt or the Giver of the Torah, but rather God the Most High, Maker of heaven and earth. But, despite all of this, or perhaps because of all this, each person who prays has his own God, who is also the God of us all, and likewise the God of our ancestors, as well as the God of Avraham, the God of Yitzchak, and the God of Yaakov.

We are yet to explain the special connection to Avraham specifically, in addition to the relationship with the other forefathers. Certainly, in light of my explanation, it is possible to view Avraham as the first of the firsts. If what makes the forefathers special is their primacy, then Avraham is the most primary of them all. It seems to me, however, that we must delve deeper in explaining what lies behind the *chatima* "*Magen Avraham*," Shield of Avraham, which, according to the midrash cited earlier, was promised specifically to Avraham in the first prophecy in the age of Judaism.

Chapter 4

Avot: Fathers (II)

In the previous chapter we explained the connection between the first blessing of the *Amida* and the forefathers. We explained that the first blessing presents the God whom we address in prayer. The God of prayer is the God of the fathers in several respects:

Elokei harishonim: God of the forebears, who discovered God on their own.

Elokei hayechidim: God of the individuals, each of whom paved his own, original path to God in order to serve Him, and each of whom had a unique connection with God.

Elokei haavot: God of the fathers who preceded Sinai, whose connection to God is not a result of revelation or command, but rather stems from man's own search, from the image of God entrenched within him. In this context we noted the presence of Malki-Tzedek king of Shalem, who is Shem son of Noach, and whose God is E-l Elyon, God the Most High.

1. *MAGEN AVRAHAM*: SHIELD OF AVRAHAM

We must explain the special emphasis on Avraham out of all three of the forefathers. Why, in the *chatima*, is Avraham alone mentioned, "Shield of Avraham," even though the blessing is called the blessing of the fathers?

In order to explain this, we must return to the source of the term "Shield of Avraham." Immediately after Avraham defeats the four kings and returns Lot from captivity, and after he meets Malki-Tzedek, God appears to him and promises: "Do not fear, Avraham, I shall be your Shield (*Magen lekha*), your reward is very great" (*Bereshit* 15:1). God declares Himself to be the "Shield of Avraham." The question is, of course, what was Avraham afraid of, and why does God have to reassure him? The Midrash responds to this dilemma with several suggestions:

I shall be your Shield: R. Levi explained this in two ways, and the Rabbis in one.

> R. Levi explained: For Avraham was anxious and said, "Perhaps there was one righteous or God-fearing man among those troops whom I killed..."
>
> R. Levi gave an alternative: For Avraham was anxious and said, "Perhaps the sons of the kings whom I killed will gather troops and come and wage war against me..."
>
> The Rabbis explained it thus: Avraham was anxious and said, "If I descended into the fiery furnace and was saved, and waged war with the kings and was saved, then perhaps I have already received my reward in this world and have nothing for the World to Come..." (*Bereshit Rabba* 44:4)

The question of the Midrash, what is it that Avraham was afraid of, is only sharpened by the fact that this took place *after* the successful completion of the war. Prior to the war, a war against four superpowers that had conducted a campaign of conquest along the entire Jordan River, there is no hint that Avraham was afraid, and God certainly did not come to reassure him. Avraham went out to fight without hesitation the moment he heard that his kinsman had been captured. Only after the spectacular victory do we find that Avraham is afraid. The Midrash's response – we won't dwell on the details of each explanation but rather the general impression – is that Avraham's reaction should be seen not as fear (*pachad*) in the usual sense but as anxiety (*hitpachadut*).[1] What

1. The Hebrew verb *mitpached* is a rabbinic neologism used only for Avraham, and once

does it mean to be anxious? This is not fear of a particular enemy from whom one is fleeing, but rather, in modern terms, anxiety and emotional distress. Avraham suffers from lack of self-confidence: perhaps the defeated kings have sons, perhaps there was a righteous person among the dead, or perhaps he has no merits left for the World to Come. When the enemy stood before him, he acted instinctively, without recoil, and only now when there remains no imminent threat on the horizon does Avraham imagine all sorts of threat.

Why? Simply put, these points are dependent on one another. Avraham is truly the very first, without foundation or tradition and without guidance. He was not commanded by God to go to war against the kings, but rather acted of his own volition for he knew, deep down, that it was the right thing to do. The midrashim on the book of *Bereshit* emphasize that Avraham always acted according to his own understanding and only afterward received confirmation from God that he was indeed correct. Consequently, despite his resolute determination, and perhaps precisely because of it, Avraham suffers from anxiety, from doubts, from inner angst. At the end of the day, he has nothing to rely upon in his decision making, no Torah, no ancestral tradition, and no direct prophetical instruction. As one who lives, by his own choice and by his free conscience, alone and prior to everyone ("Walk *before* Me and be perfect"), Avraham is constantly subject to uncertainty and anxiety.

In response to this state, God says to him, "I am your Shield (*Magen*)." The Shield of Avraham is the shield of him who has nothing else to rely on but God Himself. When man feels that he has no other source who can support him, no tradition, no family, no patron in his society, that he has nothing else in his world to rely upon and which he can look to for support, he needs the "Shield of Avraham" to save him. Does this sound familiar? We explained in the exact same way in the first chapter that this is the essence of "*avoda shebalev*," serving God with the heart – prayer. It is the sense that we have nothing else to rely on but God Himself, that everything comes from Him, and that there is no other

---

for Yaakov. The form of the verb is reflexive, and therefore I interpret it as "making oneself fear" rather than fearing; i.e., experiencing an underlying unfocused disquiet and unease.

source but Him. The first blessing, therefore, places us right before the God of prayer, the Shield of Avraham. As individuals and lone beings, with full, deep recognition of our loneliness, we turn to Him who will take us under His wing, to the Shield of Avraham.

We will come back to ascertaining the special significance of the name "*Magen*," Shield; however let us first analyze the other descriptions of God that appear earlier in this blessing.

2. *GOMEL CHASADIM TOVIM*: WHO BESTOWS GREAT ACTS OF KINDNESS

After we have addressed our God and the God of our fathers, we reach a phrase which is borrowed from Malki-Tzedek: "*E-l Elyon koneh hakol*," "God the Most High who creates all."[2] In the middle of this phrase an additional phrase has been inserted: "*Gomel chasadim tovim*," "Who bestows great acts of kindness."

One could understand "*gomel*" to mean "who rewards," in which case "acts of kindness" are not the acts of God, but the actions of man which He is rewarding. However, this is unlikely, as this point is mentioned later on in our blessing: "*Vezokher chasdei avot*," "Who remembers the kindness of the fathers." This is the concept of *zekhut avot* (the merit of the fathers). Therefore, "*Gomel chasadim tovim*" must have a different meaning.

It would seem that "*gomel*" here means to bestow, and "great acts of kindness" is the object of said bestowment: God performs acts of kindness for us. What does this mean? What are the great acts of kindness? *Chesed*, kindness, refers to an act which is performed outside of the world of obligation and recompense, and great acts of kindness are those actions which exemplify this characteristic in the strongest of terms. The ultimate kindness is the act of creation, as the Sages expounded on the verse "*Olam chesed yibbaneh*," "The world is built out of kindness." God's creation of the world was not an appropriate response or justified act engendered by some previous event, for the simple reason that there was no previous reality. It was simply altruistic benevolence, pure

2. Originally in *Bereshit* as "*E-l Elyon koneh shamayim vaaretz*," "God the Most High who has made heaven and earth."

chesed. This being the case, "Who performs great acts of kindness" is an explanation of "Who creates all." However, by placing this phrase in the middle of Malki-Tzedek's phrase, the Sages effected a subtle change in the meaning. When Malki-Tzedek said "God the Most High who has made heaven and earth," he was expressing thanks to God for granting victory to Avraham. However, gratitude is inappropriate in the first blessing; gratitude merits its own blessing at the end of the *Amida*. When we say "Who performs great acts of kindness," we are not establishing our relationship with God within the framework of thankfulness, of gratitude for all the various things that God has done for us, but rather within the framework of ownership. God has done everything for us, including the act of creation itself, as absolute kindness, and therefore He owns everything – *Koneh hakol*. Consequently, He owns us too. This fact has practical ramifications – we are His servants and belong to Him, and therefore we are bound to serve Him.[3]

3. *ZOKHER CHASDEI AVOT*: WHO REMEMBERS THE KINDNESS OF THE FATHERS

"Who remembers the kindness of the fathers" – here the blessing begins to transform, from a universal meaning to a Jewish one. God remembers the kindness of the fathers of the Jewish people. What was the "kindness of the fathers"? The answer is alluded to in the continuation – "And brings a redeemer to their children's children for the His name's sake, with love." If indeed God remembers the kindness of the fathers, why is His redemption of their descendants accomplished for His name's sake, rather than for the sake of those kindnesses of the fathers? An additional question: Why does the concept of *zekhut avot* (the merit of the fathers) specifically focus upon kindness, and not on the mitzvot that the fathers performed in all areas of their righteousness? It seems that the "kindness of the fathers" is not a general term for the mitzvot or good deeds that they performed, but specifically acts of kindness.

---

3. This idea was cited in the name of R. Yona in the first chapter. R. Yona identified the Exodus from Egypt as the reason for our servitude, meaning that we are dealing specifically with Jewish servitude. In contrast, my claim is that at this stage in the *Amida* the servitude is universal, and its cause is creation, the ultimate *chesed*.

The "kindness of the fathers" means the acts of kindness that the fathers performed for God, in proclaiming His name in the world, and accepting Him as Master over them. The forefathers created a reality in which God is the God of "the people of the God of Avraham," and His name is proclaimed in the world. The Sages describe an existence in which God was absent from the world, hidden, and exiled. The Sages say about Avraham that he "mended the tear" (*Bereshit Rabba* 39:3). The first thing that Avraham did upon arriving in the Land of Israel was to call out in the name of God (*Bereshit* 12:8). *Zekhut avot* is not merely a matter of delayed reward, paid out to the children for the earlier deeds of the fathers, but rather a merit that exists because the reality that the forefathers created continues to be realized through the fulfillment of the children.

The relationship between a Jew and God is not merely a relationship of a creature and his Creator, but also of a subject and his Master, of a people and its King. The relationship includes the forging of a unit, the identification of God with the people who bear His name. All of this is a result of the actions of the forefathers. It is for this reason that God brings a redeemer to their children's children, who continue this reality, *for His name's sake*, for the sake of His name whose existence in the world is only through Israel. The "kindness of the fathers" and "for His name's sake" are one and the same, for the kindness of the fathers was their proclaiming His name in the world. Their children's children are the continued realization of that proclamation, which continues to be fulfilled through them.

With this we can return to understanding the special significance of "*Magen*," Shield. "*Melekh Ozer uMoshia uMagen*" – "a King, Helper, Savior, and Shield is the Shield of Avraham. The blessing does not speak of the fact that God comes and rescues man from suffering into which he has fallen. That is the theme of the following blessing *Gevurot*, mighty deeds "Supporter of the falling, Healer of the sick, and Freer of the captive," and of course, above all else, "Reviver of the dead." A shield does not rescue man from suffering into which he has fallen, but rather prevents the suffering from befalling him at all. If you are shielded, you are not in danger at all, and may not even be aware that a threat exists.

> Fear not the dread of night, the flying arrow by day,
> The plague that roams in the dark,
> the scourge that plunders at noon.
> At your side a thousand may fall, and a myriad to your right –
> but it shall not reach you. (*Tehillim* 91:5–7)

These verses do not refer to the salvation of God when we call out to Him, but rather the fixed state by which we are under God's protection, and not even aware of the existence of danger. When Avraham was anxious, God did not promise to save him from all of those imagined foes, but rather said to him that the threat did not exist at all, that he is immune and protected in advance. Since we are with God, the bearers of His name, and He therefore dwells in our midst, remembering the kindness of the fathers, a state of "the Master and His servants" is created. We are granted shelter by God, and consequently we merit His constant protection. This is what God said to Avraham. You need not be wary each day of a new danger, for you are My servant, you are Mine, I am your Shield. Avraham is a beneficiary of the shelter of God, who is King, Helper, Savior, and Shield.

With this we have come full circle. Returning to the beginning: The Jew turns to God in prayer, just as Avraham did, just like the forefathers. This is the foundation of service and servitude. Avraham, the first of the servants of God, stood alone in the world, without support, anxious yet active, laying the basis for the proclamation of God's name in the world, and he therefore merits the blessing of *Magen Avraham*, God being his only support. Since we, as the children of Avraham, Yitzchak, and Yaakov, are servants of God, a unit of "a King and His people" is formed. In this framework, God is not only the Creator of the world whom it is fitting to serve, but rather a King, Helper, Savior, and Shield, who provides shelter for His people and protects them because they are His and the bearers of His name. The service of prayer instantly forms a special relationship with God, not an external relationship of creature with his Creator, but rather an internal relationship with a member of the same unit, in which there are servants and a Master who rules over and protects them.

4. *BEAHAVA*: WITH LOVE

There remains one word which we have yet to explain. God "brings a redeemer to their children's children for His name's sake, *with love*" – what is this love and what is it doing here?

In another context, I once heard from my master and teacher Rabbi Joseph B. Soloveitchik an explanation of the phrase recited in the *Musaf* prayer on Rosh HaShana, "And also Noach You remembered *with love*". The Rav explained that God needed to choose someone to save from the flood so that it would be possible to renew the world afterward. It is for this reason that two of each animal were saved. This being the case, two humans, any two humans, could have entered the ark. But besides this, Noach, as an individual personality, found favor in God's eyes, and was saved for that reason. The blessing of *Zikhronot* (remembrances) on Rosh HaShana speaks of the running of the world – "Who to war and who to peace" – and also of individual providence. With Noach both of these points are reflected: the remembrance was not only for the purpose of managing the world but also personal, for Noach himself. This is the meaning of "with love."

In a similar vein, in our blessing, God brings a redeemer to their children's children not only due to an obligation of recompense to the forefathers. The redemption is for the sake of His name, which we the children bear. Will redemption come because an attack on the children will constitute a desecration of God's name, as Moshe said, "Why should the nations say..."? I believe that there is another point here. As was emphasized before, we constitute a part of the unit that is God's presence in the world, and this is God's name that we bear. Therefore, God is connected to us and loves us. God identifies with us because He is our partner and we are His. Not only is there no contradiction between "for His name's sake" and "with love," since we, the object of the love, also bear His name, but on the contrary – "for His name's sake" means "with love." Carrying the name of God, the strong connection between it and the Jewish people, and love, are all different names for the same idea.

In summary: From "And remembers the kindness of the fathers" begins the building of a joint unit for the Master and His servants, which is expressed by God's being a Helper, Savior, and Shield. This relationship originates from the relationship between Avraham and God, who was a Shield for him. At the beginning of the blessing, we recognize the greatness of God, who is universal, and relevant to all mankind. In the continuation, we accept His kingship and forge a servant-master relationship. This relationship is the kindness of the fathers, with Avraham at the head, and it forges the unique bond of Israel and God.

Chapter 5

Gevurot: Mighty Deeds

אַתָּה גִּבּוֹר לְעוֹלָם, אֲדֹנָי
מְחַיֵּה מֵתִים אַתָּה, רַב לְהוֹשִׁיעַ
מַשִּׁיב הָרוּחַ וּמוֹרִיד הַגֶּשֶׁם / מוֹרִיד הַטָּל
מְכַלְכֵּל חַיִּים בְּחֶסֶד, מְחַיֵּה מֵתִים בְּרַחֲמִים רַבִּים
סוֹמֵךְ נוֹפְלִים, וְרוֹפֵא חוֹלִים, וּמַתִּיר אֲסוּרִים
וּמְקַיֵּם אֱמוּנָתוֹ לִישֵׁנֵי עָפָר.
מִי כָמוֹךָ, בַּעַל גְּבוּרוֹת, וּמִי דּוֹמֶה לָּךְ
מֶלֶךְ, מֵמִית וּמְחַיֶּה וּמַצְמִיחַ יְשׁוּעָה.
וְנֶאֱמָן אַתָּה לְהַחֲיוֹת מֵתִים.
בָּרוּךְ אַתָּה יהוה, מְחַיֵּה הַמֵּתִים.

You are mighty forever, God.
You give life to the dead and have great power to save.
(You make the wind blow and the rain fall.)
You sustain the living with kindness,
and revive the dead with great compassion,
Support the fallen, heal the sick, release the imprisoned,
And keeps His faith with those who sleep in the dust.
Who is like You, Master of mighty deeds,
and who can compare to You,
A King who kills and revives, and makes salvation grow?
You are faithful to revive the dead.
Blessed are You, God, who revives the dead.

The second blessing of the *Amida* prayer is named by the Sages "*Birkat Gevurot*," the blessing of mighty deeds.

Upon comparing it to the first blessing, the distinction and development are clear. The first blessing defines who God *is*, whereas the second blessing describes what He *does*. This makes sense in light of what we highlighted in the first chapter, that prayer is first and foremost a request for our needs. If so, it is appropriate that, before the requests themselves, there should come an explicit declaration that God can fulfill them, that He has the ability and strength to heal the sick, to support the falling, and to free the captive. All of man's needs are in God's hands, and He sustains life with kindness.

However, inspection of the language of the blessing reveals a strange focus on one particular "mighty deed," one that is, in terms of our daily lives, seemingly irrelevant, or is at least something that we do not typically request. According to the analysis of the text itself, the blessing of mighty deeds is, first and foremost, the blessing of the resurrection of the dead.

As we explained previously, the *chatima* of each blessing summarizes the essence of that blessing. The *chatima* of the blessing of mighty deeds is "*Barukh mechayeh hameitim*," "Blessed are You who revives the dead." Halakha mandates that before the *chatima* there be a summary, a "*me'ein chatima*." In our blessing it is phrased as "*Vene'eman Ata lehachayot meitim*," "You are faithful to revive the dead." These two points should be sufficient to convince us that the theme of the blessing is *techiyat hameitim*, the resurrection of the dead.

In this case, however, we are not limited to the formal criterion of the *chatima* alone. The formulation of the blessing is riddled with references to the resurrection. The blessing opens with a general statement, "You are mighty forever, God," and then immediately exemplifies this by stating, "You revive the dead." Five examples of "mighty deeds" follow, one of which is "Reviver of the dead with great compassion." The "mighty deeds" are concluded with a summation of the same nature, that God "keeps His faith with those who sleep in the dust." This is followed with an exclamation of wonder, "Who is like You, Master of mighty deeds?!" And with what is this exclamation exemplified? "A King who kills and revives, and makes salvation grow." In the conclusion, as mentioned earlier, appear the *me'ein chatima* and the *chatima* which deal with the resurrection. Clearly, it is wholly justified to conclude that this is a blessing whose theme is the resurrection.

The question, now, is: What is so important about the dogma of the resurrection of the dead that it should be placed at the start of the *Shemoneh Esrei* and merit its own blessing? What is the connection between this fundamental belief and the service of God in prayer?

This question goes beyond the boundaries of prayer. The resurrection is one of the thirteen principles of faith listed by Rambam. Rambam's entire discussion of the principles of faith arose from the Mishna in Chapter *Chelek*, which counts one who does not believe in resurrection as one of those who do not have a portion in the World to Come. The question that we asked about the importance of the resurrection in prayer can be similarly asked about the dogma itself. Why is belief in resurrection so important as to constitute a fundamental principle of Judaism, and the denial of which excludes one from the promise that "all of Israel have a portion in the World to Come"? A little self-reflection can help crystallize my question. Aside from the formal mention that some are accustomed to reciting after Shacharit, when was the last time that you devoted any thought to the principle of faith in the resurrection of the dead? How would your life, belief system, and religious experience change if you were to suddenly discover that really there is no doctrine of resurrection in Judaism? I suspect that the answers to these questions would leave belief in resurrection, even if accepted wholeheartedly, far from the center of our religious experience, and consequently on the periphery of the living Judaism of the individual. The fulfillment of a prophecy about some future event does not turn the content of that prophecy into one of the principles of faith; if that were the case, belief in the war of Gog and Magog would be the fourteenth principle in the Rambam's list of the principles of faith. It is therefore incumbent upon us to understand the religious significance of the proclamation of the resurrection, and its importance in our lives and experiences. In so doing, we will also understand its significance and role in our daily prayer.

I would like to propose the following: The significance of belief in the resurrection of the dead by God is belief in the total, ultimate victory of God and the good over creation and nature.

Allow me to explain:

God created the world with wisdom. Everything in the world is in accordance with His will. Nonetheless, there exist in this world phenomena which surprise us, contravene our expectations, and do not conform to our understanding of the goodness and wisdom of God. The prophet Yirmeyahu already asked, "Why does the path of the wicked succeed?" (12:1). This is the problem of evil, the most persistently difficult issue in the history of religious thought. Jewish religious philosophy does not deny the existence of evil, and it tries, in various ways, to cope with it. For the man of faith, addressing the problem of evil requires confronting anomalous phenomena that seemingly contradict the Divine plan. God created land, yet sometimes it quakes; God created clouds and rain, a worldwide irrigation system, yet sometimes it floods and destroys rather than sustaining life. For one who believes in God's hand in creation, these phenomena are phenomena which diverge from – in the eyes of one who believes in a natural order that reflects God's will – the expected natural order supervised and controlled by the hand of the good and merciful God.

Regarding the phenomenon of death, however, this is not the case. Death is not an exceptional anomaly of nature, but rather nature in its quintessence. In the natural world, a created world, death is universal. Thinkers of antiquity associated anything that is created with the concept of decay. Anything that comes into being must deteriorate. On the contrary, we would see eternal life as an open miracle. There is nothing more certain than death. In contrast to the implied exegesis of the verses in chapter 2 of *Bereshit*, the midrashim at the beginning of the Torah define the essence of the lower beings (in contrast to the angels) as fruitful and fertile yet mortal. Death is the most natural phenomenon, virtually the hallmark of natural life. The universal natural progression is always from life to death, and never, without exception, in the reverse order.

This one-directionality is not just a law of nature, but also a moral-religious necessity. God created the world within which there is free will. Free will is not an inadvertent side-effect of creation, but rather a central – perhaps the most central – purpose of creation. According to the majority of our Sages, the world, or at least man, was created so that through his free will he could reach out and discover God and ascend in the virtue of goodness, and thereby realize his destiny as one created in the image of God. This forms not just the basis for the success of man, but also the basis for God's presence in the world.

However, if there is free will, there will also be sin, for "there is not a righteous man in the world who does only good and never sins." Since there is sin, there is also death, for death is the inexorable result of sin. Man exists through the realization of the Divine image in which he was created. Sin, the destruction of the Divine image, demands the cessation of one's existence. Therefore, death is an integral part of the created world, not *despite* the fact that it was created by God, but rather *because* it was created by God. Death is not only a natural phenomenon in the realm of biological life; it is also natural in the sphere of metaphysics. This is because it is the salient expression of sin, evil, and inadequacy, inherent properties of a world created with the principle of free will.

However, God has promised that eventually, in this world with its natural laws, there shall be a final victory of the good. At that time, the prophecy "He will destroy death for eternity, and the Lord God will wipe away tears from all faces" (*Yeshayahu* 25:8) will be fulfilled. Although free will is at the heart of creation, nevertheless, ultimately, God promises a final victory for the good over evil. This is the victory of God *over* creation, over His own world. God is not just a mighty Warrior who conquers those powers who oppose Him; He even conquers nature itself, the world itself. Even though man is part of nature, ultimately nature is not sovereign, just as death is not sovereign. "Death, you shall die." It is within God's ability to redeem man from the very essence of the natural order. The importance of the principle of resurrection is the belief in the ultimate victory of the good over evil, of life over death, of God over the natural order which He created.

This is the meaning of the term "*gevurot*," mighty deeds, in the blessing of *Gevurot*. The mighty deeds are the conquering actions of God. This blessing is not about miracles, in the sense of wondrous deeds which dazzle and amaze those who witness them. Nor is this blessing about God's Divine providence within nature, which raises the sun in the east, brings about the night, draws plants out of the ground, and breathes air into the lungs of man. The blessing is about the might of God,

God's ability to overcome nature, to overcome even the laws which He Himself invested in nature in His wisdom, to overcome creation itself, in order to enthrone the good over nature. God can even overcome the logic and the rudimentary law of creation, which decrees that the sinner is doomed to death. For although the decree is given, and the law promulgated, God revokes the law and tears up the decree.

If we look at the examples given in this blessing, we see that they are all situations where God in His power saves man from his existing predicament. *Gevura*, might, is a redeeming revolutionary trait, which turns back the wheel which already is turning. There is a natural state and God comes and changes it. If man falls, overcome by the force of gravity, God supports him; if man is sick, his life fading, God heals him; if man is imprisoned, bound in chains which he cannot break, God breaks the bonds which hold him. The blessing is not teaching us the principle of providence, that God is responsible for all that occurs to us (which is, of course, true), but rather that no situation, no matter how final, fixed, or irreversible it seems to be, cannot be undone and resolved by Him. In other words, God can overcome any situation, because He is a mighty One of the world, who revives the dead, and is abundant in salvation. The ultimate final state, overcoming man, is death. Death may be seen as the negation of the world and of life – and it is in this sense that we say, "God kills." However, in a deeper sense, one must understand that death is inherent in the world, and that God not only "sustains the living with kindness," but also with that which transcends nature, He "revives the dead with great compassion." From this we can conclude that there is no natural state which God's might cannot overcome and nullify. Even if a sharp sword rests on one's neck, he should not give up hope for salvation.

Therefore, we pray to Him – and *only Him*. As was mentioned several times, prayer is directed to the one to whom everything belongs, from whom everything emanates, other than whom there is no savior. Moreover, we declare in this blessing that not only is there no other source of salvation, but also that there is no situation from which He cannot save us. God, the ultimate Good, has total control over the laws of nature. Everything is within His capability, and nothing is in the hands of anyone other than Him. Only once we have become convinced of this dual equation can we continue to pray and request our needs. "You are mighty forever," *forever*, God, You are He who "revives the dead," who overturns the most elementary laws of nature, and are "abundant in salvation," constantly providing deliverance, from a resolute, infinite source, a revolutionizing salvation which knows no bounds. We pray to the infinite, almighty source of good, to the fusion of good and strength. One whose eyes turn to God in such an exclusive manner is truly able to pray, to be a servant of God.

It is important to note an interesting phenomenon in our blessing. Twice the concept of *faith* is mentioned in relation to the resurrection. God is described as one who "keeps His *faith* with those who sleep in the dust," and similarly in the *me'ein chatima* adjoined to the *chatima*, we declare that "You are *faithful* to revive the dead." What is the relevance of faith in this blessing?

There is, of course, an essential difference between all the examples of mighty deeds – healing the sick, supporting the falling, freeing the captive – and the ultimate example, the resurrection of the dead. We all have experienced the former in our lives, but we have not ever witnessed the latter. On the other hand, all of the former examples are partial. They do not demonstrate the totality of the Divine might. The essence of the blessing is the infiniteness of God's might, His absolute supremacy over every situation and all of nature. This cannot be fully reflected in the examples taken from the experienced natural world. Other, non-Divine powers can also succeed, to a certain extent, in healing the sick or supporting the falling. In order to see that God is truly powerful and mighty over all of nature, one must venture out of the natural world by using the eyes of faith, to behold the resurrection of the dead. This is what we do at the end of the blessing. With the eyes of faith within us, we look and behold that, indeed, "You are faithful to revive the dead."

This situation is unique from a halakhic perspective. The *Birkhot HaShevach*, blessings of praise – and the blessing of mighty deeds is part of the unit of the blessings of praise – come as a response to a human experience that elicits a response.[1] We know at all times that God's might fills the world, but only after hearing thunder do we recite the blessing of "Whose power and might fill the world." It is clear that God created

1. See *Chiddushei HaRamban, Pesachim* 7b.

the world, yet we do not recite the blessing of "Who does acts of creation" without an experience that brings God's creation to the forefront at this very moment in time. In our blessing we praise God for His might which uproots nature, up to its ultimate exemplification, the resurrection of the dead, but this phenomenon cannot be seen with natural eyes. This is not accidental – natural eyes are incapable of seeing that which exceeds nature. In the blessing of mighty deeds, we are responding to and praising a phenomenon which we see and experience with eyes of faith. Using eyes of faith is the precondition for reciting this blessing, for otherwise the blessing would be detached from an experiential cause.

We have learned something deep and revolutionary about prayer in general. The Sages taught that one must recite the blessing of the fathers and the blessing of mighty deeds before the requests in prayer. Our blessing states that he who has only natural eyes, eyes of this world, cannot pray at all. To whom will he pray when the world closes in on him and threatens to strangle him? When the water rises up to his neck, and the weight on his shoulders drags him down to the abyss, to whom shall he turn? If his natural world should betray him, who will he rely upon? Prayer is not addressed to one who is of this world, not to kings or powers of nature, for that is idolatry. Prayer is offered only to Him who is above nature; to Him who "kills and revives"; to Him who "makes salvation grow"; to Him who can bring about things which are an impossibility to the man of the present. Prayer is based upon a faith reality, rather than upon natural reality.

We now understand a singular aspect of this blessing. Before the *me'ein chatima* there appears a sentence that is neither a request nor a straightforward expression of praise. "Who is like You, Master of mighty deeds, and who can compare to You!" is an exclamation, an expression of wonder, the likes of which does not appear elsewhere in the *Shemoneh Esrei*. An expression such as this must come as a response to something surprising, something wondrous that shakes us to our very core and unleashes from within us a spontaneous reaction. According to our explanation above, the process is understood. Before praying we stood with natural eyes, and as religious people we viewed the actions of God within the natural world. In our eyes, God was part of the natural order, of course greater than all, yet still part of that system and within which He operates. All of a sudden, our eyes have opened, and we see with eyes of faith that God is above and beyond the natural order, that He can undo the entire natural order, that the basic rules of nature, even death itself, are in His hands.

Marveling at this revolutionary discovery, which contradicts our regular way of life, we exclaim, "Who is like You!" There is none like You! There is no such comparison in all of our natural experiences. "Who is like You…who makes salvation grow," You sow the seeds of salvation within the world of decay! This new perspective changes our perception of the entire world and of our approach to God – and now we can pray to Him.

To conclude, let us return to the midrash which stood at the base of the previous blessing, the blessing of the fathers. God told Avraham that his children would recite a blessing in his name, and in the name of Yitzchak and Yaakov. "You shall be a blessing" – we conclude with you, we say "Shield of Avraham." The midrash concludes:

> R. Yudan said: I will give you a blessing in the *Shemoneh Esrei*, but you do not know if Mine comes first or if yours comes first. R. Achveya said in the name of R. Ze'ira: Yours comes before Mine, for first one says, "Shield of Avraham" and afterward "Reviver of the dead" [i.e., first "fathers" and then "mighty deeds"]. (*Bereshit Rabba* 39:11).

What does this enigmatic midrash mean? The blessing of the fathers, "Shield of Avraham," is called "your" blessing, and the blessing of mighty deeds, "Reviver of the dead," is called "My" blessing. Is Avraham the theme of the first blessing? The theme is the *Shield* of Avraham, and this is a name for God, just as "Reviver of the dead" is a name for God. In light of our explanation, the midrash is clear; the first blessing describes God in relation to the world, and specifically in relation to Avraham, for God is the Shield of Avraham. The second blessing describes God as one who overcomes the world, conquering it. The blessing is wholly "Mine."

Considering this, what is the solution to the question of who precedes whom? What is the meaning of the answer that "yours comes before Mine?" The midrash's answer, which is also our daily answer in our *Shemoneh Esrei,* constitutes a revolutionary, unique position for Judaism. Judaism states that first one must establish a relationship and connection with God; to discover God, just as Avraham did; to "create" an existence of God within the world and within providence. Only afterward can the power of God emerge and overturn the world. The heavenly kingship, a state in which "all wickedness will vanish like smoke," arrives only after the individual has called in God's name and formed a reality of the God of Avraham, the God of man. The reason for this is simple (though the theology behind it is most certainly not). God's triumph over the world is not a result of His opposition to the world – after all, He is the one who created it. God is not at war with the world. The world is not a mistake, depraved, or corrupted beyond hope. The world is the arena which God has built, in which the great drama of good and evil, of man's free will, and *tzelem Elokim,* is played out. The presence of God within the world, which is based on man's service, on the two-sided covenant, and on the kindness of the fathers, is a necessary condition for God's triumph over the world. There must first be a God "who remembers the kindness of the fathers and brings a redeemer to their children's children for His name's sake, with love"; only afterward can there be "a King who kills and revives, and makes salvation grow."

This is precisely the message that God was giving to Avraham when He promised him that there would be a blessing in his name. "*Lekh lekha me'artzekha,*" go for yourself, from your land – commence the long journey of founding the Jewish people, receiving the Torah, and establishing God's kingship. This is the basis for everything: the first blessing, the blessing of Avraham. Only after that can the blessing of God's mighty deeds be recited. The path to "He will destroy death for eternity" begins with "*Lekh lekha,*" go for yourself.

Chapter 6

Kedusha: Holiness

1. *DAVAR SHEBIKEDUSHA*: A DECLARATION OF HOLINESS

The third blessing is called "*Birkat Kedusha*," the blessing of holiness. In contrast to the previous blessings, fathers and mighty deeds, whose names required elucidation, in this case the name of the blessing is clear. A cursory glance instantly reveals that the blessing in its entirety indeed addresses the topic of holiness. Our question here is different, not textual but philosophical, and touches upon the meaning of holiness. Precisely what do we mean when we declare that God is holy? If the blessings of praise are a response to lived experiences, what is the experience to which we respond in this blessing? Similarly, we need to understand the blessing's placement in the *Shemoneh Esrei*. Within the context of the *Shemoneh Esrei*, the request for man's needs, why did the Sages enact a blessing about holiness – and why here, at the beginning of the *Amida*?

To answer these questions, we shall first examine the halakhic concept of "*davar shebikedusha*," declarations of holiness. Understanding this concept will also help us to understand the formulation of the blessing and the *Kedusha* that is recited during public prayer within this blessing. The halakhic category of *davar shebikedusha* refers to liturgical recitations, including the recital of Kaddish, *Barekhu*, and most importantly for us, the *Kedusha*. The Gemara teaches that "*davar shebikedusha*, declaration of holiness, cannot be recited with less than ten present."

The *Kedusha* opens with a declaration: "Let us sanctify Your name in the world just as they sanctify it in the heavens above."[1] Immediately afterward, we fulfill our intention by proclaiming:

> Holy, holy, holy, God of hosts, His glory fills the entire earth.

The term "*devarim shebikedusha*" implies that they are matters which deal with sanctity. It is tempting to think that the term refers to prayers that are about sanctity and holiness, such as the *Kedusha*, which begins "Holy, holy, holy." The problem is that none of the other *devarim shebikedusha* speak primarily about holiness. The same holds true for the final two verses of *Kedusha* itself as well:

> Blessed be the glory of God from His place.
> Hashem shall rule forever your God, Zion, for generation upon generation, praise God!

In *Barekhu* we simply say, "Blessed be God, the blessed." The central line of the Kaddish is the refrain, "May His great name be blessed forever and for all eternity." It seems that the common theme of these prayers is not an explicit reference to holiness, but "*barukh*," blessedness, benediction. But what, you may ask, is the connection between holiness and blessedness? Even more to the point, why is not every blessing, a hundred of which we recite daily, all containing the phrase "Blessed are You, HaShem," considered a *davar shebikedusha*?

2. *KIDDUSH HASHEM*: SANCTIFYING GOD

"A *davar shebikedusha* cannot be recited with less than ten present" (*Berakhot* 21b). This law is derived in the Gemara from the verse "And I shall be sanctified in the midst of the children of Israel" (*Vayikra* 22:32). In

1. In this book I will use the Ashkenazic version. In general, the differences in formulation are not significant for our purposes. In the following chapter, which deals with the content of the *Kedusha* itself, I will also address the difference between the formulations.

his commentary to *Berakhot,* R. Yona remarks that this principle cannot be taken at face value, for:

> Undoubtedly the recitation of the *Shema* is included in the category of *davar shebikedusha* since there is no greater *davar shebikedusha* than the acceptance of the yoke of heavenly kingship, and even so it is not included in this principle, for one is permitted to recite it in private. (Talmidei R. Yona, *Berakhot* 13a in *Rif*)

R. Yona assumes that *Keriat Shema,* despite not including in it any explicit reference to the concept of holiness, is not only a *davar shebikedusha,* but the *davar shebikedusha* par excellence – nothing is more of a *davar shebikedusha* than *Shema*! What is the definition of *davar shebikedusha* upon which R. Yona's statement is based?

R. Yona is convinced that *Keriat Shema* is a *davar shebikedusha* as it contains "*kabbalat ol malkhut shamayim,*" acceptance of the yoke of heavenly kingship. In several places in Tractate *Berakhot,* the Sages affirmed that the recitation of *Keriat Shema* is an act of accepting the kingship of God. R. Yona explains that there are two kinds of *davar shebikedusha* – those that require a *minyan* of ten and those that do not – but both exemplify accepting the yoke of heavenly kingship. This is the key for us to understand this halakhic concept.

In Judaism, the kingship of God is not understood as static, fixed, and absolute. God's kingship is dependent upon our act of acceptance, that of His people, Israel. Accepting the yoke of heavenly kingship is not just an act with which we are charged, which establishes our status as God's subjects and by way of which we *recognize* His kingship; rather, it is an act of coronation, an act which *creates* and establishes His kingship. This notion is explained by an ancient saying: There cannot be a king without a people. It is true that, in the absolute sense, God is King as an aspect of His existence, before the world's creation and after it ceases to exist. God is King, God was King, and God shall be King forever and for all eternity. "I am first, and I am last, and besides for me there is no God" (*Yeshayahu* 44:6). However, in another sense, God is only King in relation to the world which reflects His kingship, and in relation to people who accept His rule and abide by His will. The attribute of kingship is a relative one by definition; there cannot be a king without a people. This concept, when applied to the eternal King of kings, is liable to engender amazement, and most of the world's religions would reject it. Yet, amazingly enough, it is an idea sung by nursery children as well as adults in communities all over the Jewish world:

> *Adon olam asher malakh…*
> Master of the world who ruled before any creature was created. When everything shall be done according to His will, *then His name shall be called King.*

It is true that God was King before anything was created. On the other hand, however, only when everything is done according to His will and by His word, only then shall His name be called King in the true sense of the word. The full sense of the kingship of God is dependent on human actions.

There is no other attribute of God which exhibits this dependency upon man's actions as clearly as kingship. This is one of the basic themes of Rosh HaShana, the day on which we actively crown God as our King. The Sages emphasize that the blowing of the shofar is an act of coronation, and the prayers are filled with this concept. The Jewish people, mortal flesh and blood, mere dust and ashes, are the ones who "will grant You the crown of kingship."

This idea, however, is not limited only to God's kingship. All of God's attributes, as exhibited within the world (rather than in their absolute, transcendental state), are dependent on the world, namely, on the actions of man. If no one calls on God's name, then His name is not found in the world. If His name is not found, He is, so to speak, not present. The manifestation of God's presence in the world is dependent upon someone who will bear it. This is the explanation of the saying of the Sages which I cited regarding the blessing of the fathers, that Avraham "mended the tear."[2] Prior to Avraham calling on the name of God, His presence had been absent from the world. Avraham's actions mended the tear between the lower and upper worlds. The significance of the

2. *She-*icha *et hakera.*

concept of holiness in the world is that the Divine manifestation in the world is dependent upon man's willing acceptance of God's presence.

What an astonishing idea! God, the absolute and supremely transcendent Master, Creator and Destroyer of worlds, is dependent on our blessing regarding His presence in the world which He Himself created. My master and teacher Rabbi Joseph B. Soloveitchik explained that this is the meaning of all blessings. "Blessed are You, HaShem, our God, King of the world" means that we indeed add power and glory to the presence of God by revealing Him and recognizing Him in the world. This idea awards new meaning to our explanation that prayer is an act of service of God – service of Him who needs not our service. When we turn to God, to Him who has everything, yet who needs nothing, to the only one who can fulfill our many needs, we are adding to His great name, to His presence and glory in the world. So said King David, writer of psalms for Israel (*Tehillim* 104:1), "My soul, bless God," and immediately continued, "HaShem my God, You grow very great, You are clothed with beauty and majesty."

This is the meaning of the concept of holiness. God told the Jewish people, "I shall be sanctified in the midst of the children of Israel." Holiness means the presence of God. Nothing created has holiness in its own right. God alone is called holy. A place, a time, a person, is holy only because they bear the name of God, the Divine presence, or rather, because through them the name of God is revealed in the world and the presence of God is strengthened. Therefore, the way to sanctify is to bless God – to bless God, that is to increase His revealed holiness, for without our blessing His holiness will not be revealed. We generate this holiness in its revealed existence by the act of blessing, by reciting "*Yitgadal veyitkadash*," "May His great name be magnified and sanctified." His name is literally magnified and sanctified in accordance with this recitation, and through this magnification the world is sanctified.

This aspect, God's holiness *in the world*, is called by the Sages "the *name* of God." A name is what someone is called by others. The name of God, as opposed to God Himself, is found in the mouths of those who bless Him. Thus, the act of sanctity is in reciting "May His great name be blessed forever and for all eternity" in Kaddish. In Tanakh this idea is also called "*kevod HaShem*," God's honor or glory. Honor is something that appears in reflection, as something given by others. When the *Mishkan* was built, it was filled with the honor of God – "And the honor of God filled the *Mishkan*" (*Shemot* 40:35). And so we say in the *Kedusha*, "His honor fills the world." It is also the meaning of "*malkhut*," kingship, as understood by R. Yona. The acceptance of God's kingship is the ultimate act of sanctification, of creating holiness. So does the *Kedusha* conclude, "HaShem shall rule forever, your God, Zion, for generation upon generation." In *Keriat Shema*, which R. Yona labelled the *davar shebikedusha* par excellence, we add a sentence which joins all these terms together: "Blessed be the *name* of the *honor* of His *kingship* forever and for all eternity."

3. *MINYAN*: A QUORUM OF TEN

R. Yona expanded the category of *davar shebikedusha* to include prayers such as *Keriat Shema* which do not require a *minyan* of ten. However, he did not define the criterion for establishing when a *davar shebikedusha* requires a *minyan* and when it does not. Why is *Kedusha* recited only with a *minyan* whereas *Shema* is recited by an individual?

A similar question is raised by the *Rishonim*, including R. Yona, with regard to the *Kedusha* that appears in the blessing of *Yotzer Or* before *Keriyat Shema* and with regard to *Kedusha DeSidra*, the *Kedusha* that appears within *UVa LeTziyon*. There are *Rishonim*[3] who required a *minyan* for reciting these prayers as well, and they ruled that a person praying alone should skip those paragraphs. Most *Rishonim* ruled, however, that an individual may recite them, as is our practice. What is the difference between the *Kedusha* of *Yotzer Or* and the *Kedusha* of the *Amida*? The basic answer, as it more or less appears in the various *Rishonim*, is that in the blessing of *Yotzer Or* we are merely quoting the verses which describe how the angels recite *Kedusha*. In the *Amida*, however, we ourselves are the ones sanctifying.

In light of what we have explained above, the difference is clear. The recital of *Kedusha* is an active and actualizing process, in which

3. See Rambam, *Hilkhot Tefilla* 7:17. The *Kesef Mishneh* ad loc. brings in the name of R. Avraham b. HaRambam that Rambam later retracted this ruling.

we actually sanctify the name of God and realize the immanence of God's presence in the world. To recite the *Kedusha* is to create a chariot for the Divine presence, and to actualize a process of sanctification in the world. This role, described in the verse "And I shall be sanctified in the midst of the children of Israel," can only be performed by a community, by an entity which constitutes a unit of "the children of Israel." The job of supporting God's presence is given to Israel as a whole, not to the individual Jew. Those prayers designated as a *davar shebikedusha* are prayers which create *kedusha,* holiness, and holiness cannot be created without a *minyan* of ten, without the entity which represents Israel as a whole.

When I recite the *Shema* privately, on the other hand, I am not turning outward or effecting a change in the world and in the majesty of God therein. Rather, I turn inward. On a daily basis, twice a day, I have a duty to reaffirm my loyalty. Of course, the act of acceptance of God's rule adds automatically to the reality of the rule; but this is not the purpose of the affirmation. The purpose of the recitation of *Shema* is not to perfect the world, but to perfect myself. I do not attempt to act upon God's presence, but to act upon myself. In the wider sense, every mitzva I perform will bring about an increase in *kedusha* and the presence of God. But the category of "*davar shebikedusha*" is designated for those acts which directly relate to the glory and kingship of God, for those mitzvot whose fulfillment lies in man's capability to actually increase *kedusha* in the world. "May His great name be magnified and sanctified in the world that He created according to His will" – it is a cardinal belief of Judaism that the name, glory, and kingship of God can be made greater in the world. And when I make an effort to make His name greater, that is a *davar shebikedusha,* something which cannot happen with less than ten.

There are prayers which describe this process but they themselves are not the act. This is the status of the *Kedusha* recited before the *Shema* and the *Kedusha DeSidra.* We quote in them the *Kedusha* recited by the angels (which we will address in the next chapter), but we ourselves do not sanctify. Therefore, these prayers may be recited, like *Keriat Shema,* by one who is praying alone.

4. HUMANISM OR THEOCRATIC MONISM?

There are two dominant answers to the question, what is the source of value in the world? Secular humanism answers that man creates value and is the source of value. Human experience is the basis for its own "sanctity." Theological monism states that God, who resides outside of nature and transcends it, is the only source of value and sanctity. Man, like all things created, cannot be the source of value.

Judaism, following what we explained above, stakes out a different position, not so much in the middle as on both ends. On the one hand, God is the only source of value. Only absolute value, metaphysically transcendent, whose source lies outside of the world, can be the source of holiness. However, this world is, by definition, not metaphysically transcendent. The world is necessarily defective, lacking, imperfect, and at times even corrupt. In this world there exists not absolute value itself, but rather the striving toward absolute value. Our world, the world of man created in the image of God, reflects the absolute by virtue of the fact that God is the target of our aspirations. Holiness in this world is found in the process of perfecting (*hishtalmut*), not in the state of perfection (*sheleimut*). The process of perfecting is inherently meaningless if it is not directed toward the absolute perfection that we call God; yet, conversely, it can also only exist in a place where God is not absolutely present. Absolute Divinity is the source of the ever-revealing Divine presence, but the revelation of the Divine presence, the process of perfecting, is performed by mankind, bearers of *tzelem Elokim*, God's image.

The Midrash expresses this idea in a wonderfully clear yet paradoxical form:

> R. Shimon said: When the Holy One, blessed be He, came to create the first man, the angels divided into two camps and two parties. Some said: He should not be created; and some said: He should be created.... Kindness said: He should be created, for he will do acts of kindness; but Truth said: He should not be created, for he is completely false.... What did God do? He took Truth and flung him to the earth, as is written, "You flung truth to the earth" (*Daniel* 8:12). The angels said to God: Master of the worlds, how can You degrade Your royal seal (truth being

> the "seal" of the kingdom of God)? [God answered:] Let truth rise from the earth, as is written, "Truth shall grow from the earth" (*Tehillim* 85:12). (*Bereshit Rabba* 8:5)

There is no more absolute and more demanding value than truth. A little falsehood is totally false. Truth allows no compromise, for that would undermine its very nature. For absolute truth, man cannot exist, for he is "completely false." Thus God, to create man, threw Truth down. The angels, who think logically, cry out: Without Truth there is no kingdom of heaven, so there is no point in creating man. God answers: There is another, different kind of truth to that in the upper heavens, one which grows and arises from the earth. There is a truth that develops from out of the earth, from a reality of falsehood and strife, from deficiency and imperfection. That truth, albeit incomplete, is also truth, and also contains *kedusha*, a holiness of the process of perfecting. The angels, masters of the perfect yet static reality, do not understand God's answer. But this truth is not divorced from the Divine truth; it is the truth of heaven itself that grows out of a bed of lies, aspiring to return and reflect the clear and pure truth of God.

All value and holiness in this world are from man, but they must reflect the absolute holiness of God and aspire toward it.

God commanded, "They shall make Me a Sanctuary, and I shall dwell in their midst." We must make the Temple. God does not dwell on the mountain, but in the Temple that man builds. Then, and only then, does God dwell in man. God dwells in the midst of those who build. The Torah emphasizes that the Sanctuary itself dwells with them, "in the midst of their impurity" and imperfection.[4] My teacher Rabbi Soloveitchik explained this to be the difference between Mount Sinai, which has no residual sanctity, and Mount Moria, which is sanctified for all generations even after the destruction of the Temple. The former was sanctified by an act of God, and therefore, once the cloud has lifted, the mountain returns to its original state. The latter, on the other hand, was sanctified by the Jewish people, by the construction of its walls and through their festive pilgrimage, and therefore, its sanctity is permanent.

4. *Vayikra* 16:16.

Chapter 7

Nekadesh: Let Us Sanctify

In the previous chapter, I attempted to define the concept of *kedusha*, sanctity, in light of the halakhic category of "*davar shebikedusha*." I spoke of the cyclic paradox of holiness – it is, properly speaking, a transcendent attribute only of God, but it is found, in actuality, in our imperfect world; we create it by reflecting the presence of God in our lives and by striving toward absolute heavenly perfection. In this context, I quoted the midrash which states that in order to create Man, God cast Truth down to the ground, declaring that truth grows from the earth. Holiness, I explained, grows from the earth back to from whence it was cast – heaven. We shall now see how understanding this concept sheds light upon the text of the *Kedusha* prayer recited in the public repetition of the *Shemoneh Esrei*.

The core of every *Kedusha* in the *Shemoneh Esrei* consists of three verses:

> Holy, holy, holy, God of hosts, His glory fills the entire earth. (*Yeshayahu* 6:3)
> Blessed be the glory of God from His place. (*Yechezkel* 3:12)
> HaShem shall rule forever, your God, Zion, for generation upon generation, praise God! (*Tehillim* 146:10)

1. JEWS AND ANGELS

The *Kedusha* opens with a call from the *chazan* to the congregation to recite *Kedusha*. Although there are several versions of this introductory line, depending upon the custom and time of recital, they all include more or less the same point: We are about to recite the *Kedusha* "just as" it is recited by the angels in heaven before God. This concept is based on the Biblical description of the prophets hearing the first two verses of the *Kedusha* emanating from the mouths of the angels before God's throne. "Let us sanctify Your name *in the world* just as it is sanctified *in the highest heavens*."

If you remember the midrash about the creation of man that I mentioned earlier, you will surely ask: Does this not contradict everything that we have said? *Kedusha,* I explained, is something uttered specifically within the incomplete, imperfect world. *Kedusha* is recited only by man, who adds sanctity and actualizes the Divine presence in the world. This is not possible in the world of angels, a world in which the sanctity is absolute and perfect to begin with, nor by the angels themselves, who are neither evolving nor in a process of perfection, and therefore not increasing in holiness. Accordingly, if the angels recite *Kedusha,* the main concept is missing – magnification and sanctification.

My answer is – that is quite correct. The angels cannot sanctify. Although we derive the contents of the *Kedusha* from the prophets' visions of the angels, real sanctification – "*Yitgadal veyitkadash*" – can only be recited by man. The Sages express this idea in their typically concise manner:

> The ministering angels do not recite song above until Israel has recited it down below, as it is said (*Iyov* 38:7), "When the morning stars sang together," and only then, "And all the sons of God shouted for joy." (*Chullin* 91b)

The angels, it turns out, cannot initiate the recital of *Kedusha*. They can only echo our *Kedusha*. Initiative, genuine creativity, is in the hands of humans, despite their inferiority and distance from holiness. We might go so far as to say – *because of* their inferiority and distance from holiness.

Then what, you will ask, is the meaning of the angels' role here? Why do we state that we are going to do that which they do (or rather, what they will do after we begin)? The answer is rooted in the dialectical nature of *kedusha,* as I explained previously. Sanctification in our imperfect world is the uncovering of perfection within imperfection. Real, absolute holiness is the true presence of God. We bring out the absolute, its reflection, within this relative world. *Kedusha* is not expressing our own ideals, but rather is our attempt at the realization of the absolute ideals. We do not offer up a halting, hesitant, imperfect version of Divine sanctity; we aspire to reach the state of the angels, and therefore we do our best to reach out to perfection, sanctifying just as they sanctify, namely, just as they describe the *Kedusha.* If our ideal, our goal, is not in the realm of the angels, then our *Kedusha* is not the sanctification of "the great Name." *Kedusha* is in our striving, in our growth, but only when we strive to reach that which is found properly and absolutely in the highest heavens. If you sever the connection to the absolute vision of the angels, you will be left with merely human values, values which are not only imperfect but also are not in the process of perfecting. On the other hand, if you leave sanctification to the angels alone, you wind up with "*kadosh,*" holiness, but no "*yitkadash,*" the process of increasing holiness. And then, asks the Gemara, what is the point in the angels reciting *Kedusha,* for what can they add to the independent holiness of God?

In summary: The content, the vision, is that of the angels, of the absolute; the act is man's alone, who is imperfect yet in the process of perfecting. With this idea in mind, we can now understand the verses of the *Kedusha,* all of which revolve around the paradoxical dialectic of *sanctification.*

2. THE TEXT OF THE *KEDUSHA*

I. *Kadosh, kadosh, kadosh*: Holy, holy, holy, God of hosts, His glory fills the entire earth

The word "holy," taken by itself, means separated, as Ramban describes at the beginning of *Parashat Kedoshim* (*Vayikra* 19:1). When the term "holy" is applied to God, it means that He is transcendent, above and beyond this world. Holy, holy, holy, tripled into three *Kedushot,* means that God is above and beyond all concept, all relativism. In Ancient Hebrew there is no word for "infinite." The noun from the Middle Ages, "*Ein-sof*," is very useful in philosophical discourse, but it is obviously misleading, because it relates to the concept as a defined entity, as something comprehended. Infiniteness is not a defined entity, rather something that is always beyond the definable. One can point to a certain boundary and state that God is beyond it, and beyond the next boundary, and beyond every boundary. The way to express this is not through a noun, but through a direction. This is precisely the meaning of the triplet "Holy, holy, holy" – above, and above, and above further still. The phrase indicates a continuous, never-ending direction. God is above everything, and specifically there is where His absolute holiness is found.

Yet – His glory fills the entire world. Glory ("*kavod*," honor), as we saw in the previous chapter, refers to God's presence in the world, to that which is reflected by those who honor Him. God is wholly other and transcendent, yet His glory fills the world and rests upon the *minyan* of the community of Israel who sanctify Him.

The custom is to rise up on one's toes when reciting the words "Holy, holy, holy." According to the *Midrash Tanchuma* (*Parashat Tzav*), the source for this is the verse "With two [wings] he [the angel] would fly" (*Yeshayahu* 6:2). One who recites *Kedusha* is imitating an angel. But notice in which specific aspect we imitate the angels – by attaching wings to our feet. When we recite the *Kedusha*, and specifically when we recite "Holy, holy, holy," we try to detach ourselves from the ground, and fly – to stretch heavenward. "Truth shall grow from earth" – in order to recite *Kedusha*, you have to reach, yearningly, for the stars.

II. *Barukh kevod*: Blessed be the glory of God from His place

On Shabbat, the *chazan* appends an introductory line to the different verses of the *Kedusha*. Before the verse "Blessed," we find the following introduction:

> His glory fills the world,
> His servants ask each other,
> "Where is the place of His glory?"
> They say to each other, "Blessed."

This question, "Where is the place of His glory?" is based on the Gemara in *Chagiga* (13b): "Blessed be the glory of God from His place – from here we learn that no one knows where His place is." The Gemara understands that "Blessed be the glory of God from His place" means that the place of His glory is His place, the place of God, and no one else has a part in it. Therefore, even the angels ask, in wonder and ignorance, where is the place of His glory, and they cannot point to it. The glory of God is from His place, His private realm that is hidden from and transcends all else.

This declaration is the opposite of the previous verse. We said that His glory fills the entire earth, yet where is the place of His glory? From where does it derive, what is the basis, the root, the home of that glory? It fills the world, but what is its source, where does God's glory belong? The answer – from His place, a place so transcendent that even the lofty angels are not familiar with it. The glory of God which fills the whole world, created by the free acts of human beings, their strivings and their yearnings, is nonetheless the glory of God, the reflection of absolute perfection. The blessing ("Blessed") is in this world, but it is *from* the other world, the world where God is exalted alone, with the sanctity of "Holy, holy, holy." We must not forget, even for one moment, that God's glory which we magnify and sanctify is rooted in an existence wholly outside of us and which transcends us. We exalt and recite "Blessed," and bless the glory of God – but it must be from His place, from the place of God alone.

The transcendent holiness of God ("Holy, holy, holy") is reflected in His glory which fills the whole world, and this immanent glory is rooted in a place so high and transcendent, that only God knows it. The circle revolves from pole to pole and back again. In the *Kedusha,* man is required to hold on to the two ends of this equation, as diametrically opposed from one another as heaven and earth. Only then can man truly crown God as King over the world – the ultimate meaning of *kedusha.*[1] In order to simultaneously hold on to these two almost contradictory extremes, we come full circle, from top to bottom and back up again, beyond all limits.

1. Remember the words of R. Yona which I cited in the previous chapter: "There is no greater *davar shebikedusha* than the acceptance of the yoke of heavenly kingship."

III. *Yimlokh*: HaShem shall rule forever, your God, Zion, for generation upon generation, Praise God!

This is not a descriptive statement of fact, but a proclamation. In crowning the king, the people cry out, "Long live the king!" (*Shmuel Alef* 10:24; *Melakhim Alef* 1:25; ibid. 1:39; et al.). We are actually coronating God, and this is the *Kedusha*, the formation of a chariot for God's presence in this world.

The proclamation has two parts. "HaShem shall rule forever" is a general statement – God is King, and King forever. The second part, "Your God, Zion, for generation upon generation," is a particular statement about the Jewish people. God's rule over Zion is God's rule over Israel, in the royal capital, Jerusalem. When the Jewish people declare God as King in Zion, this has immediate religious-political significance. We are no longer talking universal theology here, but politics, genuine Jewish politics – God is our King.

Since this proclamation has immediate significance, and is not merely declaratory but actively effective, there is an immediate change in the actual presence of God's kingship in our midst. We have succeeded in increasing the holiness and the kingship of God. Our experiencing this new reality engenders in us an exclamation of praise in response – *Halleluya*, praise God! This last word of the *Kedusha* is our response to the reality created by the previous words of this verse, for the previous words truly succeeded in effecting a new reality. A King has been crowned in Zion, now, at this moment – praise God!

This verse, unlike the first two, is not a quote from a prophetic vision. It was not recited previously by the angels and revealed to us in prophecy. In fact, in two other recitations of the *Kedusha*, which according to the accepted opinion in halakha are not our active *Kedushot* but rather a description of the angels' *Kedusha* (the *Kedusha* of "*Yotzer*" recited before *Shema* and the *Kedusha DeSidra* in "*UVa LeTziyon*"), this verse is not found. One should note that there is a different verse there – "*HaShem yimlokh le'olam va'ed*," "God shall rule forever."[2] This substitution in place of "HaShem shall rule forever, your God, Zion,

2. In *UVa LeTziyon* it appears immediately after the prophetic verses, whereas in the blessings of *Keriat Shema* it appears only after *Keriat Shema*.

for generation upon generation" is, in my opinion, the best proof for the claim that these *Kedushot* are not actual creations of sanctity but only declarations that the process exists. We, the people of God, have the ability to declare "Your God, Zion, for generation upon generation," and thereby actually crown God. The angels do not have the ability to actually crown. The angels simply state, as a matter of fact, that God shall rule forever. *We* are the ones with the right and the obligation to actually crown God, and therefore there cannot be any source in the heavens for us to copy. It is not in heaven – this kingship does not exist at all without our actions. Therefore, this line we had to discover on our own. It is not taken from a book of prophecy, but rather from a book of personal inspiration, from *Tehillim*, the psalms of King David of Israel.[3]

3. *KETER*: A CROWN

The opening introductions to the weekday *Kedusha*, and at Shacharit on Shabbat and in the Ashkenazic tradition at *Musaf* as well, are all according to the format described above. We recite the *Kedusha* in this world, just as (i.e., with the same formulation and content as) the angels recite it in the heavenly realms. However, at *Musaf* in the Sephardic tradition, there is a different introduction, essentially distinct from the usual formulation.

---

3. The *Divrei Chamudot* (*Berakhot* 2:23) innovated the ruling that the permission granted to answer the *Kedusha* at a point in prayer where one is only allowed to interrupt "out of honor and fear" is limited to the first two verses alone, which are based on a prophetic vision of the angels' *Kedusha*. "*Yimlokh*," "HaShem shall rule forever," is not based on a prophetic vision, and therefore one may not interrupt at a point where only limited interruptions are allowed. His assumption is that "*Yimlokh*" is not really a part of the *Kedusha*. This ruling was adopted in the *Mishna Berura* (66:17) as well. From the simple understanding of the words of the *Rishonim* who did not differentiate, despite the general term "*Kedusha*" clearly implying all three verses, it seems that the verse "*Yimlokh*" is also included in the *Kedusha* and it is permitted to recite it at points where one is allowed to interrupt "out of honor and out of fear." According to my explanation of the essence of the *Kedusha*, and especially in light of R. Yona's statement regarding the centrality of accepting the yoke of heavenly kingship to the concept of *davar shebikedusha*, it seems to me that "*Yimlokh*" is the most important part of the *Kedusha*, and one should be particular in reciting it even more than the verses recited by the angels.

> *Keter…*
> A crown will be given to You, HaShem our God
> By the angelic host above with Your people Israel gathered below,
> Together all of them will present You with *Kedusha.*

There are two unique changes here. The first is that we are declaring from the start that the purpose of the *Kedusha* is kingship, presenting a crown. The connection between *kedusha* and kingship is not surprising, as we know from the conclusion of the *Kedusha,* and as we saw in the words of R. Yona. However, we usually only reveal God's kingship once we have already emphasized the cyclical journey from God's transcendent holiness to the world being filled with His glory and then back to His place, whereas here we are, from the very outset, explicitly defining our act as one of coronation, of presenting a crown.

The second point – and this is significantly unique – is that here we are not imitating the angels but joining them. Not "Just like the angels sanctify Him in heaven," but "Together all of them will present You with *Kedusha.*" The crown is presented not only by us, in accordance with what I explained that we alone, and not the angels, are able to crown and coronate, but rather by "the angelic host above with Your people Israel gathered below."

The Gemara in *Chullin* that I quoted above, stating that Israel's *Kedusha* comes before the angels' *Kedusha,* presents an additional difference between the two *Kedushot*:

> Israel are adored by the Holy One, blessed be He,
> more than the ministering angels,
> For Israel recite song at all times,
> whereas the ministering angels only recite song once a day.
> And some say once a week,
> And some say once a month,
> And some say once a year,
> And some say once a Sabbatical cycle,
> And some say once a Jubilee cycle,
> And some say once ever.

I do not believe that there is any other place in the Gemara where there exists such a list of "and some says" appearing one after the other. Clearly, this is not a real dispute between different opinions of anonymous *Tanna'im*, but a process; as it were, whenever the *Tanna* tries to state that the angels can only recite *Kedusha* at rare intervals, immediately there arises a claim that the interval must be rarer and rarer, until reaching once ever. It is clear that the principle here is what I explained above – that the true *Kedusha* does not belong to the angels, yet it seems that the Sages retain the tradition that, nonetheless, the angels will eventually recite this praise. At the very end of the universe, there will be some sort of ultimate union of the worlds, truth will grow from the earth and will reach the heavens, will join together the worlds with God's kingship, and the purpose of creation will be fulfilled. The *Kedusha* of "*Keter*" is referring to the ultimate kingship, when "on that day God will be One and His name One." This is only possible when, in some sense, the division between the upper and lower worlds will be closed, and all of God's creatures will join together to crown Him King. The closing of that circle and its unification – "together all of them will present You with *Kedusha*" – is the ultimate kingship.

Perhaps Shabbat, an imitation of the World to Come, is the time when we taste this potential. At the *Musaf* prayer, a prayer which represents the special Shabbat sacrifice, we allow ourselves to look forward to the possibility that our *Kedusha* will be so effective that it will bring us to unification with the "perfect" *Kedusha* recited in the heavens.

Thus far we have dealt with the formulation of the *Kedusha*. We are yet to examine the actual blessing in which the *Kedusha* is embedded: the third blessing of the *Shemoneh Esrei*, the blessing of *Kedusha*, holiness.

Chapter 8

Ata Kadosh: You Are Holy

אַתָּה קָדוֹשׁ וְשִׁמְךָ קָדוֹשׁ
וּקְדוֹשִׁים בְּכָל יוֹם יְהַלְלוּךָ סֶּלָה.
בָּרוּךְ אַתָּה יהוה, הָאֵל הַקָּדוֹשׁ.

You are holy and Your name is holy,
And holy ones praise You daily, *sela*!
Blessed are You, Lord, the holy God.

After dedicating two chapters to the *Kedusha* – a general introduction to the concept of holiness and a discussion regarding the recital of *Kedusha* in the repetition of the *Amida* – we return to the third blessing of the *Amida* itself: *Ata Kadosh,* You are holy.

The explanation of the first line, with its two components, follows easily from the principles discussed in the previous chapters. "You are holy" – God is intrinsically holy, in and of Himself. "And Your name is holy" – Your name on our lips and Your presence on earth are also holy. God's holiness is reflected within the imperfect yet evolving world of man, and this reflection is holy as well.

The line which requires special attention here is the second one: "And holy ones praise You daily, *sela.*" Firstly, who are the "holy ones"? Moreover, if the theme of the blessing is the holiness of God, why is the holy ones' praise relevant, and what is the connection between the praise of God and His holiness?

1. HOLINESS AND MIRACLE

In his book *Peirush HaTefillot VeHaBerakhot*, R. Yehuda b. R. Yakar[1] explains this line by reference to a midrash about the splitting of the Sea of Reeds.

> "Holy ones praise You, *sela*." This language refers to the *Mekhilta*: "R. Meir says: If for Adam the first man, who was alone, I made dry land, as is written, 'God said, let the waters gather'" – *Explanation: Just as I am alone and One, so man was alone and one* – "For the holy congregation shall I not turn the sea into dry land!?" – *Explanation: Since I am holy*. This must be the proper interpretation of the *Mekhilta*, for if the explanation were that they are many and Adam only one, it should simply have said "If for the lone man I perform this act, shall I not do so for the many?" Why were they called "the holy congregation"? Rather, it must be as I have explained. Therefore, we pray and say: Just as He did miracles for us since we are called "holy" as He is, so too we should praise Him since we are called "holy" as He is. (*Peirush HaTefillot*, 43)

This enigmatic explanation raises more questions than it seems to solve. R. Yehuda b. R. Yakar explains the performance of miracles for Israel as a function of their being called holy as God is. This connection is reciprocal, for just as God acts for the sake of His holy ones, so too we praise God for that very reason, namely our being called holy as He is. R. Yehuda b. R. Yakar has clearly extracted from this midrash an answer to our first question – the "holy ones" are Israel.[2] However, what is the connection between holiness and miracle? What is the connection between holiness and prayer? Finally, what is the meaning of the equative "just as" clause which, in his words, means: Just as God performed miracles for the sake of the holy ones, so too the holy ones should praise God?

---

1. R. Yehuda b. R. Yakar was Ramban's teacher. He authored one of the first books dedicated to the explanation of prayer.
2. And not the angels, as other commentators explain.

2. HOLINESS AND NATURE

In the previous chapters we explained that *kedusha*, holiness, is an attribute which, by its very essence, is otherworldly. Holiness is the attribute of perfection and necessarily transcends the world. Holiness in and of itself is above and beyond this defective, lacking, and imperfect world. Holiness *in the world* is a result of man's ability to transcend himself and embark upon a process of perfection and completeness. Holiness exists when man aspires to be more than he is, to transcend his natural state. Nature is a system of laws at whose source lies the law of conservation – the whole is equal to the sum of its parts. No natural object in this world can transcend itself. But man, the image of God (as we explained in chapter 2), is defined as one who aspires to be like God, to strive upward, and to transcend himself. This is the essence of holiness – holiness which is the transcendence of God above the world on the one hand and, on the other hand, the transcendence of man above himself, his nature, and the entire natural world. With holiness, the whole produced is more than the sum of its parts.

This is precisely what a miracle is. When there is a breach in the law of causation in the world, and something is created without natural causes, we view it as the revelation of God's power. If the law of causation were absolute, there would be no such thing as a miracle nor would there be holiness. Holiness is to the world of values as miracles are to the world of action. Therefore, the midrash explains, according to R. Yehuda b. R. Yakar, that there exists a direct connection between the increase in holiness, namely, the increase in the Divine presence in nature as a result of man's actions, and the phenomenon of miracles, the presence of God's power, acting freely beyond the confines of natural cause and effect.

This point must be understood on two levels. Firstly, the fundamental holiness of the "holy ones" constitutes a reality of God's presence. The holiness of man, that is, holiness by way of man, is really the holiness of the Divine presence, as we emphasized in the previous chapters. Therefore, it is to be expected that an increase in the Divine presence will also result in an intensification of God's power, as Moshe requested after the sin of the spies: "And now, may the power of God intensify, as You have spoken" (*Bemidbar* 14:17). Secondly, as I have explained, there exists a parallel between the profound concept of human holiness, as a transcendence over one's own nature, and the phenomenon of the miraculous, as a Divine triumph over nature. When the law of holiness functions, the law of nature subsides and, thus, there can be an actuality of miracle.

3. HOLINESS AND PRAISE

The second part of the equation is now equally clear, as it is expressed in our blessing. Since we are called holy like God, we should praise Him who is the "holy God." Praise and blessing, as we have seen, are themselves acts of sanctification. The "holy ones" praise God daily, for this is an expression of their holiness. They are not holy by virtue of their righteousness, exceptionality, or asceticism in comparison to their fellows, but rather by virtue of their carrying God's name in the world and being the ones who bless Him. Holy ones pray to God every day, therefore there is holiness in the world, and therefore they are holy. Since He is described in terms of holiness, and they align themselves to Him, then they too are described in terms of holiness. Should they cease to praise Him, their holiness would disappear.

Therefore, the blessing concludes, "Blessed are You, the holy God." This is a realization of what we have described – the holy ones praise and declare, "Blessed are You, the holy God." A circular relationship is formed – and, as we saw in the explanation of the *Kedusha* in the *chazan*'s repetition of the *Amida*, holiness is always circular: the holy ones praise the Holy One, therefore they are holy, and therefore they praise the Holy One. The theme of this blessing is indeed the holiness of God – but the holiness of God *in the world* is the holiness of God in the mouths of those who praise Him, who are holy, that is to say bearers of holiness, because they bear the name of God on their lips. The imminent holiness of God is the same as – and dependent upon – the reality of "and holy ones praise You daily, *sela*."

4. MIRACLE AND PRAISE

R. Yehuda b. R. Yakar claimed that the holy ones' praise of the Holy One is based on the "just as" clause, namely, on the performance of miracles by the Holy One for the sake of holy ones.

It seems to me that he is addressing here specifically the verb "*hallel*," praise ("they shall praise You"). Halakha ties the obligation of *hallel* to miracle, as is explained in the Gemara in *Pesachim* 117a, referring to the Song of the Sea, recited after the splitting of the sea:

> Who initially recited this *hallel*?... The prophets among them instituted that Israel should recite it on every appropriate occasion, and for every suffering, may it not come upon Israel, that when they are redeemed, they recite it over their redemption.

In contrast to the praise of *shevach*, the praise of *hallel* is a reaction to something exceptional that has befallen us, which we have personally experienced. In the blessing of thanks at the end of the *Shemoneh Esrei*, we recite, "We thank You and recite *tehillatekha*, Your praise ... for Your miracles which are with us each day, and for Your wonders ... at all times." In contrast, until now in the first three blessings, the theme is general *shevach* of God's eternity, without any exceptional current experience. *Shevach* to the mighty God who is abundant in salvation is always relevant, whereas *hallel* requires a current experience of the hand and power of God.

According to R. Yehuda b. R. Yakar, the foundation of the recital of *hallel* is rooted in the fact that through holiness one feels the power of miracle. Since we are holy and sanctifiers, we transcend our own nature and bring down holiness into the world, we experience the power of miracle, the transcendence over the natural forces which is buried deep in the presence of God. Two people stand side by side: The first, holy and sanctifier, rising and sanctified, therefore sees before him the miracle and is able to give *hallel*-praise. The second, unsanctified, a natural being, is chained to natural forces and to his own nature, and therefore sees before him only a world organized and run by the laws of creation. He sees not the power of God – and rightly so, for the power of God is missing from before him. The former gives *hallel*-praise, and through this praise he sanctifies even more, whereas the latter is silent.

It is regarding this that it says, "And You are holy, enthroned upon the praises of Israel." God's holiness rides upon the praises of Israel.

5. *ME'EIN CHATIMA*

In the Sephardic tradition, there is a third line, after "And holy ones praise You daily, *sela*." Before the conclusion, they recite, "For You are a great and holy God and King."

This is a classic *me'ein chatima*. In most of the blessings of the *Shemoneh Esrei*, before the *chatima*, there appears a line in the form of "For You are Master of a quality about which I am blessing," such as "For You are a Pardoner and a Forgiver," "For You are a strong Redeemer," and finally, "For you are a Hearer of prayer." In the Ashkenazic tradition, however, this line is absent, and it appears that the *me'ein chatima* is missing, for the previous line, "And holy ones praise You daily, *sela*," lacks any explicit reference to God's holiness. This omission must be addressed.

According to our explanation, however, the answer is clear. The statement that holy ones praise God is, in fact, the *me'ein chatima*, and there is no more fitting *me'ein chatima* than this. "And holy ones praise you daily, *sela*" does not refer to the holiness of Israel, but rather the holiness of God, the very same holiness that the holy ones create with their praise. The theme of the blessing is not the absolute, transcendent holiness of God, but rather holiness which aspires for perfection, that of "*Naaritzekha venakdishekha*," or, more precisely, the unification of both *Kedushot*. There is no need, therefore, for a more explicit *me'ein chatima*.[3]

6. *LEDOR VADOR*: FOR GENERATION UPON GENERATION

There is an additional version of this blessing. In the Ashkenazic tradition it is recited every day in the *chazan*'s repetition, and in the Sephardic tradition it is reserved for the repetition of *Musaf* on Shabbat.

---

3. The question of the additional line was already addressed in the *Rishonim* and is not originally related to Sepharad or Ashkenaz. Abudraham, the Spanish sage, cites this formulation, but he nonetheless notes that the masses do not recite it. Similarly, R. Yehuda b. R. Yakar cites the additional line as the French tradition. On the other hand, it is written in the *Tur* and the *Zohar Chadash* (*Parashat Teruma*) that the blessing of *Ata Kadosh* contains fourteen words, which works if we count the words of the blessing without the additional line.

For generation upon generation we shall recite Your greatness,
And for all eternity Your holiness we shall sanctify,
And Your praise, our God, shall never ever leave our lips.
For You are a great and holy God and King.

Despite the numerous changes throughout the whole text, the general theme is similar and analogous to the one we have already discussed. The centrality of the worshipper's role as the basis for the concept of holiness is emphasized even more. There is, however, one striking theme not found in the regular version of the blessing, which repeats itself throughout the blessing. Three times this blessing emphasizes the *eternal nature* of praise: "*Ledor vador*," for generation upon generation; "*ulnetzach netzachim*," and for all eternity; and "*le'olam va'ed*," forevermore. This seems to be the main point of the blessing in this version, and its repetition and the placing of expressions of eternity at the head of each line emphasizes this theme even further.

If we understand the thesis that I have been advancing in an exclusive manner, namely, that the *only* basis for holiness and the existence of God's presence in the world is the act of man's sanctification of God, then the affirmation of the eternal constancy of the sanctification of God becomes palpable and crucial. As mentioned, the blessing is not about praise or the obligation of man to praise his Creator; rather, it is about holiness and the redemption of the world from secularity. This holiness is dependent upon praise of God. If, however, the world would have no sanctity, if it would not reflect the holiness of God, if there were no place in the world for God's majesty at all, then how could it exist? Clearly "there is none other than He," and nothing can exist outside of God's presence. This being the case, it is not only the world's holiness that is dependent upon the deeds of man, but also its very existence. Hence, we declare and pledge our commitment (rather than merely describe, as is the case in the regular version) that this process of praise and sanctification shall be constant, for all generations. If the blessing were referring to the obligation of praise, then it may be fitting that this obligation be discharged once a day, or once a week (or once a month, year, Sabbatical cycle, or Jubilee cycle – as the Gemara suggested regarding the praise sung by the angels), when one is not fulfilling other important duties. But if we are discussing the only basis for sanctity in the world, then not even for one second can one imagine a world which is devoid of the praise and sanctity of God. We are not responding to the kingship of God; we are affirming it. The onus for the presence of God in this world rests upon our shoulders; hence it "shall never ever leave our lips."

There is a fine paradox in this affirmation. If there is one quality that we should most fear to attribute to man most, other than holiness itself, it is constancy. As Coleridge stated, "Constancy lives in realms above." *Netzach,* eternity, is seemingly not an attribute that we should dare attribute to man! The explanation for this lies in the relationship between these two qualities. If holiness is attributed to man, then eternity must be too, for holiness allows no compromise. If we do not aspire to establish and affirm a reign that is eternal, then we do not aspire for transcendence, and there is therefore no sanctity at all. Either you reflect the holiness of God, transcendent and Divine, eternally King, or you reflect no more than yourself, devoid of growth, without transcendence, deprived of unlimited striving, and without *kedusha.* Therefore, *ledor vador,* for generation upon generation!

7. *HAMELEKH HAKADOSH*: THE HOLY KING

In the Ten Days of Repentance, God sits on His royal throne. In order to express the unique connection between these days and God's kingship, we change the *chatima* of two blessings in the *Shemoneh Esrei.* One blessing is *Birkat HaMishpat,* the blessing of judgment – "A King who loves righteousness and judgment" becomes "The King of judgment." This change is understandable: the Ten Days of Repentance are days of verdict and judgment. On these days, God's kingship is revealed in His judgment.

The second blessing is *Birkat HaKedusha,* the blessing of holiness – "The holy God" becomes "The holy King." In this case, the change is surprising: Why is the blessing of holiness different from all the other blessings in the *Shemoneh Esrei*? Why should the blessing of holiness be changed in the days of kingship? What is the connection between holiness and kingship?

The answer is clear. The kingship of Rosh HaShana is one in which we coronate God and accept His kingship upon ourselves. The shofar is a declaration of God's kingship, and we bestow upon Him the royal crown. This is, as we have defined it, the whole principle of *kedusha,* holiness: Man generates God's kingship and presence in the world. God as King within the world is *haMelekh hakadosh,* the holy King. *Malkhut* and *kedusha,* kingship and holiness, are two sides of the same coin.

Chapter 9

Daat: Knowledge

אַתָּה חוֹנֵן לְאָדָם דַּעַת
וּמְלַמֵּד לֶאֱנוֹשׁ בִּינָה.
חָנֵּנוּ מֵאִתְּךָ דֵּעָה בִּינָה וְהַשְׂכֵּל.
בָּרוּךְ אַתָּה יהוה, חוֹנֵן הַדָּעַת.

You grant man knowledge
and teach mortals understanding.
Grant us from Yourself knowledge,
understanding, and perception.
Blessed are You, Lord, who grants knowledge.

The first three blessings of the *Shemoneh Esrei* are defined as blessings of praise.[1] The concluding three are defined as blessings of thanks.[2] The middle blessings are the *Bakashot*, blessings of request. Each blessing expresses and hence defines a human need. According to the Sages' formulation of the *Shemoneh Esrei*, the first need is knowledge. One could explain the precedence of knowledge in terms of logical order in requesting one's needs, as the *Yerushalmi* states, "If there is no understanding, there is no prayer" (*Berakhot* 5:2). However, it seems more compelling to view the placement of knowledge as the first request as an expression of the importance of knowledge among the needs of man,

1. *Berakhot* 34a, Rambam *Hilkhot Tefilla* 1:4.
2. Rambam, ibid.

as his foremost important need, as declared in the Gemara (*Nedarim* 41a), "In the west they say: One who has this [knowledge] in him, has everything in him. One who does not have this in him, what is in him?"

1. *CHANINA*

The blessing opens with an affirmation of praise, "You grant (*chonen*) man knowledge." The root "*chonen*," to grant, repeats itself in the main body of the request, "Grant us (*chonenu*) from Yourself knowledge, understanding, and perception," and also in the *chatima*, "Who grants (*chonen*) knowledge." Clearly, according to the Sages, this is the fitting verb for knowledge. The phraseology of the blessings is taken from the language in the Tanakh. *Chanina*, to grant something, and especially to be granted something by God, is a common verb in the Tanakh. However, not once in the whole of the Tanakh does *chanina* appear in the context of knowledge.

The *Rishonim* (R. Yehuda b. R. Yakar and Abudraham) found a source for the first line of our blessing in the verse "He who teaches man knowledge" (*Tehillim* 94:10). There is no doubt that this is indeed the source; the verse is similar to the blessing, including the use of the word "man" (which is not to be taken for granted in Jewish prayer). This source highlights the Sages' deliberate decision to change the verb from "teaches" to "grants."[3] Substituting the verb from the source verse would, in any event, require explanation; but substituting it for a verb which has no connection to knowledge anywhere in the entire Tanakh is most astonishing. What is the motive for this substitution? To broaden the question – what is the true meaning of the verb "*chonen*," to grant?

Typically, the verb "*chonen*" appears in the Tanakh not only without the object "knowledge," but without any object at all. The most notable example appears in the priestly blessing – "May God shine His face upon you, and *yechuneka* [often rendered as "be gracious to you"]" (*Bemidbar* 6:25). The vast majority of this verb's other appearances follow suit.[4] Why did the Sages attach this general verb to

3. Note that "teaches" appears in the second line: "And teach mortals understanding."
4. E.g., *Bereshit* 43:29, *Tehillim* 4:2, and many more.

a specific object in their coining of the phrase "*Chonen hadaat*," "Who grants knowledge"?

The key, in my opinion, lies in an additional phrase in this blessing, which is also unique and does not appear in any other blessing. The request for knowledge from God is formulated thus: "Grant us *from Yourself* (*me'itekha*) knowledge, understanding, and perception." In what sense is knowledge granted "from Yourself," from God's self? We do not find that we request health from His self, or wealth from His self, nor even forgiveness from His self. Only knowledge, understanding, and perception are from God's self.

The formulation of this blessing is affirming that knowledge is different from all other things that we ask of God. God *creates* health and wealth, salvation and redemption, in order to give them to us. These are entities that are created, and are vital to the survival of mankind. Knowledge is not created, but shared. God shares with us knowledge, His knowledge. Knowledge is a Divine trait, a supreme attribute of God. Knowledge is, in the words of the prayer, "from Yourself," from God's own self.

This is, I think, the explanation for the use of the verb *chonen* in the request for knowledge. Consider the meaning of the verb in the priestly blessing, "May God shine His face upon you, and *yechuneka*." It seems that, just as in the case of "shine upon you" the aim is not the gain of a specific object, but rather a state of radiance upon us, the blessed direct contact with God, so too with "*yechuneka*," the *chanina* from God is the radiance of shining His face upon us, the opening up of Himself to us. It does not signify an object being given, but rather a *relationship*, a relationship of love and intimacy. There will be of course a result from this *chanina*, which is reflected in our lives. In what sense? Our blessing holds the answer – if there is *chanina*, it is reflected in "*de'ah bina vehaskel*," knowledge, understanding, and perception.

The *Midrash Rabba* on the priestly blessing (*Bemidbar Rabba* 11:6) asks: In what way are we granted (*chanunim*)? This is not a question about God and what He grants, for *chanina* has no object. "*Chonen*" is not a synonym of "*noten*," giving. Rather, the Midrash is asking about the recipient of the *chanina* – in what way are they *chanunim*, how is it expressed? The Midrash answers:

> From where do we know that they are granted (*chanunim*) even with knowledge and understanding?
>
> Because it is written "*viychuneka*," as we pray, "You grant man knowledge, and teach mortals understanding."

The Midrash asks from where we know that they are granted knowledge, and answers: from the verse "*viychuneka*." Obviously one who does not already know that *chanina* includes knowledge will not find a hint in this verse to knowledge. This, I believe, is exactly the point – it says "*viychuneka*," without any additional object; therefore, *chanina* is the actuality of the shining of God's face, of being illuminated with God's radiance. It was obvious to the Sages that God's light is knowledge, understanding, and perception.

The Midrash brings a proof for its supposition from the *Shemoneh Esrei*. It is unusual, to say the least, to find such a case, where the proof for a Biblical interpretation is brought from the text of Rabbinic prayer. The reason for doing so here is that knowledge does not mean the act of *chanina*. The definition of *chanina* does not include an object. It is the result of *chanina* as experienced by man, of being a partner in the Divine actuality itself, of being illuminated by it, of experiencing its blessing. The answer is not found in a linguistic check of Biblical language but in our own lives, in the human experience. For such an idea, prayer, the spiritual experience of the Jewish people, constitutes a valid source. We pray, "You grant man – knowledge."

Hence, *chanina* is "from Yourself," from within Yourself. We are not asking for something as a gift, we are not requesting a precious object, but rather that God should grant us a measure of Himself, literally share with us a Divine value, knowledge. Beyond the content of this grant – that we should have knowledge – we are seeking the experience from which knowledge emanates – and this is the root of all religious experience, cleaving unto God (*deveikut*). Knowledge is a need of man, even on the simply daily level, but beyond this at its very root exists the ultimate religious experience, cleaving unto God Himself. This *deveikut*, the *chanina* "from Yourself," results in knowledge and wisdom.

The reason for this is the deep-rooted Jewish belief that true human wisdom is the wisdom of God. Sometimes we hear the seemingly modest claim that man's intellect is respectable but merely human, pragmatically useful but not Truth. As part of the natural world, man is not a partner to the supernatural truth, and cannot grasp the transcendent. Judaism rejects such "intellectual self-effacement." It teaches that man can be a partner in the Divine wisdom, and that no other wisdom exists. Rambam famously identifies the "image of God" with the intellect.[5] Man's intellect is not a creation of God, like the other elements of the heavens and earth, but rather the image of God, and in the use of which man partakes in the Divine knowledge.

Even Ramban, who disagrees with Rambam in terms of the value of intellect in the religious life of man, agrees that wisdom is participation in God's wisdom. The Gemara states:

> Since the day that the Temple was destroyed, prophecy has been taken away from the prophets and given to the Sages. Is a Sage not a prophet? This is what we mean: Even though it was taken away from the prophets, it was not taken away from the Sages. (*Bava Batra* 12a)

The difficulty is clear – if the Sages are prophets, what does it mean that prophecy was taken away from the prophets? Rashi explains that prophecy was taken away from the prophets who were not Sages but remained with the prophets who are also Sages. Ramban asks: Can there be such a concept, a prophet who is not a Sage? Surely "the Divine presence only rests on one who is wise, mighty, and wealthy." Ramban answers that there are two types of prophecy:

> Even though the prophecy of the prophets was taken away, which is through vision and foresight, the prophecy of the Sages, which is through wisdom, was not taken away; rather, they know the truth through the holy spirit that dwells within them. (Ramban, *Bava Batra* 12a, s.v. *ha*)

5. In the previous chapters I presented a different explanation for the image of God, but this does not detract from the current point.

Wisdom is itself a type of prophecy, the action of the holy spirit residing within the Sage, and it was not taken away even after the destruction of the Temple. Wisdom is not a neural synapse in the brain, but the immanence of the holy spirit, God's presence, upon man. This is the *chanina* granted from His self, God's radiance.

A succinct expression for this concept, that wisdom is not just from God but from within God, and that this is the intent in our blessing, is found in the Midrash:

> The upper beings saw that the Holy One, blessed be He, had passed the Tetragrammaton to Moshe, and recited, "Blessed are You, God, who grants knowledge (*chonen hadaat*)." (*Pirkei DeRabbi Eliezer* 47)

To pass over the Tetragrammaton is to pass over a part of God's essence, for His name, and especially the explicit Tetragrammaton, symbolizes the essence of that which it relates to. Specifically the passing over of the Tetragrammaton led the angels to the blessing of *Chonen Hadaat.* The notion that mere mortals can attain the wisdom of God itself, and that it functions within them, is a novel idea for the angels.

2. THE INTERNAL ORDER OF THE BLESSING

This blessing is formulated in reverse, compared to the other blessings of request in the *Shemoneh Esrei.*

The other blessings open with a request and conclude with words of praise. These words of praise function as a *me'ein chatima* summation adjoined to the blessing's conclusion, and typically adopt the formulation "For You are Master of that which I am requesting."[6] The blessing of knowledge reverses the order – opening with praise, (that) "You grant man knowledge," and only afterward turning to request, "Grant us from Yourself knowledge." What is the explanation for this reversal?

One might claim that this is merely stylistic enhancement, resulting from the placement of this blessing – the first in the order of requests.

6. Sometimes the *me'ein chatima* is assimilated into the request itself, for example, "And return us in perfect repentance before You."

The blessing of knowledge is an opening to the middle section, and it seems more polished to begin with a statement of praise, and only afterward mention the egotistic request. This may certainly be true. However, in light of what we have just explained, I think there is another explanation. In all the other requests, we ask God to provide what we lack. There is no question of our ability to receive if God chooses to give. If God decides to grant our request for health, then of course we shall be healthy. If He gathers us from the four corners of the earth, then our feet will undoubtedly be placed at the gates of Jerusalem. But in the case of knowledge, it is not that simple, for knowledge is not a created gift, but is God's wisdom itself. The idea that we can have supreme knowledge is presumptuous. How can mere mortal man, finite and limited, share in the infinite, transcendent wisdom of God? "For the heavens are raised high above the earth, so are My ways raised high above your ways, and My thoughts above your thoughts!" (*Yeshayahu* 55:9). Hence, before such an audacious request, we must first state – and indeed convince ourselves – that it is indeed possible and appropriate, for we know that "You grant man knowledge, and teach mortals understanding." In this case, the praise is not the reason why we want God to grant the need in question (as is the purpose of the praise in the other requests), but rather is the basis and sine qua non for the possibility of its provision. Without this statement, the request is absurd!

This question – the reversal of the order of praise and request in the blessing of knowledge – also appears in a fascinating note of the *Bach* on the *Tur*. The *Tur* (115) cites the Gemara's question (*Megilla* 17b), "Why did they see fit to recite [the blessing of] wisdom after [the blessing of] holiness?" The *Bach* asks, surely the requests come after the three blessings of praise, and therefore it is obvious why wisdom, the first of the requests, should come after holiness, the last of the blessings of praise. On the other hand, the question cannot be why wisdom is the first of the requests, for this has a different answer ("If there is no understanding, there is no prayer"). The *Bach* answers that the Gemara's question refers to the opening of the blessing of knowledge, which is not a request like the other middle blessings, but praise, "You grant man knowledge," similar to the opening of the previous blessing – "You are holy, and Your name is holy." The *Bach* claims that the reason for establishing this order was the desire to connect the blessing of knowledge to the previous blessing. "It wishes to say, since You are holy and Your name is holy, included in this is the fact that You grant man knowledge, as this emanates from that, and therefore I ask that You grant us from Yourself knowledge etc." In other words, the Gemara's question is: What is the source for the idea that wisdom emanates from holiness.

The *Bach*'s explanation as to the style of the blessing of knowledge, and its concatenation with the blessing of holiness, is understood in light of our explanation about the granting (*chanina*) of knowledge, and our explanation in the previous chapters about the concept of holiness. The holiness on which the third blessing is based is the reflection of God's transcendence in the actions of man; it is the presence of God which arises from the free act of one who was created in His image. It is therefore obvious why holiness leads to knowledge, for knowledge is the very wisdom of God.

It is now clear that knowledge and wisdom are "drawn" from holiness. If holiness runs through our veins, if God's presence rests upon us – not as something external, but as a reflection of absolute perfection within the process of perfecting – then the first expression of this should be understanding, the intellectual enlightenment of man. If God is not present *within* the world, then there is no understanding and man cannot grasp God's wisdom. If man himself is a chariot for the Divine presence, if he himself is holy ("And holy ones every day praise You, *sela*"), then he can share in the wisdom of God and be granted (*mechunan*) with knowledge, understanding, and perception.

The Gemara in *Megilla*'s answer to the question of the connection between the blessing of holiness and of knowledge refers to the adjoining of the verse "And they shall sanctify the Holy one of Yaakov, and the God of Israel they shall exalt" (*Yeshuyahu* 29:23) to the verse "And those who err in spirit will know wisdom" (ibid. 24). This is not merely a connection between holiness and wisdom, but a connection between the *act of sanctification* and the wisdom of those who err in spirit. Notice that it is not just the sanctification of God that is being addressed, but also the sanctification of "the Holy one of *Yaakov*" and "the God of *Israel*," transforming ourselves into the bearers of God's holiness, who is called the Holy one of Yaakov, that teaches mortals understanding.

3. *DE'AH BINA VEHASKEL*: KNOWLEDGE, UNDERSTANDING, AND PERCEPTION

In most explanatory books on prayer, the bulk of the commentary is devoted to explicating the various synonyms for wisdom in the blessing and the differences between them. They typically clarify the difference between "knowledge (*de'ah*), understanding (*bina*), and perception (*haskel*)" in the Ashkenazic tradition and "wisdom (*chokhma*), understanding (*bina*), and knowledge (*daat*)" in the Sephardic tradition. In Rambam's tradition, neither perception nor wisdom are omitted; the formulation is, "Grant us from Yourself knowledge (*de'ah*), understanding (*bina*), wisdom (*chokhma*), and perception (*haskel*)." There exists a more developed formulation, which I have not found in any *siddur*, yet appears in the *Sifrei* on the priestly blessing: "*Viychuneka*: With knowledge (*daat*), wisdom (*chokhma*), perception (*haskel*), morals (*musar*), and understanding (*bina*)." The starting point for understanding the specific implication of each of these expressions is the Mishna in *Pirkei Avot* (3:17).[7] There is, of course, special significance in the realm of mysticism for these names as well, each of which relates to a different *sefira* (heavenly realm). This task I leave for others to complete. For our purposes, I think it is appropriate to concentrate on "*daat*," knowledge, which is singled out in the *chatima* on its own – "*Chonen hadaat*," "Who grants knowledge." We typically think of *daat* as knowledge, as information. I think, though, that it does not so much refer to factual information as to grasping the essence of something. For example, the Sages regularly refer to "*yode'a et Kono*," which means one who "knows" his Creator. This does not mean that he has memorized a biography of God, but rather that he has a deep inner sense of awareness of God's presence. The most famous use of the word "*daat*" in this sense does not refer to intellectual knowledge at all – "And Adam knew (*yada*) Ḥava his wife." It is specifically in this sense that I claim that *daat* is "from Himself," from within God Himself. We want to transcend the superficial gathering of sensory information and get to the essence of things, to perceive them as God

7. See, especially, Rambam's commentary ad loc.

perceives them. True *daat* requires the vantage of God. A prayer for *daat* is a prayer that God Himself become part of our minds, that He grant us of Himself.

Now, having requested to be brought into the direct presence of God, we must immediately address the serious issue which opposes such a reality – sin.

Chapter 10

Teshuva: Repentance

הֲשִׁיבֵנוּ אָבִינוּ לְתוֹרָתֶךָ
וְקָרְבֵנוּ מַלְכֵּנוּ לַעֲבוֹדָתֶךָ
וְהַחֲזִירֵנוּ בִּתְשׁוּבָה שְׁלֵמָה לְפָנֶיךָ.
בָּרוּךְ אַתָּה יהוה, הָרוֹצֶה בִּתְשׁוּבָה.

Bring us back, our Father, to Your Torah.
Draw us near, our King, to Your service.
Lead us back in perfect repentance before You.
Blessed are You, Lord, who desires repentance.

The fifth blessing of the *Shemoneh Esrei* is the *Birkat HaTeshuva,* the blessing of repentance. The request for repentance raises a problem. What exactly are we asking for? Clearly, repentance is something which we must do ourselves if it is to have any meaning. If God performs the repentance for us, if He "leads us back in perfect repentance before Him," then this is not our repentance. Hence, what exactly are we requesting Him to do in this blessing?

The formulation of the blessing, at least in the *chatima,* reflect a sensitivity to this question. Every other request in the *Shemoneh Esrei* has a fixed *chatima* in the form of "Blessed are You, who performs that which we have requested." If I request healing, the *chatima* is "Who heals the sick of His people Israel." If I pray for the building of Jerusalem, the *chatima* is "Blessed… who builds Jerusalem." The blessing of repentance has a unique *chatima,* "Blessed… who *desires* (*harotzeh*) repentance."

The *chatima* does not establish what God does, but only His attitude toward the topic of the blessing. Following the usual formulation, the *chatima* should be "Blessed ... who leads us back in repentance," like the *me'ein chatima*; however, the Sages seemingly saw this as impossible and inappropriate. It is impossible to request of God that He perform the repentance for us. However, this only sharpens our question. What are we really asking of God in this blessing? And now that we have seen the unique formulation of this *chatima*, what is the connection between our request and God's will (*ratzon*)?

I would like to suggest four answers to this question. The answers do not contradict one another; on the contrary, they complement one another. In order to understand the blessing, we shall examine the concept of repentance, and we will present repentance as an idea composed of four layers. Of course, we will not succeed in exhausting the entirety of this important topic, to which whole books have been devoted. It is my hope that, at the very least, we will succeed in clarifying those aspects of the principle which are relevant to understanding the blessing in the *Shemoneh Esrei*.

1. REPAIRING A RELATIONSHIP

Normally, when one repents, he is hoping for forgiveness and atonement. But that is clearly not the focus of this blessing, for one very simple reason – it is the theme of the following blessing. Forgiveness is granted its own blessing. So, what is the intended result of the request in the current blessing?

Repentance is not merely an internal process of regret and reformation of character. Sin objectively destroys the relationship between us and God. This is true metaphysically – sin corrupts the image of God in which man was made – but even more so socially. Man's relationship with God is a personal one, and this relationship is damaged when man sins: "Your iniquities have separated between you and your God, and your sins have hidden His face from you, so He does not hear" (*Yeshayahu* 59:2). One who sins is, in Rambam's words, "separated from HaShem God of Israel ... he calls out but is not answered ... he performs good deeds, but they are torn away before him" (*Hilkhot Teshuva* 7:7). Moreover, he is "estranged before God, repulsive and cast away and an abomination" (ibid. 6). Therefore, the purpose of repentance is not that man should merely change his ways and reform himself, but that he should repair the relationship between himself and God as well, mending the tear between them. After repentance, man is "loved and pleasant, close and a friend" (ibid. 6), he "is joined to God's presence… he calls out and is answered immediately… he performs good deeds, and they are received with enjoyment and happiness" (ibid. 7). In this request in the *Amida*, we are not seeking help with an inner psychological process, but rather that God should bring us close, through repentance, to Him once more.

> Bring us back, our Father, *to Your Torah,*
> Draw us near, our King, *to Your service*

This phraseology is not a figurative way of saying bring us back to the path of Torah and mitzvot, but rather to literally bring us back to Your Torah, and to bring us close and accept us into Your service. In other words, take us back into service of You and count us among Your faithful servants once more. In Rambam's words, and to use the same verb as in our blessing, "Repentance *draws near* those who are distant" (ibid. 6).

That is seemingly the reason why in this blessing (and in the next blessing, of forgiveness) God is called by the title "our Father," which is found in no other blessing in the *Amida*. In the other requests, we are appealing to the all-powerful God, to the mighty King, who has the power to do great things. Here, however, I do not need power and I do not appeal to the King. I appeal to our Father and request that He take me back. When, in the continuation of the blessing, we address God with the title "King," this does not mean the King who commands a certain act, but the King who takes man back into His service.

Since the relationship is personal, it is not automatically repaired by our deciding to repent. The relationship depends on both sides. Actually, it depends mostly on God's side, for it is a relationship of holiness which is based on man's being in the image of God, a "chariot for His presence," and a basis for His holiness. We are requesting to be admitted into the holy community[1] and to have the impurities in our hearts replaced by the presence of God.

Therefore, we do not refer to God who "does something," but to God who desires repentance. The key to reacceptance into His service depends directly on God's will and not on His might. If He wishes it, I will be reaccepted, without need for further action. Given that the request here is to accept our repentance, we conclude the blessing with "Who desires repentance," which is the precise source for the possibility of the fulfillment of our request. God desires our repentance, namely, He desires *us*, ourselves, when we repent, and He is satisfied with us and with our repentance. Therefore, we are able to pray that this should indeed come to pass, and our actual act of repentance results from our free will.

2. THE WORLD OF ACTION AND THE WORLD OF WILL

There is a second level in which the desire and will of God are crucial to our ability to freely repent. R. Yitzchak Hutner *zt"l*, in his work *Pachad Yitzchak* on Yom Kippur, elaborates on the idea that repentance is based on the principle that "uprooting of the will results in the uprooting of the action." Judaism insists that repentance means much more than a decision not to sin anymore. Repentance causes the sin itself, as a historical fact, to be destroyed, nullifying its existence. The reason that Judaism grants repentance such an ability is rooted in the understanding that sin is not merely a historical action, but also a flaw and a corruption of the soul, a form of poison which spreads within the recesses of the soul of the sinner, tarnishing and destroying it. Repentance uproots from the soul the sin and its damaging effects, turning it into non-fact; it annuls the sin's historical existence. Now clearly, in the natural world, this is impossible. In the world of action, what is past is past and cannot be undone. The entire edifice of repentance is based on a miracle, a miracle which goes against the inexorable flow of time in the natural world. What man has the power to do, naturally, is to undo his will. He can change his desire to do

1. Which was mentioned in the midrash that was brought in the chapter about the blessing of holiness.

wrong. The success of repentance depends on an act of God which assimilates the *world of action* to the *world of will,* such that uprooting our will to sin is instantly reflected by the uprooting of the sin itself. In the world of will, the existence of sin is dependent on the continued affirmation of will, the sin must be sustained by the will of the sinner. Cut off from its life support of human desire, the sin withers and dies, it deteriorates and ceases to exist. The historical fact of yesterday's sin disappears in the world of will.

What precisely is this world which R. Hutner calls "the word of will," the world where reality is no more than the will of the individual? It is, of course, the world of God, of "He who spoke and the world came into existence." In the act of creation, God's will is equivalent to reality. For the Creator, there is no gap between will and reality. For the uprooting of our will to sin to result in the disappearance of the sin itself, we would have to be like God, not created man. Therefore, to whom can we appeal for this miracle to take place? To the God of the world of will, to Him who *desires* repentance. We appeal not to God who "does," but to God who "wills" (*rotzeh*), because if God wills repentance, then our repentance will constitute the uprooting of the action of sin itself, and thus the true cleansing of our soul.

As with the first answer, the actual act of repentance is not the theme of the blessing. That is something which we must do ourselves. But the result of repentance, in this case the uprooting of the act of sin, is in God's hands. We appeal to Him that He should "will" repentance, for His will is equivalent to action.

3. HELP IN REPENTING

Despite what I stated above, that man cannot seek help for the actual act of repentance because it is dependent on him alone, our Sages did indeed teach that man needs the aid of God in repenting, just as he does in all his other endeavors. The question, of course, is: How is this possible without suspending man's free will which lies at the very heart of repentance?

The answer must be that man initiates the first step. Only after man makes the first move is it stated that "he who comes to purify himself, is aided."[2] The blessing teaches us that this help, which is relevant to the continuation of the process, is essential for the first step as well. Man's ability to take the first step is dependent on his ability to sense the reality of the process of repair in the relationship. This notion is true both psychologically and metaphysically.

Psychologically: True repentance is not performed only out of a desire to observe mitzvot, or to avoid punishment for disobeying God's will. The real motivation for repentance arises from man's desire to be better, namely, to become closer to God. The feeling, half intellectual and half intuitive, that by correcting my behavior I am actually changing the meaning of my life, entering into the presence of God, and sensing the closeness of holiness, is the motivating force behind deep and revolutionary repentance. This is the meaning behind the choice of words in the saying of the Sages I quoted above: "He who comes to *purify himself*, is aided." If one performs good deeds but does not feel the purity and holiness in the move, he will not be able to continue to climb and perfect himself. The "help" granted to one who comes to purify himself is purity and sanctity. This result of repentance is the most important factor in maintaining the path to repentance. God's acceptance of our repentance, as was described in the previous explanations, is a necessary condition for man's ability to motivate himself to repent.

Metaphysically: This "help" is not merely a quirk of human psychology, a humanistic need of man for encouragement and support. The closeness to God is a real, metaphysical necessity for successful repentance, for repentance is a genuine creation of man. The repentant man transcends his own natural ability, creating good that did not exist in him previously. This fundamental idea – which constituted a basic principle in our understanding of the concept of holiness – is what sets repentance apart from man's other decisions. The ability to be better than you are is not something inherent in one's present, natural condition, because by definition you are becoming better, greater, than you are presently. From where, therefore, does one obtain this ability to perfect himself, to transcend himself? This is the principle of the "image of God,"

2. *Yoma* 38b.

which I explained a few chapters ago: Man is not limited by some fixed program, for the image and design in which he was created is nothing less than God. Man's ability to transcend himself emanates not from within his actual, concrete self, but from his connection to God, from his cleaving to his spiritual destiny, from his ability to reflect God. The Midrash explains the verse "He made us and to Him we are" (*Tehillim* 100:3) as follows: "To Him we perfect our souls" (*Bereshit Rabba* 100:1). Repentance is the creation of good by man, and therefore it is a reflection of Divine perfection. As we emphasized in the chapters about holiness, the process of perfecting (repentance) cannot be real if it does not draw strength from absolute perfection. Therefore, if the act of repentance is toward God, it can succeed, because this coming closer empowers the act. The result is what empowers the action.[3] Hence, God must come close to us, so that we can truly change and better ourselves. This closeness, which depends on man's will, is what enables the miracle of transcendence, the breach in the law of causation, and the creation of more value and more holiness.

This is what we are praying for. We pray that God, who desires repentance, should bring Himself close to us so that we can return in complete and true repentance. Without this help, which is actually the continuation of the repentance process, we would not be able to make the first move.

4. THE WILL OF CREATION

There is an additional meaning to the importance of God's will in repentance, which is a continuation of the previous idea. God's desire for repentance is not merely a particular desire which God conveys to the repentant man at a certain moment, but rather is the universal character of God's will in all of creation. When we describe God's actions, we have many titles, and the blessings in the *Shemoneh Esrei* represent only some of them – He who grants knowledge, who forgives and pardons, who

3. This goes against the Aristotelian principle that the cause must precede the effect, but this is precisely the uniqueness of the image of God within the natural world. God, the purpose and goal, is the causative factor in the creation of man, who was made in His image.

redeems Israel, who gathers the remnants of His people Israel, etc. But there is only one title based on God's will – "*Harotzeh bitshuva,*" "Who desires repentance." The reason for this is that repentance is possible only because it is rooted in the reason for creation itself. The world was created out of God's desire and wish that man create more good and more value, from his own free will. God does not want us to be good, for then He would have created us so, but rather that we be better, namely, that we grow, develop, improve, and ascend the ladder of good, thereby coming closer to God. Repentance, turning freely to the good, is therefore a reflection of the deepest will of creation. The world, we might say, was created for the sake of repentance – or, in the language of the Sages, repentance was created before the world was created (*Bereshit Rabba* 1:4).

The significance of this is that God's desire for repentance is the basis of His relationship with the world. This basis is why repentance is possible. If, God forbid, God were to "give up" on man and his chance to repent, then repentance would be impossible, for the world's existence would be based on God's will that we be good – and all that is not good would no longer be able to exist. One who is bad now and comes to repent exists and succeeds in his repentance only because he lives in the light of Him who desires repentance, and this desire sustains the entire world. Indeed, one who repents must surely bless, "Blessed... who desires repentance."

What is the meaning of the phrase "perfect repentance" in our blessing? Imperfect repentance, I would suggest, is the psychological, internal repentance of the individual, in which he corrects and changes his desire from now on, going forward. Perfect repentance is the repairing of the relationship between man and God, and man's restoration to the line of God's servants, to His service, and to His Torah. The first step must be taken by man entirely on his own, at least on the level of preliminary initiative. For the second we appeal to God, to the uncovering of His will and desire for our repentance, for our drawing near and our cleaving unto Him.

"Lead us back in perfect repentance *before You*": Given that repentance is not an internal affair alone, but a repair of the relationship between man and God, it can take place only if man is "connected" to the power and goodness of God. Logically, this is possible only *after* one has repented, because sin actually distances man from God and separates them from one another. Despite this, we pray that we can return *before Him,* in His presence, that He will bestow upon us some of this closeness so that we can return to Him. If the repentance is not "before Him," it will not succeed in being "to Him." Here, "before Him" means that we stand before Him, in God's presence, at the time when we are repenting.

Chapter 11

Selicha: Forgiveness

סְלַח לָנוּ אָבִינוּ כִּי חָטָאנוּ
מְחַל לָנוּ מַלְכֵּנוּ כִּי פָשָׁעְנוּ
כִּי מוֹחֵל וְסוֹלֵחַ אָתָּה.
בָּרוּךְ אַתָּה יהוה, חַנּוּן הַמַּרְבֶּה לִסְלֹחַ.

Forgive us, our Father, for we have sinned.
Pardon us, our King, for we have transgressed;
For You are a Pardoner and a Forgiver.
Blessed are You, Lord, the gracious One who greatly forgives.

After repentance comes forgiveness.

In the previous blessing, we asked for help in the act of repentance and success therein; in this blessing we ask for forgiveness and pardon. The Sages chose to separate these two requests. Based on what was explained in the previous chapter, the request for repentance is a request for God's closeness, for healing and repairing the tear formed between God and us. The need that the blessing comes to fulfill is the divide, spiritual emptiness, and estrangement vis-à-vis the world of holiness. The current blessing responds to a different need, and asks for a different solution. Sin is bad and engenders punishment. Sin is not just the negation of inner holiness but also an injury to God's kingship and laws. Divine justice mandates a response, for it cannot be that "the Judge of the whole world will not do justice." Hence, man needs to be saved from punishment and from God's wrath, for the proper sentence of a sinner is death. Because these are two very different requests – one based on man's internal spiritual welfare and lack of holiness, and the other referring to our physical well-being and success in the material world – the Sages wanted it to be clear that we should not confuse the two. As we have emphasized previously, the middle blessings are based on the needs of man, each blessing representing a distinct need. It is important for man to understand that the need to be close to God is wholly independent of the need to be spared from punishment. More so, one should note that the need to be close to God precedes the need to be spared from punishment.

The formulation of the blessing itself is very straightforward, but I would like to comment on a few points.

1. *SELICHA, MECHILA, KAPPARA*: FORGIVENESS, PARDON, AND ATONEMENT

The three terms in the title are, in our minds, virtually inseparable. In the Yom Kippur prayers, these three terms always appear together – "*Selach lanu, mechal lanu, kapper lanu,*" "Forgive us, pardon us, atone for us." In our blessing in the *Shemoneh Esrei,* however, atonement is absent. In order to understand why, we have to understand the significance of each term.

1. *Selicha,* forgiveness: When one forgives, he no longer holds a grudge. Forgiveness is required when someone is personally affronted. If I see someone acting improperly, but his sin does not affect me personally, then there is no place for forgiveness on my part. Only the person who was affronted is able to forgive. To ask God for forgiveness, therefore, is to ask Him not to be angry with us; we are asking God to change His attitude toward us, even though that attitude is justified. Why is God angry at one who sins? How can one entertain the possibility that God is "affronted" by sin? Judaism does not embrace the philosophical assumption that man's actions do not affect God. Every sin is an affront, a personal affront, to God, who is Creator and King of the world. This does not mean that God has a fragile ego, God forbid, or that He is easily insulted;[1] the affront is not subjective, but objective. Sin is an act

1. Although there are also sources which are willing to explain the verse "And He was saddened in His heart" (*Bereshit* 6:6) close to its simple meaning.

of rebellion against God's kingship, of throwing off the yoke of heaven. We, mere mortals, in our subjective psychological lives, experience wrongdoing against us as a personal affront. This has an objective parallel – an affront against good and justice. Sin has a personal aspect, for God has a personal relationship with His creations who were created in His image, and especially with His children, to whom He gave His Torah and with whom He forged a covenant. The Biblical metaphor of father and son is transformed in the literature of the Sages into a central principle in understanding sin. The Sages constantly compare one who sins to the son of a king who goes astray. This idea is expressed in this blessing and in the previous blessing. Notice that only in these two requests do we appeal to God with the title "our Father."

Aside from the objective wrongdoing, there is a personal sin against God. In this sense, God is different from a judge in a court of law, who dispenses justice without any personal stake in the matter. God is personally involved in the conflict, and He presses His complaint against us – "Hear, O mountains, the case of God, and you firm foundations of the earth, for God has a case against His people, and a suit against Israel" (*Mikha* 6:2). As a remedy to this issue, man asks for forgiveness, he requests that God not let our actions affect His feelings toward us.

2. *Mechila*, pardon: Pardon is different from forgiveness. "*Mechila*" is a word borrowed from a legal context, from monetary law. If a person owes someone money, but he waives the need to repay, this is called "*mechila*."[2] It does not interest us how the creditor feels about the debt, but only whether he waives his right to collect it. Similarly, there does not have to have been a personal affront from the outset. Debts can arise in a purely civil context – for example, if one borrowed money – and in this scenario, too, the creditor can waive the debt. Whenever one has the right to demand redress or payment from someone, he has the ability to waive that right, thereby pardoning the debtor from paying the debt.

2. Given the legal connotation of "*mechila*," a better translation might be "remission," a word rarely used in religious context in modern English.

In the context of sin, pardon refers directly to the punishment. This is based on the idea that the punishment is inherent in the sin itself, and a direct result of it. Just as borrowing generates an obligation of repayment, so too sin generates a punishment. This is the principle of pure justice – punishment as a restoration of the equilibrium which was upset by the sinner. We feel this when we read of someone who has committed a crime and has managed to avoid ever paying for it. Our hearts tell us that something is wrong here, something requires correction. Enlightened people will sometimes call this feeling a desire for revenge, but that is incorrect. This feeling exists even when we have no connection to the sin whatsoever and have not been affected by it. It is in this sense that *mechila*, pardon, is different from *selicha*, forgiveness. Forgiveness is based on a personal affront to God, whereas pardon is based on a breach of the principle of justice. God, in this picture, acts as the creditor, who pardons the debtor from having to pay. Forgiveness amends God's attitude to man; pardon amends the obligation of punishment itself. God does not change His attitude; He exempts us from the debt which we owe Him.

3. *Kappara*, atonement: Atonement is fundamentally different from the previous two terms. It is easy to notice the difference if we note that forgiveness and pardon are also human actions, whereas atonement is relevant to God alone. If I offend someone, I can – and must – request that he forgive me and pardon me for my debt to him, but I cannot ask him to atone for me. The object of atonement is not God's attitude to man (as in forgiveness), or God's demands of man (as in pardon), but man and the sin itself. Objects which have been defiled by sin need atonement. We find atonement even with regard to inanimate objects. On Yom Kippur, the High Priest atones for the Holy of Holies and the altar. The cause of defilement there is the actions of man, but it is the altar that requires rectification. Man, too, is defiled from his sins, and therefore he requires atonement, like an object tarnished by sin. Atonement is a form of purification, as we find in the verse which concludes the Yom Kippur service: "For on this day *He shall atone for you to purify you* from all your sins, before God shall you be purified" (*Vayikra* 16:30). R. Akiva had the following saying:

> Fortunate are you, Israel, before whom are you purified and who purifies you – your Father in heaven, as is written, "And I shall pour over you pure waters and you shall be purified" (*Yechezkel* 36:25). And it is written, "The hope (*mikve*) of Israel is God" (*Yirmeyahu* 17:13). Just as a *mikve* purifies the defiled, so does the Holy One, blessed be He, purify Israel. (*Yoma* 85b)

The aspect of sin which requires forgiveness is the personal affront to God; the aspect of sin which requires pardon is the breach of justice which requires recompense; the aspect of sin which requires atonement is the internal defilement of man's soul, the corruption of the image of God. A person who sins has a corrupted personality, a tainted character, and a polluted soul. He has not only performed sin; he is immersed in sin. Atonement is healing, it is the rehabilitation of the sinner. It is essentially a miracle, an act of re-creation – and therefore it requires God's power. When man asks for atonement, he is essentially asking for redemption from sin, to be saved from a contamination that has conquered his inner being.

Hence, I believe, atonement is not mentioned in the current blessing, not because it is not important, but because its proper place is in the next blessing, *the blessing of redemption*. As we shall see in the next chapter, the request for redemption includes redemption from spiritual trouble no less than redemption from political oppression and personal tribulation.

Why do the Sages separate forgiveness and pardon from atonement? The answer lies mainly in understanding the next blessing, but the main idea is understandable even now. As we emphasized in the explanation for separating repentance from forgiveness, the defining principle for determining the contents of each blessing is the *need*, not the result. Although sin underlies all three of the processes, from the perspective of the need of man the need for atonement is very different from the need for forgiveness and pardon. The latter two arise from man's need to ensure his welfare and happiness, to save himself from punishment and merit life. Atonement arises from man's inner spiritual need to be healthy in spirit; there is no external threat of punishment or justice. Man who seeks atonement is looking not for security, but wholeness. Therefore, these two requests, which refer to two completely different aspects of man's personality, are placed in two separate blessings.

2. *KI CHATANU*: FOR WE HAVE SINNED

We seek forgiveness "*for* we have sinned," and pardon "*for* we have transgressed." At first glance, the role of the word "for" here is wholly different from the role of the word "for" in "*For* You are a Pardoner and a Forgiver." The latter phrase explains why God can forgive. Is sin the explanation for God's response to our request? The simple explanation is that we are explaining why we need forgiveness, and not the reason that God should forgive us. "For we have sinned" is the reason for our request, and not the reason for God's response.

However, it seems that the Sages actually understood "for we have sinned" to be the reason why God should forgive us. We find this idea in *Bemidbar Rabba* (20:13), where it is explained that Bilam rushed to declare "I have sinned" because he knew that "any person who sins and admits 'I have sinned' – no angel is permitted to touch him." This idea is explained in the *Yerushalmi* as follows:

> "And Shmuel said: We have sinned to God" (*Shmuel Alef* 7:6). Shmuel wrapped himself in the cloak of all of Israel. He said before Him: Master of worlds, do You judge a man for anything other than his saying before You "I have not sinned"? As it says, "Behold, I will bring you to judgment for saying, 'I have not sinned'" (*Yirmeyahu* 2:35); but they are saying before You, "We have sinned." (*Yerushalmi Taanit* 2:7)

The Sages teach us a fundamental concept regarding the sinner's relationship to God. At least with regard to punishment ("the angels are not permitted to touch him") and to judgment ("You judge a man"), the essence of God's reaction is rooted in man's refusal to recognize the fact that he has sinned. Self-delusion, masking oneself in the guise of righteousness, is what brings on a powerful and wrathful response more than anything else. This is the reason why, in the *Viduy* (confession) prayer, we begin with "For we are not so *brazen-faced and stiff-necked* as to say before You that we are righteous and have not sinned." So too, in *Para-*

shat Vayigash, the dramatic reversal takes place when Yosef's brothers free themselves from denial with the admission, "*Indeed,* we are guilty" (*Bereshit* 42:21). So long as man stands before God and insists upon his righteousness, there is no option for forgiveness and pardon. Forgiveness and pardon in such a scenario will only strengthen man's attachment to his sin. Release from the necessity of punishment can only come as a result of inner recognition of the truth.

According to this explanation, the meaning of the request in our blessing is: Forgive us, our Father, for we (*admit that we*) have sinned.

3. *HAMARBEH LISLOACH*: WHO GREATLY FORGIVES

The *chatima* of the blessing is, "Blessed... who greatly forgives." The question is obvious. Why specifically in this blessing do we not use the regular *chatima* formulation, "Blessed... who performs that which we requested," but instead recite, "Blessed... who *greatly* performs that deed?" This question brings us to a more basic question – what exactly is the meaning of "Who greatly forgives"?

The phrase is based on the verse in *Yeshayahu* (55:7): "Let the wicked man leave his way, and the sinful man his thoughts, and let him return to HaShem and He will have mercy on him, and to our God *for He will greatly forgive.*" The verse seems to imply that "He will greatly forgive" is the persuasive justification for the wicked person's return to God, as if to say that if God would *simply* forgive, and not *greatly* forgive, then the wicked person would not have sufficient reason to turn to Him.

There are those who explain "Who greatly forgives" in the numerical sense. God forgives, and forgives again, repeatedly, even regarding a person who asks for forgiveness and then sins again. This is the explanation of the Baal HaTanya, for example, in *Iggeret HaTeshuva*: In contrast to man – regarding whom if asked to forgive again a person whom he had already forgiven in the past and who then repeated the offense again, even if he forgives the sinner, the forgiveness will not be fully unqualified and there will remain a sense that the first forgiveness was wasted – God forgives again without there being any difference between the first time and the one-thousandth time. Each act of forgiveness is complete and wholly sincere, just like the first time.

Another explanation that I once heard sees "Who greatly" as a quantitative notion. God forgives with abundant excess. According to the letter of the law, forgiveness is meant to match the request for forgiveness, just as God said to Moshe: "I have forgiven *according to your word*," as you requested. This is highly logical, for without a request for forgiveness it would be unwise to forgive. But, at the end of the day, God greatly forgives. God grants forgiveness in a greater amount than requested. The cup of forgiveness is bountiful and overflowing with the forgiveness that was poured into it.

The need for this attribute is rooted in the fact that it is difficult for a person to recognize and evaluate the full effect of his sin, and consequently he does not request sufficient forgiveness. Even one who admits with full sincerity "I have sinned" does not recognize all the defects, all the destruction and devastation that he has caused by sinning. Psychologically, it is hard for him to internalize the magnitude of the devastation, and metaphysically, as a finite mortal being, he is wholly unable to comprehend the depth of the ramifications in the upper and lower worlds, in the realm and the fabric of spiritual existence, which were harmed and damaged by his actions. But the compassionate God abundantly forgives, even more than what was requested by the penitent man.

These explanations are enlightening and also undoubtedly correct. However, I would like to add another idea, not to contradict, but to further deepen these two explanations.

In my opinion, "Who greatly forgives" means that God's ability to forgive is endless, infinite. Not only does God forgive more than is requested, and every time anew, but this forgiveness draws, at its foundation, from an infinite source.

Now, the more metaphysically inclined among you will surely protest that none of God's attributes are limited. God's power is infinite, in all respects. What is so special or noteworthy about forgiveness?

Theology has taught us that all of God's attributes are unlimited. Yet, when we appeal to God with a specific request, we do not ask for the use of infinite power. In order to give man financial sustenance, a finite amount of power is needed, according to the person's needs, and similarly with regard to the building of the Temple and the ingathering of the exiles. Since the world is finite and its inadequacies are finite, all that is required in correcting the state of the world is a finite amount of power. An infinitude of power was required only for the creation of the world, which was *yesh me'ayin,* ex nihilo, something out of nothing. There, there was no proportion between the problem (non-existence) and the solution (the world). But since creation, all problems are finite problems, and God solves them with finite power, as is necessary. Hence, man need not appeal to the infinite Healer, or the infinite Judge, or the infinite Subduer of the enemy, in order to request his needs.

There is, however, one exception to this sweeping generalization. There is one problem within the world which, in order to successfully solve it, we require an infinite source of power – and that is the problem of sin.[3]

Since man has free will, he is capable of unlimited good. As we have stated previously, the upper limit of man's development is nothing less than God, in whose image man was made – i.e., infinity. But the necessary balance between the possibilities of good and evil which results in man's freedom of will implies that the lower limits of his depravity be also unlimited. Just as we regularly declare that no matter how far man has fallen, he can still repent and return, so too, no matter how far he has fallen, he can fall further still. If there were a lower limit to man's depravity, he could not repent (freely) at that point either. Hence, evil in this world is, in principle, potentially infinite. Therefore, the answer to our own evil must be infinite. Accordingly, God is called "Who greatly forgives," who holds for us a boundless, limitless supply of forgiveness. The forgiveness which I am seeking now is drawn from an unlimited fount; otherwise, this forgiveness would not be able to correct my evil, which also derives from an unlimited fount.

Forgiveness for even one small sin derives from an unlimited resource of forgiveness. This is true for two reasons:

---

3. Back in the second blessing, I explained the phrase "*abundant* in salvation" (*rav lehoshia*) as referring to the fact that God's salvation is not of this world, but above and beyond anything within the world. That was in a general introductory blessing, where I explain to myself who God is. In the individual requests, however, there is no need to address God as Infinite when bringing a finite problem to His attention, and therefore there is no place for "abundance" or "greatly" (*rav* or *marbeh*), with the exception of the blessing of forgiveness.

1. Every sin, even a "little" one, results from man's infinite ability, as an image of God, to commit evil.
2. When man utilizes free will to sin, it calls into question the very creation of the world and turns back the clock to a pre-creation reality. Everything that exists, exists because God wills it. In principle, nothing can exist against God's will. Yet – evil exists. Logically, the existence of sin should result immediately in its non-existence, for by going against the will of God it negates its own metaphysical basis. R. Hutner explained the doubling of God's name (the *Shem Havaya*), "HaShem, HaShem," in the thirteen attributes of mercy this way. According to the Gemara,[4] "I am God before man sins, and I am God after man sins." R. Hutner explains that God's name (the *Shem Havaya*) is what brings all the worlds into being. I am HaShem before man sins – yet, once he has sinned, all of creation should revert to non-existence. The first name cannot overlook the sin, and a further act of creation is required, a further *Shem Havaya* which brings all the worlds into being, to renew a world in which sin exists. Therefore, any sin, even the smallest transgression, requires an infinite power, which holds the power of creation ex nihilo, because the pre-sin world has no capability to sustain the world post-sin.

It is clear, therefore, that the Baal HaTanya was correct, and the fact that God "greatly forgives" means that He forgives and forgives again, without deficit. It is similarly clear that the moment that the act of forgiveness commences, it does not stop at the "vessel" formed by the request, but overflows on all sides, like a river bursting its banks. These two ideas are a direct result of the fact that every act of forgiveness derives from the actions of an infinite power within creation.

---

4. *Rosh HaShana* 17b.

Chapter 12

Geula: Redemption

רְאֵה בְעָנְיֵנוּ, וְרִיבָה רִיבֵנוּ
וּגְאָלֵנוּ מְהֵרָה לְמַעַן שְׁמֶךָ
כִּי גּוֹאֵל חָזָק אָתָּה.
בָּרוּךְ אַתָּה יהוה, גּוֹאֵל יִשְׂרָאֵל.

Look upon our affliction, fight our cause,
And redeem us quickly for Your name's sake,
For You are a powerful Redeemer.
Blessed are You, Lord, who redeems Israel.

The seventh blessing is *Birkat HaGeula*, the blessing of redemption. The Gemara (*Megilla* 17b) asks why the blessing of redemption precedes the blessing of health, unlike the order that appears in the Tanakh, "Who forgives all your sins, who heals all your ailments, who redeems your life from the pit" (*Tehillim* 103:3–4). The Gemara answers that there is special importance in placing the blessing of redemption as the seventh blessing, because according to tradition the Messianic redemption will take place in the seventh year of the process of redemption. Rashi points out that the theme of this blessing is not the future national redemption, but the redemption of the individual from personal suffering. He explains that the Gemara's answer is merely a reference to a general context of redemption.

It is obvious to Rashi that "redemption" in our blessing is a synonym for salvation and rescue from all sorts of personal sufferings which may befall a person. The main reason for this is, undoubtedly, the context: all the opening blessings, from "Who grants knowledge" through to "Who blesses the years," deal with the provision of needs to the individual worshipper. The requests in the *Shemoneh Esrei* can be divided into two distinct sections: firstly, private requests,[1] and afterward, from "Who gathers the remnants of His people Israel" through to "Who causes the horn of salvation to grow," national requests which refer to the future redemption of the Jewish people. Hence, it is clear that our blessing, which appears in the middle of the first section, is also dealing with needs of the individual in his current life, and not with the hopes for the Jewish people's national future.

In light of this assertion, the question is: What are we asking for here? More accurately, the question is what is the problem which the redemption in this blessing comes to solve? Surely one could define the subject of any other request as redemption. If one is hungry, does he not need redemption from hunger? If he is unintelligent and foolish, does he not require redemption from ignorance? Is not the theme of the blessing "Who shatters enemies and subdues the iniquitous" redemption from enemies and foes? In other words, what is the specific problem for which the blessing of redemption was designated?

1. *RE'EH VEONYENU*: LOOK UPON OUR AFFLICTION

The blessing opens with an extraordinary request: "Look upon our affliction." This is truly astounding. Why do we need to request of God that He make a special effort to recognize the problem before He proceeds to solve it? There is no phenomenon like it in any other blessing. We do not ask that God should look upon our financial difficulties before requesting that He grant us sustenance, nor do we ask that He look upon our ignorance before He grants us knowledge – there is no need for such a request! It is obvious that God recognizes our situation, and nothing is hidden from Him. If so, why does this specific blessing commence with the request of "Look"?

1. Phrased in the plural form, of course, but referring to the needs which emanate from problems of the individual.

The origin of the formulation "Look upon our affliction" is in the redemption from Egypt. In *Parashat Bikkurim*, the bringing to the Temple of the first fruits (*Devarim* 26:5–11), between the verse which describes the slavery in Egypt and the verse which describes the Exodus, appears an entire verse which describes an intermediate stage, a stage that preceded the redemption itself: "And God saw our affliction and our toil and our burden." It is safe to assume that the aim of the recital which accompanies the bringing the first fruits is not to point out the causes for the Exodus from Egypt, but rather to praise and thank God who brought us to "this place, and gave us this land, a land flowing with milk and honey." In other words, "And He saw our affliction" is not the cause of the redemption but a part of it, and it constitutes an independent stage in the development of redemption which serves as an independent unit of praise. This actual "seeing" of our affliction includes a dimension for which we thank and praise God.

It would seem that looking upon our affliction is not for the purposes of obtaining information. In the *parasha* for bringing the first fruits we are not thanking God for being up to date with our sorrow, and this is not what we are asking for in prayer. Note that we are not asking that God look upon our predicaments, but that He look upon our affliction. Affliction denotes inner tension and psychological suffering, a feeling of loss of control. Such a person's state is one where "the water has risen up to his soul" and he appeals to God "from the depths." All of these are not descriptions of specifically the objective scenario, but rather the subjective state which a person enters as a result of a particular objective situation. "Look upon" is not a request that God pay attention to a particular predicament, that He be aware of the objective scenario, but rather that He recognize the anguish and inner suffering in which the person is engulfed. God sees our affliction, our burden, and our toil. We ask God to take our suffering "to heart." Clearly, such a recognition of suffering is not merely informative, but involves partaking in the suffering itself. "Look upon our affliction" is essentially a request that God identify with the worshipper's suffering.

Can this really be?! Can a person truly request such a thing, that the King of kings identify with his sorrow so much so that He actually partakes in it?

> "Advance, O God, and may Your enemies be scattered, and may Your foes flee." Now what have all the nations of the world and all the kingdoms of the earth done, that they should be referred to as enemies and foes to God? Rather, anyone who acts as an enemy and a foe to Israel it is like he has acted as an enemy and a foe to God, and he is also an enemy of God, as it says, "And I will make an enemy of your enemies and I will oppress your oppressors" (*Shemot* 23:22). Yet, you do not know if it pains Him or not; thus, when it says, "I am with him in suffering" (*Tehillim* 91:15), you learn that, whenever Israel is suffering, God is also suffering with them, so to speak. And similarly, you find that when Israel were subjugated in Egypt, God's presence was only revealed to Moshe out of suffering and from within the burning bush.... And similarly, it says, "Whom You redeemed for Yourself from Egypt, a nation and its God" (*Shmuel Bet* 7:23). R. Akiva said: He said to them: Just as you were subjugated, the subjugation was, so to speak, before Him. And similarly, it says, "One who touches you, it is as if he touches the pupil of His own eye" (*Zekharya* 2:12); R. Elazar son of R. Yose HaGelili says: It is as if he pokes his finger into his own eye and gouges it out. (*Sifrei Zuta*, 10)

The midrash emphasizes God's complete participation in the suffering of Israel, so much so that Israel's suffering is described as causing God actual physical pain, so to speak. One might have posited that such a participation applies only to the suffering of all of Israel and not to the suffering of the individual. But the basis for all of the sayings in the "I am with him in suffering" genre is the mishna which relates to the suffering of the individual:

> R. Meir said: At the time when a person suffers, what expression does God's presence use, so to speak? My head is too heavy for Me, My arm is too heavy for Me. (Mishna *Sanhedrin* 6:5).

The root of God's participation in Israel's suffering is His participation in Israel's pain, and His identification with that pain is to such a level that "My head is too heavy for Me," that God's head, so to speak, aches.

Commencing the blessing of redemption with a request that God identify with man's suffering opens before us the path to understanding the theme of this blessing. "Redemption" is not synonymous with "solution." Man has many problems which require a solution, but this cannot be called redemption. Redemption is required in a situation where man is lost, "over his head," where the harsh waters are sweeping him away and he is losing control. When man is trapped by forces over which he has no control, when he is lost and devoid of all hope, then he seeks redemption.

The legal term "*geula*" is used in the Torah for the redemption of a slave, or for redeeming one's portion of land after it has been sold. The slave cannot free himself from bondage, but someone can come from outside to redeem him. The field is in the hands of someone else, it has left your legal control, but you bring it back to where it should be. That is the feeling, the need, that underlies the prayer for redemption – I am lost, overwhelmed by relentless waters, on the verge of defeat, and there is no one who can save me other than the redemptive arm of God.

The paradigmatic archetype redemption in Judaism is the Exodus from Egypt. The acme of the redemption, the moment that was engraved in the collective-historical memory of the Jewish people, is the parting of the Sea of Reeds – the people are fleeing, still slaves in their self-consciousness, and find themselves trapped between the sea before them and Pharaoh's army behind them, enclosed on all sides. There is no route of possible escape – and then God's outstretched arm appears, and the path of salvation opens, breaching the imprisoning walls. We replicate the expression of this feeling every single day: "For God has rescued Yaakov and redeemed him from a hand mightier than him."

This blessing emanates not only from the objective suffering which befalls us, but mainly from the sense of helplessness and doom that encompasses us. Therefore, we open with "Look upon our affliction," that God should perceive this inner distress and identify with it, take it upon Himself. The redemption from Egypt began with this very expression: "And God looked upon the children of Israel, and God knew" (*Shemot* 2:25). God saw, and He knew, meaning He understood and absorbed the inner sense of their predicament – not their slavery, but the groan which resulted from the oppression.[2]

Thus, the request for redemption is first and foremost a recognition of the state of despair of the human condition without God, and the hopelessness therein; an admission that we desperately need God and rely upon Him. The request arises from our own understanding of our "affliction," which is reflected in the opening of the blessing where we appeal to God to look upon "our affliction," so that He can redeem us from it.

2. *KAPPARA*: ATONEMENT

In the previous chapter we saw that atonement does not appear in the blessing of forgiveness, and I claimed that its proper place is here, in the blessing of redemption. It is now clear what the basis for this claim is. Redemption refers at its base to one's mental state, to a psychological affliction which is the result of a misfortune. In contrast to forgiveness and pardon, which refer to God's attitude to us, atonement refers to the state of our souls. Atonement comes to save us from an internal corruption which contaminates our internal existence. Therefore, atonement is a part of the process of redemption. God's seeing our affliction applies to sin no less than to external troubles; and what a sinner needs is redemption from sin – this is what we call atonement.

3. *VERIVA RIVENU*: AND FIGHT OUR CAUSE

Understanding "fight our cause" stems from our explanation of "look upon our affliction." We are interested, of course, in the final outcome – that God should expel the oppressor who fights us and attacks us; but the formulation of the request "Fight our cause" emphasizes not just the outcome, but also the medium – that God should rally to our side and fight our battle. The meaning of "Fight our cause" is that God should not only feel our sufferings and our pain, but rather He should also see our problems as His own problems. God's being on our side, with

2. "And the children of Israel groaned from the work, and they cried out … and God saw" (*Shemot* 2:23–25).

us in suffering, is no less important to us than destroying the enemy – "I am with him in suffering" (*Tehillim* 91:15). "And God looked upon the children of Israel, and God knew" – knowledge that comes as a result of seeing is a knowledge of *deveikut,* of empathy and communion. We are not seeking relief from afar, although God's relief from afar is no less effective. We are seeking help that comes through solidarity, joining with us closely; this kind of help will redeem us of both the inner distress of the soul as well as the external distress of the enemy.

Given that redemption comes from empathy, from "looking upon us," it exists even when there is no objective justification for it. God is not the United Nations, whom we have to convince of our righteousness, but is an ally, participating in the affliction from the outset. Our suffering is His suffering, and our pain is His pain. We find this regarding Yorovam son of Yoash:

> In the fifteenth year of Amatzyahu son of Yoash king of Yehuda, Yorovam son of Yoash king of Israel became king in Shomron for forty-one years.
> And he did what was evil in God's eyes; he did not depart from all the sins that Yorovam son of Nevat had caused Israel to commit.
> He restored the territory of Israel from Levo Chamat to the Arava Sea, in accordance with the word that HaShem, the God of Israel, had spoken through His servant, the prophet Yona son of Amitai from Gat Chefer. (*Melakhim Bet* 14:23–25)

The contradiction between the second and third verse is glaring. If he committed evil no less than Yorovam son of Nevat, how did he manage to restore the territory of Israel to the largest dimensions? The following verse answers this – and note the resemblance to the language of our blessing:

> For God saw the affliction of Israel, very bitter, with neither bond nor free left, and with none to help Israel. And God resolved not to blot out the name of Israel from under the heavens; and He delivered them through Yorovam son of Yoash. (Ibid. 26–27)

From a linguistic perspective, the phrase "Fight our cause" is based on other verses,[3] but in terms of content, it seems to me that the verses about Yorovam on of Yoash express the essence of our blessing more than any other verse. God saw Israel's affliction, and hopelessness, without any chance of relief, and this mandated redemption in spite of all the sins that Yorovam had caused Israel to commit. God empathizes with the mental distress, which leads to His partaking in Israel's battles, not because this is a reward that they are deserving of, but because He fights our cause – His cause.

4. *GE'ALENU MEHERA LEMAAN SHEMEKHA*: REDEEM US QUICKLY FOR YOUR NAME'S SAKE

What is the connection between God's name and redemption? The answer is obvious – God's name is borne by Israel. The usual explanation given for the connection between God's name being placed upon us and His aiding of us is the desecration of God's name in the eyes of the nations – "Why should the nations say, 'Where is their God?'" (*Tehillim* 79:10). According to this explanation, it is enough that the nations think that God is associated with Israel for it to constitute a desecration of God's name, even if this is not the case. However, I believe that "For Your name's sake" refers to a genuine desecration of God's name through Israel's downfall, wholly unrelated to what the nations say. Even if were obvious to everyone that the misfortune is not due to Divine impotence, nonetheless the disaster is a diminution in God's name, because Jewish existence is, in reality, the bearer of God's name. This is an additional outcome of the empathy with which the blessing began. We appeal to God to identify with His name that we bear by our existence. God's presence and holiness in the world is synonymous with Jewish existence. "Act for Your name's sake and sanctify Your name on those who sanctify Your name," as we recite during the High Holy Days,[4] is not a request that God reward our good deeds, nor is it merely advice to God that He prevent scandal and ignomy in the field of public relations; rather, it

3. Such as, "For God will fight their cause" (*Mishlei* 22:23), "And I will fight your cause" (*Yeshayahu* 49:25), "Fight my cause and redeem me" (*Tehillim* 119:154).
4. Introduction to *Kedusha* following *UNetaneh Tokef.*

is a reminder of the congruity between His name in the world and our situation. If He is with us in suffering, His name is tarnished, as it were. "For His name's sake" is the inner kernel of our redemption.

The *Rishonim* found the Biblical source for "For Your name's sake" in the verse, "Our Redeemer, God of hosts is His name" (*Yeshayahu* 47:4). God of hosts means the God of His multitudes – Israel. The name of God[5] is the name which includes us in it. Our Redeemer – His name is HaShem, God of Israel. God's association to Israel constitutes an integral part of His name. Therefore, He redeems His people – for His name's sake.

5. *GO'EL CHAZAK*: A POWERFUL REDEEMER

There exists a verse which is strongly reflects the formulation of the entire blessing. Yirmeyahu the prophet prophesies on Babylonia, the exiler of Israel:

> Thus says the God of hosts: The children of Israel and the children of Yehuda are oppressed together, and all their captors hold them fast and refuse to let them go. *Their Redeemer is powerful, God of hosts is His name; He shall thoroughly fight their cause* (*riv yariv et rivam*), that He may quiet the land and upset the inhabitants of Babylonia. (*Yirmeyahu* 50:33–34)

All the aspects which we have spoken about appear here. The situation is one of imprisonment, of overpowering enslavement ("Their captors hold them fast and refuse to let them go"). Redemption results directly from God's name ("Their Redeemer is powerful, God of hosts is His name"), and therefore God fights their cause, and resultantly also quiets the land and upsets Babylonia as well. This verse adds a further aspect – "Their Redeemer is *powerful*."

Strength is a peculiar attribute to apply to the King of kings; it seems to imply that God must exert Himself in order to overcome especially difficult challenges. From a theological perspective, there are no

5. God of hosts – *HaShem Tzeva-ot* – is one of the names of God which may not be erased.

tasks that require more effort or more exertion than others when it comes to the Almighty. Strength as an attribute of God is associated only with redemption. It is necessary to understand God's redemptive strength from the perspective of the person being redeemed. Strong redemption is an act of God which demonstrates special power and strength upon the backdrop of our inability to save ourselves in any other way. We are trapped and chained, and from our perspective there is no force in the world which can free us. It takes the overwhelming power and strength of God to break the shackles of our enslavement. Thus, at the redemption from the prison that was Egypt, God redeemed us "with a powerful hand and an outstretched arm." This is no less true with regard to inner affliction. To be redeemed is to behold the mighty hand of God. The transition from the feeling of hopelessness and doom – with neither bond nor free left – to the realm of freedom and the ability to act and shape the future, is what redemption is, and is what projects upon man the strength of the Redeemer's hand more than any other experience. Every redemption is from slavery to freedom, including, and perhaps primarily, in the realm of internal feelings and emotional ability. It is for this that we bless, "Blessed ... who redeems Israel."

Chapter 13

Refua: Healing

רְפָאֵנוּ יהוה וְנֵרָפֵא
הוֹשִׁיעֵנוּ וְנִוָּשֵׁעָה, כִּי תְהִלָּתֵנוּ אָתָּה
וְהַעֲלֵה רְפוּאָה שְׁלֵמָה לְכָל מַכּוֹתֵינוּ
כִּי אֵל מֶלֶךְ רוֹפֵא נֶאֱמָן וְרַחֲמָן אָתָּה.
בָּרוּךְ אַתָּה יהוה, רוֹפֵא חוֹלֵי עַמּוֹ יִשְׂרָאֵל.

Heal us, God, and we will be healed.
Save us and we will be saved, for You are our praise,
And bring a complete healing for all our ailments.
For You are a faithful and merciful God, King, and Healer.
Blessed are You, Lord,
who heals the sick of His people Israel.

Regarding all the previous requests, I asked: What is really the theme of this blessing? This time, however, the theme seems simple and straightforward. We are asking God to heal us. Everyone knows what healing is, just as we all know what sickness is. The blessing, therefore, is straightforward, and expresses a basic and essential human need. It would seem, upon first glance, that we can safely skip and proceed to the next blessing.

Upon further inspection, however, it seems worthwhile to spend some time examining the text of the blessing, which gives rise to a plethora of questions regarding the language that the Sages used when formulating the prayer for healing. I do not believe that we have yet dealt with a blessing that presents such an array of anomalous phrases requiring analysis.

1. "Heal us, God, and we will be healed" – This duplication is incomprehensible. What is the difference between the request of "heal us" and the request of "and we will be healed"? Is there ever a need to request of God that He bless us, and also that the blessing be fulfilled? In no other blessing do we find such a phenomenon, that we request that God redeem us and that we be redeemed, or that He bless us and that we be blessed.
2. "Save us and we will be saved"[1] – Why is a request for salvation placed here? Healing is a clear and defined need. Why is a general and undefined request for "salvation" appended to this blessing? What is the nature of this salvation, and how is it associated with healing?
3. "For You are our praise" – In the formulation of the requests in the *Shemoneh Esrei*, the request is usually followed by a justification of praise, commencing with the words "For You are…" In the previous blessing, for example, the request for redemption is justified with the phrase "For You are a powerful Redeemer." Since You are a powerful Redeemer, it is therefore to You that we appeal for redemption. According to this formulation, in the blessing of healing we justify our appeal to God to heal us because He is "our praise." But what kind of justification is this? Surely, we should say, "For You are a faithful Healer" – parallel to the usual formulation. How does the fact that God is the subject of our praise serve as the reason that He should heal us? This question is deepened by the fact that the expected justification indeed appears at the end of the blessing, "For You are a faithful and merciful God, King, and Healer." Why, then, do we need two clauses of justification; what is the purpose of the first justification, and what does it mean?
4. "A faithful (*ne'eman*) Healer" – What is the meaning of *faithfulness* in the context of healing? There is no other blessing of request in which God's ability to bless us is described as a faithful ability.

1. Note that the same duplication as before exists here as well.

5. "Who heals the sick *of His people Israel*" – In the previous blessing, the praise of God was attributed to His association with the Jewish people – "who redeems *Israel*." There it is understandable, since redemption is a concept which has specific meaning within Jewish history and the national relationship of God with the Jewish people. Redemption is a concept which is basic to the relationship of God with His people, the nation of Israel. But what special association is there between health and the Jewish people? Is there a special kind of healing for Jews, or special sicknesses for Jews? Earlier in the morning, before this blessing, we praised God and called Him "the Healer of *all flesh*."[2] A person's health is a universal human problem far more than knowledge (Torah), repentance, or forgiveness, yet out of all of these it is only regarding healing that we appeal to God as Healer of His people Israel specifically. This requires explanation.

1. FOR I AM HASHEM YOUR HEALER

Let us begin with the last question. That healing is a sign of the relationship between God and the Jewish people is explicit in the Torah. There, specifically health was chosen as a witness and sign to the special covenant between God and His people. After the crossing of the Sea of Reeds and the "Song of the Sea," God says to Israel:

> If you will diligently hearken unto the voice of HaShem your God, and do that which is right in His eyes, and listen to His commandments, and keep all His laws, then all of the diseases which I have brought upon Egypt I shall not bring upon you; for I am HaShem your Healer. (*Shemot* 15:26)

Moments prior, the Jews had just successfully and miraculously crossed the sea. Are they sick at that time, that God should pledge to heal them? On the contrary, the verse is clearly promising that they will not be sick. Not that they will be healed, but that they will never get sick or afflicted

2. *Asher Yatzar* – "Blessed ... who created man with wisdom .... Blessed who heals all flesh and does wonders."

in the manner of the Egyptians, who have just been afflicted with the ten plagues. The Midrash asks the following question:

> "All of the diseases which I have brought upon Egypt I shall not bring upon you." Then what is the meaning of "For I am HaShem your Healer"? Rather, God said to Israel: The words of the Torah which I have given you are life for you and healing for you, as it says, "They are life to him who finds them, and healing for all his flesh." (*Yalkut Shimoni* 257)

The midrash explains that healing here does not refer to treating illness, but to the bestowal of life and its perpetuation. If you are bound up with the Torah and live by its word, it is a source of life for you and thus you will not get sick. God is our Healer in this verse, not in the sense that He is a doctor treating specific illnesses, each illness and its own medicine; but in the sense that following in His ways, observing *all* of His laws, is the true path to a life without any illness. Not a path of treatment for the defective and the faulty, but the path of health and life itself. A person who cleaves to the Torah of life cannot become sick.

And why is this so? Not because hidden among the ways of God are secret formulas for health, but because "I am HaShem – your Healer." The connection to Torah, in the words of the midrash, or the connection to God Himself, is life. This is the message of the verse which we recite when we return the *sefer Torah* to the Holy Ark – "It is a tree of life for those who grasp it, and those who support it are fortunate." True health emanates from the spiritual power of Torah and the presence of God therein.

Within the context of *Parashat Beshalach*, I think that the explanation of the promise is as follows: The Jews have just passed through the sea, with the walls of death towering above them on either side. Normally, we tend to think of health as normal and disease as an anomaly. But for the Jews who are passing through the sea's depths, this is certainly not the case. Their world is a world of death, stretching on either side of them; they are literally walking through the valley of the shadow of death, between mountainous peaks devoid of life. Their very existence is a miracle, not a miracle of salvation from some threat, but one of life within death. They are living and breathing within the water's depths, a place where people cannot live. God says to them: If you keep My commandments, then this is how you will pass through the world, with death on either side while you remain healthy and whole, for miracle and providence will act as a healing and a safeguard for you. God, and the keeping His Torah, is the Healer from the death that surrounds us. It is in this sense that God is He who heals the sick *of His people Israel*; this attribute does not exist at all for one who is unconnected to Torah and mitzvot.

2. *REFA'ENU HASHEM VENERAFEH*: HEAL US, GOD, AND WE WILL BE HEALED

The first part of the blessing is taken, word for word, from *Yirmeyahu* 17:14, with the singular form of the verse switched into the plural. Yirmeyahu says to God, "Heal me, God, and I will be healed, save me and I will be saved, for You are my praise." Here, too, we must ask: Was Yirmeyahu sick? An examination of the previous verses clearly places this "healing" in the context we described regarding the crossing of the sea:

> God is the hope of Israel, all who forsake You shall be shamed,
> and they that depart from You shall be written in the earth,
> For they have forsaken God, a fount of living waters.
> Heal me, God, and I will be healed, save me and I will be saved,
> for You are my praise. (*Yirmeyahu* 17:13–14)

Verse 13 describes what happens when one forsakes the fount of living waters, God. All who forsake You will be shamed, will be disgraced, will wither, for without the fount of living waters it is impossible to survive. After this prophetic vision, the prophet immediately exclaims in prayer, using the first person rather than speaking in the name of the people, "Heal me, God, and I will be healed." It is clear to Yirmeyahu that God's healing of Israel is the opposite of forsaking the fount of living waters. Closeness to the fount of life, to the Torah, and to God, is health, and healing is the opposite of forsaking God.

In other words, the prophet is not praying for a cure for his illness. He is requesting that he be immersed in the fount of living waters, he is seeking closeness to God. This closeness will result naturally in physical health, vitality of strength, and vibrancy of life.

We now understand the duplication of "Heal me, God, and I will be healed." The act of healing here is quite distinct from the ultimate physical result. The "Heal me" takes place on the spiritual-psychological plane. The act of healing is not medicinal but Divine and Torah-based, through closeness to God. The result is physical health. We are not asking, as Yirmeyahu did not ask, for a particular medicine which will act against a particular malady, but rather for the act of healing in general, an acceptance of the covenant between Israel and God and its fulfillment. The result is not equivalent to the process and is not to be taken for granted. It is an expression in the physical world of an internal spiritual process, and is therefore the subject of a separate request within the framework of the blessing. *Heal me* – may You please attach Yourself to my spirit and my soul, *and I will be healed* – my flesh and my body and will be cured.

This understanding may constitute the explanation and background for Chida's exegesis of the verse in *Yirmeyahu.* Chida raised the question of duplication, and answered as follows:

> It is known that when a person has a physical malady, it is because of his transgression, and the main sickness is in his soul which has damaged a limb or sinew that corresponds to a specific commandment which he did not observe out of the positive commandments, or a negative commandment which he has transgressed, as our teacher R. Chayim Vital *zt"l* explained at length in *Shaarei Kedusha* – see there in great length. This is what is written, "Heal me" in my soul, "and I will be healed" in by body, "save me" from the hand of the prosecutor created by my transgression who stands and prosecutes in heaven against my soul, "and I will be saved" from physical suffering. "For You are my praise," and I have no redeemer other than You. (*Tzavarei Shalal* on *Haftarat Bechukotai,* 3)

Chida, based upon R. Chayim Vital's doctrine on the relationship between the body and the soul, explains the verse as requesting Divine treatment on the spiritual-psychological level, and the result will inevitably occur on the physical plane as well. We explained the source for this form of psychological treatment in a slightly different way to Chida, who speaks about sin. We spoke about the opposite element, about observance of the commandments. The point is fundamentally the same though. Closeness to God and cleaving to His commandments is the fount of living waters; physical recovery is the result.

Chida offers an additional explanation to the verse, and although it provides a different explanation for the words, it is based on the same concept. His words are based on the statement of the Zohar:

> R. Elazar commenced and stated: "Heal me, God, and I will be healed." Once he has said "Heal me," why does he say, "And I will be healed"?... Rather, all acts of healing in the world are in God's hands, but some of them are through an agent whereas others are performed without an agent. Those which are performed through an agent are healing, but after a period of time they return, whereas those which the Holy One blessed be He heals [directly] never return. (Zohar Part 3, 304)

In other words, and as Chida explains it, "'Heal me, God' – by Your hand, 'and I will be healed' – forever, 'save me, God' – by Yourself, as it were, 'and I will be saved' – and there will be no more subjugation" (Chida, ibid., 6). This is, of course, another explanation for the duplication, but it can be also explained in accordance with our thesis. The difference between healing by an agent and healing by God is the difference between a physical medicinal treatment (the agent) and cleaving to the fount of living waters. If the connection is to God directly, then the body is in a state of life. If the treatment is merely on the physical level, then a person is in a fundamental state of sickness, which he fights locally with medicine. He is prone to slip and fall at any moment.

3. *HOSHI'ENU VENIVASHE'A*: SAVE US, AND WE WILL BE SAVED

In light of our explanation, the appearance of salvation in the blessing of healing is evident. The real fundamental goal of the blessing of healing is the presence of God in our biological lives, which is expressed as health and life. Since the blessing is not limited to physical health, although health is the principal expression of life, we expand the request to salvation in general. If we attach ourselves to the fount of living waters, this will be expressed in health, but also in other achievements, in the vitality of life and the success of life over troubles. This is the salvation – hence, "And we will be saved."

4. *KI TEHILATEINU ATA*: FOR YOU ARE OUR PRAISE

Rashi[3] explains that we praise God for being our Savior and Healer. But our praise also serves as a reason for our being granted health. This is clear once we realize that the health here is a direct result of our closeness to God and not a gift which He separately grants us. Closeness to God and His presence residing within us are expressions of His covenant with us, a covenant which requires that we accept God as our Savior and King. "For You are our praise" does not mean that we praise Him, but that God is the goal of our lives and He is forever present in our experience. We identify ourselves as the people who carry God's name on our lips. "For You are our praise" means that God's name is in our mouths, and therefore we bear His name. God, the fount of living waters, is in our midst – and this is as a result of the fact that we, for our part, accept upon ourselves to praise Him, and to carry His name in our midst. If our lives are based on a connection of praise to God, then we will be full of life and healthy.

This explains the unusual use of the noun "our praise" to express that we praise Him. Healing does not come as a reward for the fact we fulfilled the commandment of reciting praise, but for ourselves being an object, a *cheftza*, of God's praise. One who prays is, in his very being, praise of God, for he is obligated to serve Him in every way he can and to carry His name and His praise in the world.

3. *Yirmeyahu* 17:15.

5. *VEHAALEH REFUA SHELEIMA LEKHOL MAKKOTEINU*: AND BRING A COMPLETE HEALING FOR ALL OUR AILMENTS

After this introduction, we add the specific request, healing for our wounds and maladies. Only after citing the praise-justification for the process of connecting to life do we return to requesting a cure for physical illness. After the specific request for healing comes a specific praise-justification – "For You are a faithful God, King, and Healer." This blessing has two separate parts, and therefore there are two separate justifications. Finally, we end with the *chatima*, "Who heals the sick *of His people Israel*," for in this blessing we are not requesting recovery from all afflictions of the flesh, which are universal to all of mankind, but rather fulfillment of the covenant and a spiritual connection with God based upon His covenant with the Jewish people.

6. *ROFEH NE'EMAN*: FAITHFUL HEALER

Unlike the other expressions in the blessing, which are closely aligned with the verses in Yirmeyahu and elsewhere, the phrase "Faithful Healer" does not have a Biblical source. In his *Peirush HaTefillot*, R. Yehuda b. R. Yakar cites a verse from the *Tokhecha*, the description of Divine retribution: "And God will make your plagues amazing, and the plagues of your seed – great and faithful plagues, *evil and faithful (ne'emanim) diseases*" (*Devarim* 28:59). In order to understand what faithful healing is, we must first try to understand what "faithful diseases" are.

Rashi (ad loc.) explains that faithful diseases are diseases which successfully fulfill the Divine mission for which they were sent. Ibn Ezra suggests that faithful diseases are diseases which have no cure, which are permanent and untreatable.[4] This would imply that faithful healing means a permanent cure which will not fail.[5] This is apparently the understanding of R. Yehuda b. R. Yakar as well; he quotes a midrash which explains the

4 "*Ne'eman*," faithful, means steadfast and strong, as in the verse: "And his hands were steadfast (*emuna*) until the sun set" (*Shemot* 17:12).

5. This explanation aligns with the words of the Zohar and Chida's explanation which were cited earlier.

significance of the two birds in the ritual cleansing of a person afflicted with *tzaraat*: "Just as [the slaughtered bird] cannot return, so too the affliction cannot return. Thus, it is written, 'For I am HaShem your Healer.'"[6]

7. THE EIGHTH – LIKE CIRCUMCISION

The Gemara in *Megilla* asks why the blessing of healing was chosen as the eighth blessing.

> R. Acha said: Since circumcision was given on the eighth [day], which requires healing, therefore they established this as the eighth [blessing]. (*Megilla* 17b)

You might claim that the connection is between health and that which occurs *after* the circumcision, in whose wake healing is required. In light of what we have learned, however, we can perhaps explain that the connection is to the circumcision itself, and it is no coincidence that they saw circumcision as a foundation of healing. As we have explained, the source of the Jewish people's healing is covenant, the affiliation to the community of God. Circumcision is a mark in the body which constitutes a physical manifestation of the circumcised person becoming a servant of God, and this parallels our explanation of the phrase "You are our praise," the spiritual manifestation of the person praying carrying God's name. True, the baby needs healing after the circumcision, but the circumcision, or "*brit*" – which literally means covenant – is also the source of healing itself. Hence, the blessing of healing was established as the eighth blessing, which parallels the day of circumcision, and not as the ninth, tenth, or eleventh, which parallel the days of recovery. Healing, like the covenant of circumcision, is a sign in the body indicating the connection to God in one's soul. One who is a member of the covenant of circumcision is also a member of life and health.

May it be His will that the faithful Healer send a complete healing to all the sick of His people, and salvation and comfort to the members of His covenant.

---

6. The midrash assumes that if God is the Healer, then the cure is eternal. It seems that this is the source for the words of the Zohar.

Chapter 14

Birkat HaShanim: The Blessing of the Years

בָּרֵךְ עָלֵינוּ יהוה אֱלֹהֵינוּ אֶת הַשָּׁנָה הַזֹּאת
וְאֶת כָּל מִינֵי תְבוּאָתָהּ, לְטוֹבָה
וְתֵן טַל וּמָטָר לִבְרָכָה / וְתֵן בְּרָכָה
עַל פְּנֵי הָאֲדָמָה, וְשַׂבְּעֵנוּ מִטּוּבָהּ
וּבָרֵךְ שְׁנָתֵנוּ כַּשָּׁנִים הַטּוֹבוֹת.
בָּרוּךְ אַתָּה יהוה, מְבָרֵךְ הַשָּׁנִים.

Bless this year for us, Lord our God,
And all its types of produce for good.
Grant dew and rain as a blessing
On the face of the earth,
And satisfy us with Your goodness, like the best of years.
Blessed are You, Lord, who blesses the years.

1. THE BLESSING OF THE YEARS

The text of this blessing does not seem to have a clear Biblical source. The *Rishonim* (R. Yehuda b. R. Yakar, Abudraham) identified just one verse as a possible source for part of the formulation of this blessing: "And I will restore (*shillamti*) to you the years" (*Yoel* 2:25).

Although only a single word ("*shanim*," years) from this verse appears in our blessing, the commentators were correct in their directing us to examine it. The word "years" is the most striking word in the blessing, and appears not only in the opening, but in the *me'ein chatima* and the *chatima* as well. Yet, its role as the object of this blessing is wholly incomprehensible. It is obvious that the theme of this blessing is success and prosperity, primarily for food, and thus the obvious object for the action of "blessing" could have been the earth (if we are thinking primarily in an agricultural framework, such as the verse "And bless the earth") or, more directly, ourselves. Unexpectedly, the Sages chose to associate the blessing with a unit of time, with *the year*. This is reflected by the standard Rabbinic name for our blessing – *Birkat HaShanim,* the blessing of the years. Why is time being blessed here, and how does the blessing of the year express itself in our material prosperity?

A second difficulty, less striking, centers on the verb that appears in this blessing. The action required of God is blessing – Bless for us, bless our year, who blesses the years. Even the noun, the object requested, is blessing – "And grant a blessing." There is nothing inappropriate about this in and of itself, until we realize that, in the same vein, we could have used the root "bless" for every other blessing – all of them are requests for blessing. We could be blessed with health, with knowledge, or with forgiveness. Yet, ultimately, only this blessing is a request for blessing per se, in a unique manner. This is the "blessing of blessing" no less than it is the "blessing of the years." On the other hand, the blessing is not detailed and there is no clear explication as to the content of the "blessing" in this blessing. Were it not for the lone reference to rain on the face of the earth, the formulation of the blessing would sound like a general request for absolutely anything. In other words, we have to ask ourselves why material prosperity and success are described simply and generically as "blessing." And if we put these two questions together, what is the true meaning of the *chatima* – "Who blesses the years?"

The initial answer to the question, why a unit of time is the unit of a blessing for prosperity, is that the Sages undoubtedly thought in agricultural terms. Agriculture revolves in a yearly-seasonal cycle, especially in the Land of Israel which is dependent upon the winter rains. One has either a blessed year or an unblessed one. This, however, gives rise to a new question: Why did the Sages choose to particularize the request to agriculture? Despite the importance of agriculture, it is not the only sphere in which we need to request material success.

2. AND I WILL RESTORE TO YOU THE YEARS

Since the blessing of the years is based upon the verse in *Yoel*, let us examine this chapter and analyze the verse in its context. This chapter describes a terrible invasion of a great army, a plague of locusts, which blots out the sun and destroys everything that stands in its path:

> Blow a horn in Zion and sound an alarm on My holy mount; let all the dwellers on the earth tremble, for the day of God has come, for it is close.
> A day of darkness and gloom, a day of cloud and fog, spread like soot over the hills;
> A vast, mighty horde, nothing like it has ever happened, and it shall never happen again through the years and ages. (*Yoel* 2:1–2)

The prophet portrays horrific descriptions of desolation and destruction, and then calls for repentance and prayer:

> "Yet even now," says God, "turn back to Me with all your hearts, and with fasting, and weeping, and lamenting."
> And rend your hearts, rather than your garments, and turn back to HaShem your God,
> For He is gracious and compassionate, slow to anger, and abounding in kindness, and renouncing punishment. (12–13)

The prophet then describes the prayer that ascends by way of repentance, and the Divine response:

> The priests, the ministers of God, shall cry between the hall and the altar, and they shall say, "God, spare Your people, and let not Your heritage be given to shame by letting the nations rule over them, why should it be said amidst the nations, 'Where is their God'?"
> And God was zealous for His land, and He pitied His people.

> And God responded and said to His people, "Behold I shall send you grain, wine, and oil, and you shall be satisfied with it,
> But I shall not permit you to be again a shame amidst the nations." (17–19)

It is clear from these verses that the agricultural failure of the Land of Israel constitutes a desecration of the name of God. The result of the loss of produce caused by the locust swarm is that the nations will exclaim, "Where is their God!" The recurring blessing, the sending of grain, wine, and oil, pledges that Israel will never again be a shame among the nations. The response to the priests' prayer is a blessing of fruit, the arrival of rain in its proper time, the filling up of the granaries, and finally – restoration of the years.

Fear not, O earth! Be glad and rejoice, for God has wrought great deeds.

> Fear not, O beasts of the field, for the pastures in the wilderness are clothed with grass, for the trees have borne their fruit; fig tree and vine have yielded their strength. O children of Zion, be glad, rejoice in HaShem your God, for He has given you the early rain in His kindness,
> And He makes the rain fall as before, the early rain and the late.
> And the granaries shall be filled with grain, and the vats shall overflow with wine and oil.
> *And I will restore to you the years* consumed by the locust and the hoppers, the grubs and the swarms,
> My great army which I sent against you. (21–25)

The conclusion of the prophecy explicitly describes the necessary association of the blessing of the land with God's presence among the Jewish people:

> And you shall eat your fill and praise the name of HaShem your God who dealt so wondrously with you,
> And My people shall never be shamed.

> *And You shall know that I am present in the midst of Israel,* and that
> I am HaShem your God and there is no other,
> And My people shall never be shamed. (26–27)

It is clear from this prophecy that agricultural success in the Land of Israel is the clear sign and expression of God's presence within the Jewish people. Agricultural failure is a mark of shame, and the return of God's presence promises – twice – that "My people shall never be shamed." A year devoid of blessing for the land is not merely agonizing, but is a deficient year, a wasted year; hence, God promises to restore the years which the locust consumed, like someone repaying a debt. The reason for this is that a year without agricultural success is a deficient year, deficient of God's presence, whereas a blessed year is a whole year, a year which sees the fulfillment of the promise "And You shall know that I am present in the midst of Israel."

3. *BERAKHA*: BLESSING

To better understand why blessing refers primarily to the blessing of the fruits of the land, we must remember that blessing means the power of growth and reproduction. The first blessing in the Torah was "*Peru urevu*," "Be fruitful and multiply." This is the blessing which concludes the creation of the world, and it was given only after creation was complete. In the act of creation, everything is created according to a plan, bound by its limits. Every created object is equal to itself and can contain no more than what was accorded to it by creation. But at the conclusion of creation, God blessed the animal world with the blessing of "Be fruitful and multiply," meaning the power to increase beyond the boundaries of creation, and thereby continuing, in a sense, the act of creation. This continuation develops and transcends its starting point. This power, to develop and multiply, is the power of creation, the power of God who creates *yesh me'ayin, ex nihilo*. The power of creation is granted to created things, to allow the continuation of true living growth and development.

Within the natural world, the place where we see this power of growth and reproduction is first and foremost in the land, which for us represents the bedrock of growth. Land, earth, and soil are metaphors for the source of growth. When we ask for prosperity and sustenance, we are not merely asking for the tangible objects we need to live on. We are not asking only for money, food, a daily quota of bread, or any other object that God can create and hand us. We are asking for blessing, the blessing of God; that is, the power to create by ourselves and to produce more on our own, to be creative and productive. To be blessed means to be endowed with creativity. This power of multiplication is the power of God Himself, and if we are blessed with it, it is only because God is present within us. A person who feels this creativity, this ability, knows "that I am present in the midst of Israel, and that I am HaShem your God…" (v. 27). Why? Not because God gave the Jewish people an abundance of food, but because "He has given you the early rain in His kindness" (v. 23). The rain which makes the fruit grow is the real blessing, rather than the fruit itself, and along with it – with the early rain – joy and delight.

This is also the key to the choice of the year, a unit of time, as the object of the blessing. Because the blessing is not the fruit itself, but growth and development, the blessing is applied to time. Growth is a process which exists in the context of time. Without time there can be no growth. A stationary object can exist without relating to time. But if I am asking for the presence of God to be expressed in the power of growth and development, then I am asking for something within the context of time, and hence – the blessing of the years. Time is not just the vessel which contains the blessing – a blessing over a period of time – but is the object of the blessing itself. I am asking to become part of a process, of something which can exist only within the sphere of time. In this blessing, I appeal to God who blesses the years, and makes things grow within time. God's presence within time is what man needs and yearns for, and this blessing of God's presence will express itself in the land.

4. *VESABE'ENU MITUVEKHA*: AND SATISFY US WITH YOUR GOODNESS

There are two versions of the fourth line of this blessing: "And satisfy us with *Your* goodness," "And satisfy us with *its* (the earth's) goodness (*mituvah*)." The first version is clearly in line with the theory that I have been presenting. We are asking explicitly to benefit from God's blessing, and that God should be active and present in our lives. In my opinion, the second version should also be understood in the same way. This will be clear if we pay attention to the verb used in this request – "*Vesabe'enu*," "And *satisfy* us with its goodness."

"*Sova*," satisfaction, means satiety. The connection between satisfaction and blessing lies at the heart of the mandate for the recitation of Grace after Meals, as appears in the verse, "And you shall eat and be satisfied, and you shall bless HaShem your God for the good land which He has given you" (*Devarim* 8:10). In this verse, and even more so in our blessing, I suggest we should not understand this satisfaction to be indicating the *quantity* of prosperity. We are not asking God to give us a specific quantity of success, a large enough amount for us to be satisfied. Satisfaction does not describe quantity, but rather a person's internal state. "Satisfy us" means give us a *feeling* of satisfaction, a feeling of gratification and completeness; this feeling is the feeling that we are productive enough to support ourselves. A person who is not creative, but has a support network, is not satisfied but needy, even if he is not currently hungry. Only a person who possesses – or has within him – an abundant and emanative source has true satisfaction. In the Shabbat *Amida* we say, in a slightly different context, "Satisfy us with Your goodness, and gladden our soul with Your salvation." This is not merely a physical feeling, but the sense of creativity and fullness of a productive life. It is the sense that one has at the end of a productive workday, a day well spent;[1] this is the feeling of productiveness – and satisfaction. The request of "And satisfy us with its goodness," the good of the land, is a prayer for an internal-spiritual connection to the physical-material goodness of this world. This goodness is itself based on the spiritual nature of blessing, productivity, and creativity.

Having said that, I admit that I prefer the version "And satisfy us with Your goodness (*mituvekha*)." The goodness of God here is not the fruit that God sends us, but the fullness of His presence in our midst, and the resultant blessing evident in our endeavors.

1. This is the exact opposite of one who sows the field, only to see it consumed by locusts.

5. THE LAND OF ISRAEL

The blessing does not explicitly mention the Land of Israel, but only "*haadama*," the land. Without a doubt, the blessing includes prosperity and success in all forms, and consequently refers to all lands. Nevertheless, it is clear to me that the blessing is hinting at the Land of Israel, as is quite clear in chapter 2 in the book of *Yoel*.[2] This should not be surprising. If the blessing is about God's presence, as manifested in the physical prosperity of the land, then clearly the correct appropriate scene for this is the heritage of God, the place of His presence, the Land of Israel. This understanding would support the accuracy of the version "And satisfy us with its (the Land of Israel's) goodness (*mituvah*)," and would essentially nullify the discrepancy between "its goodness (*tuvah*)" and "Your goodness (*tuvekha*)."

6. MIDWAY

We are halfway through the blessings in the *Shemoneh Esrei*. At this stage, the requests transition from the needs of the individual to the needs of the community in history, and from the fate of the Jew to the fate of the Jewish people. Notice the phenomenon which has been developed in the past chapters. Even though I was careful to emphasize in the introduction that the subjects of the blessings are worldly, genuine needs of the material man who lives on earth and not transcendental religious subjects, it transpires that to each of the blessings of request I have discovered a spiritual character. I have claimed that, in one way or another, we are asking for a closer relationship with God, whether this is with knowledge, repentance, forgiveness, healing, redemption, or prosperity. I admit that I did not set out with that goal at the start of the book – on the contrary, it was important for me to emphasize that the requests are based upon all the needs of man. The ideas presented here are the result of analyzing the nuances of the language, the Biblical parallels, and the Rabbinic statements. The resultant explanation is that the needs are indeed human needs as I intended, but the solution in each request was

2. This notion will be especially significant upon analyzing the next blessing; we will see there that there is in fact no specific blessing in the *Shemoneh Esrei* dedicated specifically to the Land of Israel.

God's willingness not only to provide us with our physical needs, but to also give of Himself; in this way God both forms a relationship with us and provides a response to our lack as well.

This idea seems to me now to be true and fundamental: the true, spiritual relationship between God and us is based on practical – including physical – needs of man, a creature of His handiwork. Prayer is a religious and spiritual connection, not by translating the language of prayer into something more refined, into alluding to the upper worlds and secret spiritual strivings; but because the necessities of man, who was created in God's image, are themselves only truly answered by connecting to the source of life, King of the world. When we pray, we are not asking for something not found in this world, but we are reasserting that the things of this world are all from God. We reaffirm that all our needs in this world are part and parcel of our relationship with God, and that only through accepting our necessities from God can we truly spiritualize our physical lives.

To return to the theme of the first chapter, prayer is *avoda*, service of God. Service is the centering of our needs on God, for only He can fulfill them and supply us with blessing and meaning. We truly want health, knowledge, and prosperity; yet, we realize that these things themselves are not merely earthly goods which we cannot do without, but are themselves the manifestation of God's presence and His blessing. If we obtain them elsewhere (or think that we can obtain them elsewhere), then they are no more than dust and ashes. If we realize that we are receiving them as part of – and from within – our relationship with God, from the fount of living waters, then they themselves are the basis for a religious cleaving unto the living God.

Chapter 15

Kibbutz Galuyot: Ingathering of the Exiles

תְּקַע בְּשׁוֹפָר גָּדוֹל לְחֵרוּתֵנוּ, וְשָׂא נֵס לְקַבֵּץ גָּלֻיּוֹתֵינוּ
וְקַבְּצֵנוּ יַחַד מֵאַרְבַּע כַּנְפוֹת הָאָרֶץ.
בָּרוּךְ אַתָּה יהוה, מְקַבֵּץ נִדְחֵי עַמּוֹ יִשְׂרָאֵל.

Sound the great shofar for our freedom,
And raise a mast for the ingathering of our exiles,
And gather us together from the four corners of the earth.
Blessed are You, Lord,
who gathers the dispersed of His people Israel.

The tenth blessing is the ingathering of the exiles.

Until this point, the blessings have expressed the private needs of the individual praying. From here onward, the blessings focus upon the national destiny of the Jewish people. From the blessing of the ingathering of the exiles until the blessing of "Who causes the horn of salvation to grow," every blessing deals with a different stage of the process of the future redemption; this stands in contrast to the previous blessings, which deal with the immediate needs of the individual.

1. THE THEME

This first request, the first stage of the redemption, is the ingathering of the exiles. There is a natural and justifiable tendency to see this blessing as a prayer referring to the Land of Israel. However, there is, in fact, no explicit mention of the Land of Israel in this blessing at all. It is clear, of course, that when God gathers our exiles, they will be gathered in a specific place, and there can be no question that that place is the Land of Israel. Yet, the blessing itself deals not with returning to the Land of Israel, but rather, in a clear and explicit manner, with the ingathering of a dispersed people. The blessing does not emphasize the superiority of one particular geographical location over another, but rather the importance of gathering all of Israel to *one* place in contrast to their dispersion in *many* places. It is true that, in the Sephardic tradition, the third line reads, "And gather us together from the four corners of the earth *to our land* (*le'artzenu*)";[1] but this only further emphasizes the absence of an explicit mention of the Land of Israel from this blessing. Clearly the addition of a single word ("*le'artzenu*") at the end of the sentence comes to fill this obvious void, but it does not have the power to change the clear, primary focus of the entire blessing.

Examining the blessing clearly shows us that the principal theme of this blessing is not the importance of the Land of Israel, but the "togetherness" – and gather us together. If we focus, as we did in the previous blessings, on the source of the request – on the human need and deficiency which the request comes to solve – it is clear that we are not talking about *exile*, an individual far away from his home, but rather *dispersion*, the dispersion of the Jewish people and their distance from one another. The root of this blessing is the need for unity, rather than the need to be at home, in the Land of Israel. The crucial request is: "And gather us together from the four corners of the earth." The *chatima* of the blessing is quite clear – we are addressing Him who "gathers the dispersed of His people Israel."

Before we try and understand the significance of this theme, let us, as usual, examine the language of the blessing. This gives rise to several difficulties:

1. The phrase "to our land" does not appear in the Ashkenazic version.

1. The blessing is characterized by its use of very poetic language. The ingathering of the exiles takes place with the blast of a shofar and the raising of a mast. What is the purpose of this flowery language?
2. The blasting of the shofar is "for our freedom." Why is freedom mentioned here? The blessing is about the ingathering of the exiles and not about freedom. This question is especially relevant today, when the most Diaspora Jews are not in a state of slavery; yet it seems that, regardless of the particular era, there is an essential difference between the problem of exile and dispersion and the problem of enslavement. What is the connection between ingathering of the exiles and freedom?
3. What is a "*great*" shofar? What is the difference between a regular shofar and a great shofar?
4. In the *chatima*, the dispersion of Israel is described by a new term which does not appear in the main body of the blessing – "nidchei *Yisrael*." *Niddachim* does not just mean dispersed, but rather displaced – it suggests the presence of a force which is pushing and forcing out the displaced Jews from their natural home. In the verse from *Yeshayahu*,[2] which serves as the source for the opening of this blessing, "*niddachim*," displaced ones, is used in parallel to "*ovedim*," lost ones. A displaced person is not merely *far* from home; he is prevented from returning. Why do we use this specific description in this blessing?

2. INGATHERING AND UNITY

The idea of ingathering and unity is one of fundamental principles of Jewish redemption. In Jewish thought, the disunity of the Jewish people is the antithesis of the unity of God. The creation of the world is meant to reflect the kingship and the unity of God. When there is disunity in the world, when not everything is directed toward serving God, there is a deficiency in God's kingship, and it constitutes an

2. "And it shall be on that day that a great shofar shall be blasted, and the lost ones (*ovedim*) of the land of Assyria shall come, and the displaced ones (*niddachim*) of the land of Egypt, and they shall bow down to God on the holy mountain, in Jerusalem" (*Yeshayahu* 27:13).

injury to the unity of God. On the day when everything in the world will be unified in the service of God, the unity of the world will constitute the basis for the unity and kingship of God. We proclaim this vision in the prayers of Rosh HaShana, the day on which God ascends the throne of kingship:

> And everything made will fear You,
> And all creatures will bow down to You,
> *And they will all be made into a single union,*
> *To do Your will with a perfect heart.*

And the result is:

> *On that day, God will be one and His name will be one.*

This role, establishing the unity of God in the world, is a role specifically borne by the Jewish people. Hence, the physical dispersion of the Jewish people detracts from the unity of God in the world and, primarily, from the unity of His kingship. When we are dispersed and disunified, there is no social-national vehicle to embody the kingship and unity of God. Thus, the problem is not the absence of the Jewish people from a particular place – although, naturally, the one place which is to be the locus of the unity of the Jewish people, the only place where such a unity can occur, is the Land of Israel – but rather the lack of the physical and metaphysical unity of the Jewish people. We are pleading for a solution to this terrible problem, a problem which is severe not only for us, but for the Divine presence as well. Neither the individual Jew, nor even the entire Jewish people dispersed across the four corners of the earth, can truly be the vehicle for Divine unity within the world.

There are two earthly vehicles for the majesty of God: one human-social, and one local-geographical. The former – the Jewish people – is the subject of our blessing. The latter is Jerusalem, which is the subject of a different blessing, further on. The two foci are bound together in various verses, for example in the verse which constitutes the source for the expression "dispersed of Israel": "God is the Builder of Jerusalem, He will gather together the dispersed of Israel" (*Tehillim* 147:2). The order in this verse is the opposite to that of the *Amida*,[3] yet it seems to me that the more significant difference is the Sages' decision to separate these two themes entirely in the formulation of the *Amida* and distance them from each other. This becomes even more apparent when we examine the verse which provided the language for the opening of our blessing: "And it shall be on that day that a great shofar is blasted, and the lost ones of the land of Assyria shall come, and the displaced ones of the land of Egypt, and they shall bow down to God on the holy mountain, in Jerusalem" (*Yeshayahu* 27:13). The prophet Yeshayahu emphasizes that the gathering together of Israel is for the purpose of immediately ascending to serve God in Jerusalem, the royal capital. The Sages drew on the language of this verse in formulating our blessing, but deliberately omitted its immediate continuation about Jerusalem, delaying the latter theme by inserting three other blessings between them.

The *Tur* explains the appearance of the shofar in our blessing by reference to the above verse which connects the ingathering of the exiles with service of God in Jerusalem. When offering up sacrifices, there is a requirement to sound a blast: "And on the day of your joy, and on your festivals, and on your new moons, you shall blast trumpets over your burnt offerings and over your peace offerings, and they shall be to you as a remembrance before your God, I am HaShem your God" (*Bemidbar* 10:10). Thus, explains the *Tur*, given that the purpose of ingathering the exiles is to bow before God in Jerusalem, God uses the shofar, a symbol for the sacrificial service, in order to activate the ingathering the exiles. It seems to me, however, that specifically in the blessings of the *Shemoneh Esrei* we see that this is not the case. The shofar blasts for our freedom, wholly unrelated to sacrifices. On the contrary, here the shofar *initiates* the ingathering of the exiles, whereas with the sacrificial service the shofar is a response to the sacrifice, symbolizing the manifestation of God's presence *as a result of* the service. Despite the fact that the *Tur*'s explanation lines up with the verse in *Yeshayahu*, it seems to me that the Sages saw the shofar as directly associated with the ingathering of the exiles, and the offering of sacrifices as an eventual and somewhat remote

3. Namely, Jerusalem comes before gathering the dispersed.

goal in the process of the ingathering. We must find a direct association between the shofar and the ingathering of the exiles.

As we have seen in Biblical verse, there is no doubt that the ingathering of the exiles is meant to lead to service of God in Jerusalem. This idea follows from the notion that the physical unity of the people of Israel is the vehicle for the unity and kingship of the God of Israel. The aim is one nation serving one God. Yet, as I have pointed out multiple times, the formulation of the *Shemoneh Esrei* is based on necessities and not on philosophical ideas. The building of Jerusalem, the final destination of the ingathering of the exiles, will be addressed in the continuation of the *Amida*, and it constitutes an independent need of the Jewish people. But in terms of the formulation of necessities, things which we lack, there is no clear connection between the need for Jewish unity and the need for service of God. Our blessing alludes to this final destination, because it establishes the meaning of our request, but the request stands on its own two feet. Thus, we are left with the question of what the connection is between the shofar and the ingathering of the exiles.

The shofar is the central symbol of Rosh HaShana. Not only do we blast the shofar over each of the middle blessings of the *Musaf* prayer on Rosh HaShana, but there is also an entire blessing dedicated to the shofar. What is the theme of the ten verses of *Shofarot*? Examining those verses instantly shows that the common theme is the revelation of God's presence. The first three verses address the giving of the Torah (the past), the three verses from *Ketuvim* address the presence of God in our lives (the present), and the final three verses (including the verse which we discussed, "And it shall be on that day that a great shofar is blasted") speak about the future redemption. The shofar is "the blast of the King," the fanfare sounded before the King enters. The shofar blast is not a symbol for God's hidden presence within the natural order, but rather proclaims the revelation of His presence which pierces the veil of nature and transforms it.

We now understand the use of the phrase "great shofar." A great shofar is a shofar that transforms history, whose appearance brings about not only an event of political importance, but a religious revolution, a fundamental change in the standard relationship between nature and its Creator. Today "You are indeed a God in hiding,"[4] but "on that day a great shofar shall be blasted." The shofar, namely, the revelation of God's tangible presence within the world, is what calls upon the dispersions of Israel to gather together. Consequently, there is a qualitative difference in the nature of the ingathering. The Jewish people gather together *around* the call of God, they are drawn after the sound of the shofar. An ingathering of the exiles which is not around this call is not true Jewish unity, for it is not centered on the unity of God.

This idea, that the ingathering is around God, is clearly expressed in the second line of the blessing, with the special metaphor: "And raise a mast for the ingathering of our exiles." A mast is a flagpole, a lofty banner, a flag raised on high. The raising of a mast leads to an ingathering of the exiles because they gather around it. The verse in the order of *Shofarot* which precedes "And it shall be on that day that a great shofar is blasted" is: "All inhabitants of the world and dwellers of the earth, when a mast is raised in the hills, observe; and when a shofar is blasted, listen" (*Yeshayahu* 18:3). Both the shofar and the mast call on people to follow them and to gather around them. Since God is the one blasting the shofar and God is the one raising the mast, this means that we are praying and asking for a gathering with God at its center.

To make this even clearer, the Sages added a word not found in the original verses – "*lecheirutenu*," for our freedom. Simple geographical gathering is not necessarily related to freedom. The word "*cheirut*," freedom, is parallel to the Biblical term "*deror*." This is reflected in the *Targum*, which uses *cheirut* as the translation for *deror*. R. Yehuda b. R. Yakar explains the term "our freedom" in our blessing by referring to the following verse: "To proclaim freedom (*deror*) to the captives, and liberation to the imprisoned" (*Yeshayahu* 61:1). The ingathering of the exiles is not just a geographical process but a process of liberation, because the dispersion itself is a state of Divine concealment, of hiddenness and obscurity. In our world, we cannot hear the sound of the shofar of God, the shofar of revelation. If the exiles are ingathered around the raised banner of God, the result is not only social but spiritual – spiritual freedom and redemption. In one word, a mere hint, the blessing leads us to

4. *Yeshayahu* 4:15.

seeing dispersion as a form of slavery, with the shofar a call of liberation.[5] This understanding of the ingathering of the exiles does not override the political significance, but rather reinforces it and provides the political-social revolution with a spiritual-religious significance.

We now come to the *chatima*, which presents a new concept – "*nidchei Yisrael*." The *niddachim*, as is implied from the parallel in the verse, are "lost." This is the meaning of the verse in the book of *Shmuel*: "For we will surely die, like water that is poured out on the ground and cannot be gathered up; God will not spare any soul, but makes plans so that no one shall be displaced (*niddach*)" (*Shmuel Bet* 14:14). This is verse about Avshalom, who is "the displaced of the king," not allowed in the court of King David his father, and is banished. Returning the displaced person does not just mean bringing him to Jerusalem, but rather restoring him to a proper relationship with his father. The dispersion of the Jewish people is also displacement, because when there is no unity among the people then there is no basis for God's kingship and thus no manifestation of His presence.

If the focus of this blessing were indeed the Land of Israel, then the displaced would be displaced from the land. This notion would be based on the primary natural connection of Jews to the Land of Israel, from which they were displaced by a force which conquered their natural proclivity. But since, as we have seen, this blessing is about dispersion and unity, we reach the conclusion that the displacing force is a dispersing force, and this overcomes the natural state of unity. The primary natural state of the Jewish people is one of unity and togetherness. The Jewish people are one nation in the land – one body, an organic-metaphysical unity. Thus, it is understood why the restoration of the various parts of the body to organic functioning is a return to our freedom, to wholeness, a return to the true self of the living organism that is the Jewish people.

5. This notion of the shofar as a call of liberation is, of course, the principle of the shofar of the Jubilee year. "And you shall sound the shofar blast in the seventh month, on the tenth of the month, on the Day of Atonement, you shall sound the shofar throughout all your land.... And you shall declare liberation (*deror*) throughout the land for all its inhabitants" (*Vayikra* 25:9–10).

Now, you may ask, what is the cause for the dispersion of Israel, or, in other words, what is the root of the problem that we are trying to correct? The traditional answer points to the nations as the cause – *shibbud malkhuyot*, the subjugation of the nations. Our blessing gives a different answer, one especially appropriate to our own times, when the nations are not withholding our return to Israel. The answer is – the lack of revelation, the silence of the shofar, the absence of an open call from God. This blessing includes a call for the reawakening of God's presence, so that we will be gathered around it. This connection, between the reawakening of God's presence and the ingathering of the exiles, is explicitly found in several of the chapters of *Yeshayahu* dealing with redemption. For instance:

> Awake, awake, put on strength, O arm of God; awake as in the days of old, in the ancient generations. It was you that hacked the vainglorious, that killed the crocodile.[6]
>
> ...
>
> Then the redeemed of God shall return, and come to Zion with singing, and everlasting joy on their heads; they shall obtain joy and gladness, sorrow and sighing shall flee. (*Yeshayahu* 51:9, 11)

With this blessing we are beginning a series of blessings which deal with the process of redemption. The order of the blessings teaches us about this process. The first step is to establish an organically whole society. The second step, in the next blessing, is to have that society exhibit justice and righteousness, in other words – building the institutions of a redemptive society, the basis for God's presence. Afterward, once there is one nation in the land which functions correctly, comes the downfall of the wicked, followed by the victory of the righteous, the rebuilding of Jerusalem, and the kingdom of David. In light of this, each individual praying should try to identify the point on the path of history at which he, and the Jewish people, currently reside.

---

6. The commentators understand this as referring to Egypt, the land of our captivity.

Chapter 16

Mishpat: Justice

הָשִׁיבָה שׁוֹפְטֵינוּ כְּבָרִאשׁוֹנָה וְיוֹעֲצֵינוּ כְּבַתְּחִלָּה
וְהָסֵר מִמֶּנּוּ יָגוֹן וַאֲנָחָה
וּמְלֹךְ עָלֵינוּ אַתָּה יהוה לְבַדְּךָ בְּחֶסֶד וּבְרַחֲמִים
וְצַדְּקֵנוּ בַּמִּשְׁפָּט.
בָּרוּךְ אַתָּה יהוה
מֶלֶךְ אוֹהֵב צְדָקָה וּמִשְׁפָּט.

Restore our judges as at first,
And our counselors as at the beginning,
And remove from us sorrow and sighing.
And rule over us, You, God, alone in kindness and in mercy,
And acquit us in justice.
Blessed are You, Lord,
A King who loves righteousness and justice.

1. THE THEME OF THE BLESSING

On the one hand, the *chatima* – "A King who loves righteousness and justice" – seems to unequivocally show that this blessing is about justice. But even this clear answer requires further inspection. Precisely what are we asking for? Are we asking to be judged for our actions? On the Days of Awe, we stand to be judged, and even then we primarily seek to save ourselves from justice through the attribute of mercy. Why do we ask to be judged on a regular day? Does man feel a need to be judged immediately, unable to wait until Rosh HaShana and Yom Kippur? And then, what is the meaning of the middle request in this blessing – "And remove from us sorrow and sighing"? What does sorrow have to do with justice, and why do we ask for emotional respite specifically in this blessing? We may add to these questions several questions based on an analysis of the text of the blessing.

1. The blessing opens with two requests – for the restoration of our judges and the restoration of our counselors. The two requests relate to ancient times: "Restore our judges *as at first*, and our counselors *as at the beginning*." This request, returning to a pristine state of the distant past, appears once elsewhere in prayer; it is found in connection with the rebuilding of Temple, in the *Musaf* prayer on festivals: "Build Your house *as at the beginning*." Yet, in the weekday *Shemoneh Esrei*, the phrase "as at the beginning" is not used in connection with rebuilding the Temple, but only here, referring to the reinstitution of our judges and counselors. Why? Why is it important to define the reality of justice (and counsel) as a return to an ancient state? Is the ideal of Jewish life only defined in relation to the past, rather than by yearning and looking to the future? Are all our hopes for redemption merely a desire to reconstitute the earliest stages of Jewish existence?
2. Who are the counselors? What does counsel have to do with justice?
3. "And rule over us, You, God, alone." What does God's rule have to do with social justice?
4. "In kindness and in mercy." Kindness and mercy are necessities of mankind. Yet, if the blessing is about justice and righteousness, why are we mentioning kindness and mercy?
5. "And acquit us (*vetzadekenu*) in judgment" (the Ashkenazic version). The language of the blessing is a derivation of the verse, "And I shall betroth you with righteousness and with justice, and with kindness and with mercy."[1] Aside from the order reversal, our blessing also substitutes the noun "*tzedek*," righteousness, with the verb "*vetzade-*

1. Indeed, in the Sephardic version, the text reads "With kindness and with mercy, with righteousness and with justice," as in the verse but in a different order. One could explain the change in order as a desire to conclude with "justice" so as to fulfill the

kenu," and acquit us. What does "and acquit us in judgment" mean, precisely? What is the connection between "*vetzadekenu*" and the word "*tzedaka*," righteousness, which appears in the *chatima* – a King who loves righteousness and justice?

6. This is the only blessing in whose *chatima* we refer to God as "King." Why?
7. "A King who loves righteousness and justice." As we previously noted in the blessing of repentance, every *chatima* should follow the formulation of "Blessed... who performs that which we have requested." The *chatima* defines God as the one who has the power to fulfill the request. Here, assuming that the blessing is a request for justice, the *chatima* should have read, "Blessed... who judges with righteousness," or something similar. Why does the blessing refer to God's love for justice, rather than His power to dispense it?

Most of these questions emphasize our original question. We can summarize all of the above by repeating it: What is this blessing, with its shifting themes and unclear focus, actually about? Or, in other words, what are we asking for?

2. "THEY WHO ERR FROM YOUR PATH SHALL BE JUDGED"

The Gemara (*Berakhot* 29a) provides the formulation of the *Tefilla Ketzara*, the short prayer to be recited in a time of great urgency. This shortened formulation was instituted for a person who is unable to recite the entire long *Shemoneh Esrei*. In the *Tefilla Ketzara*, a small phrase of

---

rule that a *me'ein chatima*, a quasi-reference to the theme of the *chatima*, must appear right before the *chatima*. However, R. Yehuda b. R. Yakar explained the change on fundamental grounds:

> Even though it says in the verse "With righteousness and with justice, and with kindness and with mercy," one who prays mentions kindness and mercy first, as the *Midrash Tanchuma* states: All the ways of God are kindness and truth – kindness is mentioned before truth, and righteousness before justice, as it is written (*Tehillim* 89:15), "Righteousness and justice are the base of Your throne, kindness and truth stand before You." From here we learn that we should mention kindness before mercy, because truth is the attribute of mercy, and kindness stands to the right of mercy.

a few words comes in place of each of the middle blessings. It should be assumed that each phrase captures the essence of the content of the corresponding blessing. In the *Tefilla Ketzara*, the phrase which corresponds to the blessing of justice is: "They who err from Your path shall be judged."[2] The *Rishonim* disagree concerning who will judge these errant people. R. Yona explains that God shall judge the sinners. Accordingly, this blessing is a prayer for the judgment of the wicked by God. In the text of the longer blessing, this corresponds most closely to the third line – "And rule over us, You, God, alone."

Rashi, however, explains that the sinners will be judged by Torah law. Accordingly, this is a prayer for the restoration of the Jewish legal system – the Sanhedrin and the courts of law. This explanation corresponds most closely to the first line of the blessing – "Restore our judges as at first." Other commentators offered similar ideas, such as to read it as "They who err from Your path shall *judge*" (in the active tense, rather than the passive). The explanation would then be that judges who pass judgment against Torah law will eventually return to pass judgment in accordance with Your path – according to Torah law. In terms of content, this explanation is similar to that of Rashi – a request to restore the system of Torah-based courts of law.

3. THE SOURCE TEXT

As usual, we search for the source text for our blessing in the Tanakh. The opening, as well as the conclusion, are taken from *Yeshayahu*.

> I shall restore your judges as at first, and your counselors as at the beginning;
> Afterward you shall be called the city of righteousness, a faithful city.
> Zion shall be redeemed with justice, and those that return unto her with righteousness. (*Yeshayahu* 1:26–27)

There is nothing in these verses about God ruling over us, nor is there any reference to eliminating sorrow and sighing. These verses seem to

2. *Berakhot* 29a.

support the understanding of Rashi,[3] yet if we read a few verses earlier in this chapter from *Yeshayahu,* we find God swearing an oath:

> Therefore, so says the Master, God of hosts, Chief of Israel,
> Ah, I will comfort Myself from My adversaries, and revenge Myself from My enemies.
> And I shall turn My hand upon you, and purge purely your dross, and take away all your tin. (Ibid. 24–25)

These verses are specifically reminiscent of R. Yona's explanation – God punishes the wicked. Thus, we are no closer to finding a solution to our problems.

4. THE GOOD OLD DAYS

Let us return to the first question. Why does it not suffice to ask for good judges and counselors, without asking to return to a model of the past, to our judges as at first and to our counselors as at the beginning? The answer to this question can be found if we examine the first instance of the phrase which stars in the *chatima* of our blessing – "*Tzedaka umishpat,*" "Righteousness and justice."

When God decides to destroy Sedom, he first goes to speak with Avraham:

> And God said: Am I hiding from Avraham that which I am going to do? For Avraham shall surely become a great and mighty nation, and all the nations of the earth shall be blessed in him. For I know him, because he shall instruct his children and his household after him, and they shall follow the way of God, *performing righteousness and justice,* so that God shall bring upon Avraham all that He has spoken about him. (*Bereshit* 18:17–19)

The way of God is righteousness and justice. It is the foundation of these principles in the household of Avraham that explains his being

3. In which case, we need to explain why the Sages added the additional motifs to this blessing.

chosen to be the forefather of a great and mighty nation in whom all the nations of the earth shall be blessed. "For I know him" is explained by Rashi ad loc to be "an expression of cherishment... for a person who cherishes someone brings him close to himself, becomes acquainted with him, and gets to know him well." Ramban suggests a different explanation: "I have raised him and elevated him." According to the commonality of both explanations, God explains that the basis for His personal, close relationship with Avraham is the latter's instruction of righteousness and justice. It is unsurprising, then, that the first chapter in *Yeshayahu* explains that the impending destruction is a direct result of abandoning the path of righteousness and justice. How can the destruction of Jerusalem be avoided? "Learn to do well, seek justice, relieve the oppressed, judge the orphan, fight for the widow" (*Yeshayahu* 1:17). The entire relationship of God to the Jews is based on path of righteousness and justice. The city described in that same chapter – "full of justice, righteousness lodged in it – and now murderers" (ibid. 21) – is a city that God does not "know" in the way that He knew Avraham. The rectification for this situation is presented in those verses which appear in our blessing:

> And I shall restore your judges as at first, and your counselors as at the beginning; Afterward you shall be called the city of righteousness, a faithful city. Zion shall be redeemed with justice, and those that return unto her with righteousness. (*Yeshayahu* 1:26–27)

According to this analysis, I believe that "as at first" and "as at the beginning" do not refer to a particular historical period during the First Temple era. The "beginning" here is in the sense of foundation, and it refers to the virtuous attributes of Avraham. The verses speak of returning to the very attributes upon which the Jewish people were established, to the path of God which Avraham passed on to his children and household. Those virtues are the "beginning" and the "as at first" of the Jewish people, and the marks of their relationship with God. The absence of a just society means a dysfunctional relationship between God and the Jewish people. In other words – the words of Yeshayahu – if the city is not a city of justice, God's kingship over it is impaired.

Thus, what this blessing is really about is the reconstitution of a society. Only a society which is founded on the principles of justice and righteousness can form the basis of a relationship between the Jewish people and God. The personal relationship with God is not founded on individual virtue (which Avraham surely possessed), but on social virtue. This is borne out by the verses recited daily when donning tefillin, and also constitutes a source for the text of our blessing:

> And I shall betroth you forever,
> And I shall betroth you with righteousness and with justice, and with goodness and with mercy,
> And I shall betroth you in faithfulness, and you shall know God.
> (*Hoshea* 2:21–22)

Righteousness and justice are the raw ingredients of our betrothal with God. The blessing is about a just society, but the request for a just society, in the eyes of the Sages, is an expression of yearning to return to the intense personal betrothal which characterized the relationship of God with the father of the nation, Avraham.

In the era when that virtue of righteousness and justice is absent, this yearning is felt by us as "sorrow and sighing." Aside from the feeling of need, from which arises the necessity to pray and beseech God, the request for justice arises from the internal feeling of loss, of alienation from God. We are not praying for more righteousness due to a personal problem for which the person praying requires salvation from an oppressive force, but due to a feeling of the absence of God's presence from our midst. The Sages understood this alienation to have arisen from a lack of justice and righteousness in society. Sorrow and sighing are not expressions of a physical need, like starvation or sickness, or of psychological distress due to a misfortune,[4] but are expressions of mourning, of loss of value and direction. We are mourning the current situation and pray for the restoration of our betrothal. If we can return to a society of justice and righteousness, then indeed sorrow and sighing would be

4. As we explained "*onyenu,*" our affliction, in the blessing of redemption.

removed, for we would be once again betrothed to God in kindness and in mercy, and in righteousness and in justice – and we would know God.

The emphasis of this blessing is not justice in the narrow sense of a court of law which punishes criminals, but as a basic characteristic of a society concerned about social justice. Thus, the required mediums are not only judges but also counselors, ministers, and educators – all the institutions of a properly functioning society. *Mishpat*, justice, in the Torah refers not only to "law," the legal topic studied by students in law school. *Mishpat* means balance and justice in the general sense of appropriate behavior on a societal level; *mishpat* means just distribution of the society's resources and balance among the requirements of the individual. Hence, we find in the Torah that the priestly breastplate, called the "*choshen mishpat*," rested on the heart of Aharon, which is unrelated to judgment, but rather to the presentation of all the twelve tribes united before God. This is how one is meant to understand Manoach's question to the angel, "What is to be the *mishpat* of the lad, and his actions?" (*Shofetim* 13:12). Manoach is not asking what Shimshon's punishment is to be, but rather how to educate him. What are the proper rules of conduct to teach him? This is the reason that we ask for *tzedaka* – righteousness. Righteousness exists when every person receives that which he deserves, not only as reward or punishment, but also in terms of his social and human rights. "And acquit us in judgment" is a request that we should be found innocent and not guilty, that in the realms of justice we should accomplish personal and social righteousness.

Given that our prayer for a just society is not based on national pride or political ambition, but rather on our yearning for a relationship with God on a national level, we immediately proceed to ask, "And rule over us, You, God, alone." The just society is the basis for the restoration of the kingdom of God. Human actions in establishing a just society are merely a reflection of God's rule over the world. Judaism has never believed in primitive anarchism, the dream of Jean-Jacques Rousseau, even if God directly oversees it. On the contrary, the period of Jewish history closest to that state, the era of the judges, is negatively portrayed as "There was no king in Israel, each person would do what was fitting in his own eyes." The Torah aspires to establish a society with institutions, and it speaks of appointing a king and establishing judges. Jewish rule is not contradictory to the rule of God, but rather is its true reflection and practical realization.

Thus, it is clear why we conclude specifically this blessing with a reference to God as King. The main theme of this blessing is, ultimately, the rule of God. We pray for God to rule over our society, for which we must ensure that it is a just and righteous society.

5. THE *CHATIMA*

In the blessing of repentance, I explained that the *chatima* speaks not of God's activity, but of God's desire, given that the theme of the blessing is not a request for a Divine act. Repentance is fundamentally a human act, whose success requires Divine assistance. A similar situation exists here. The just and righteous society cannot descend in perfect form from heaven. It is something we must create ourselves. The first chapter in *Yeshayahu* is a rebuke and a requirement for the performance of righteousness by the people; it is not a prophecy about redemption from heaven. If God were to lower upright judges from the sky, then justice would be done, but it would not be the basis for our betrothal with God. Society is what we make it. Yeshayahu required us to "seek justice, relieve the oppressed, judge the orphan, fight for the widow." Our appeal to God arises from our understanding that we cannot succeed by our own strength. True, God promises that He will "purge purely your dross, and take away all your tin," but first He requires that we "wash and make yourselves clean, remove the evil of your actions from before My eyes, cease to do evil" (*Yeshayahu* 1:16). Therefore, we cannot conclude with "Blessed... who performs justice," for we are not asking that God perform justice, but that He help us do justice. The commentators explain that "Who loves righteousness and justice" means who loves those who do righteousness and justice (*Bach* 118, *Pri Megadim* ibid.). This explanation lines up with Rashi's exegesis of the verse "For I know him" which we cited earlier. We are appealing to Him who loves and knows intimately those who uphold righteousness and justice, and we pray that our own commitment to righteousness and justice will restore our relationship with Him: "And I shall betroth you in faithfulness, and you shall know God."

This explains the change that this *chatima* undergoes during the Ten Days of Repentance, from "A King who loves righteousness and justice" to "The King of justice." The change from "The holy God" to "The holy King" in the third blessing is understandable, due to the Rosh HaShana period being the time for celebrating God's kingship. In the blessing of justice, however, God is already described as "King" all year round. What is accomplished by omitting "love" during the High Holy Days? In light of our explanation, the answer is clear. During this period, God indeed performs justice Himself. During these ten days, God does not love the justice that we do; rather He judges every creature and every society. On Rosh HaShana we are all individuals being judged before God's throne, and the blessing is changed accordingly.

The order of redemption which arises from these last two blessings is clear. First comes the creation of a society – the ingathering of the exiles – and afterward its establishment as a just and righteous society, as was the legacy of Avraham our forefather. "Zion shall be redeemed with justice, and those that return unto her with righteousness" – this is the basis for redemption – and we still have many more steps to go on the path ahead.

Chapter 17

Minim: Heretics and Enemies

וְלַמַּלְשִׁינִים אַל תְּהִי תִקְוָה, וְכָל הַמִּינִים כְּרֶגַע יֹאבֵדוּ
וְכָל אוֹיְבֶיךָ מְהֵרָה יִכָּרֵתוּ
וּמַלְכוּת זָדוֹן מְהֵרָה תְעַקֵּר וּתְשַׁבֵּר וּתְמַגֵּר וְתַכְנִיעַ בִּמְהֵרָה בְיָמֵינוּ.
בָּרוּךְ אַתָּה יהוה, שׁוֹבֵר אוֹיְבִים וּמַכְנִיעַ זֵדִים.

And let there be no hope for the informers,
And let all the heretics be eradicated immediately,
And all Your enemies be speedily cut off,
And speedily uproot, shatter, crush,
and subdue the kingdom of iniquity
speedily in our days.
Blessed are You, God,
who shatters enemies and subdues the iniquitous.

1. THE THEME OF THE BLESSING

The central question regarding *Birkat HaMinim* is not primarily textual but moral. It is sufficiently clear what we are praying for in this blessing. The question is: Precisely what are we asking for when we pray for the destruction of the wicked? And to whom are we referring?

The Gemara in *Berakhot* addresses the destruction of the wicked:

> There were some ruffians in the neighborhood of R. Meir who greatly troubled him. R. Meir prayed that they might die. Berurya his wife said to him: On what do you base yourself? On what is written, "Sins shall disappear from the earth"? Does it say "*sinners*"? It says "*sins*!" And furthermore, keep reading until the end of the verse – "and evildoers will be no more." When sins will cease, there will be no more evildoers. Rather, you should pray for them that they repent, and then there will be no more evildoers. He prayed for them and they repented. (*Berakhot* 10a)

Here we see that the Sages were opposed to praying for the personal destruction of sinners. Similarly, on the High Holy Days we pray that "all evil in its entirety shall go up in smoke" – evil, and not evildoers. But here, in the daily *Amida*, we ask for the destruction of evildoers, the iniquitous, heretics, and enemies. Why?

There are many textual variants of this blessing, mostly due to the fact that it was subject to multiple censorships, both external and internal, throughout the course of Jewish history. Therefore, I began by presenting one particular version. I assume that most readers do not recite this exact version, but I must pick one version. This version is the one that I recite, and it will serve my purposes in this chapter.[1]

2. *BIRKAT HAMINIM*: BLESSING OF THE HERETICS

The Sages called this blessing "*Birkat HaMinim*," the blessing of the heretics. This blessing has a unique status and history. It is essentially the nineteenth blessing. The Gemara describes its formation as follows:

> Rabban Gamliel says: Every day one prays eighteen [blessings]. These "eighteen" – surely there are, in fact, nineteen? R. Levi said: The blessing of the heretics was instituted in Yavneh [Rashi: at a later date]. Our Rabbis taught: Shimon HaPakuli arranged the

1. As I understand it, this version, which is found in the *siddur* of R. Yaakov Emden, is the closest possible one that we have to the original Ashkenazic version, apart from the opening word "*Velamalshinim*," for the informers.

> eighteen blessings before Rabban Gamliel in their proper order in Yavneh. Rabban Gamliel said to the Sages: Is there no one who knows to institute the blessing of the heretics? Shmuel HaKatan stood up and instituted it. The next year, he forgot it, and perused it [Rashi: tried to remember it] for two or three hours, but they did not remove him. (*Berakhot* 28b)

We see that the blessing of the heretics, with its formulation and content, elicits a problem not only for our generation. It elicited a problem for Rabban Gamliel the Prince as well. Rabban Gamliel had to search after the only person who was capable of drafting the language for this blessing. Even then, that same man, Shmuel HaKatan, subsequently "forgot" the blessing that he himself formulated, a forgetfulness which, I think, is testament to the difficulty in identifying with the content of the blessing. It seems that a noticeable hesitation and confusion surrounds the institution of this blessing, and there exists a fundamental difficulty with its very essence.

It is generally accepted that Rabban Gamliel was responding to the difficult conditions of his time. The Jewish community in the Land of Israel was heavily oppressed by the Roman conquerors, and heretical sects were eating away at the community from within. These are the times of the establishment of Judeo-Christian sects, which were still part of the Jewish community. It is generally assumed that the opening word "*malshinim*," informers, is a censored replacement for something more explicit. Most old texts use the word "*meshumadim*," apostates, and some explicitly state "*notzerim*," Christians. Even the term "*tzedukim*," Sadducees, which appears in some Gemara texts, is undoubtedly a common replacement for Christians or heretics.

Nevertheless, the ferocity of the imprecations in this blessing undoubtedly arouse discomfort, especially within the context of daily prayer. The blessing piles on the synonyms of destruction – uproot, shatter, crush, and subdue, removing all hope. Besides our alarm at such a fervent desire for destruction, we must remember that we have repeatedly defined the blessings of the *Shemoneh Esrei* as listing the basic needs of man. Is the destruction of the wicked really a basic need of man?

3. *MALKHUT ZADON*: THE KINGDOM OF INIQUITY

Careful analysis of the blessing indicates that it has two separate parts, which refer to two different kinds of people. This is made quite clear by the compound *chatima* – "Who shatters enemies and subdues the iniquitous." Generally speaking, there is a principle that "we don't conclude with two" (*Berakhot* 49a), meaning that there may not be two ideas in the *chatima* of a blessing. The reason that our blessing does not violate this rule is because the two ideas are apparently close enough in meaning that it is considered one theme. Nonetheless, the compound form indicates that there are two different, albeit closely related, themes here. The blessing addresses "enemies," and it also addresses "the iniquitous." This distinction is clearly borne out by the *Yerushalmi*, in the parallel discussion to that of the *Bavli* cited earlier, concerning the number of blessings in the *Shemoneh Esrei*: "One includes [the blessing] of heretics and of sinners in [the blessing of] 'subdues the iniquitous'" (*Yerushalmi Berakhot* 4:3). According to the *Yerushalmi*, there was an earlier blessing – "Who subdues the iniquitous" – to which they subsequently added references to heretics and to sinners. The blessing of "Who subdues the iniquitous" serves as host to the later addition of the blessing of the heretics. One should note that, while the *Bavli* implies that the entire blessing is an addition to an earlier framework of eighteen blessings, the *Yerushalmi* implies that the number of blessings did not change when they added the blessing of the heretics. Nonetheless, regarding the content of the blessing, the *Yerushalmi* proves our claim – there are two separate themes joined together, the blessing of the heretics and the blessing of subduing the iniquitous.

The "iniquitous" (*zeidim*) in the *chatima* are the citizens of the "kingdom of iniquity" (*malkhut zadon*) referenced in the text of the blessing. However, most versions of the blessing today have the phrase "and the iniquitous" in place of "and the kingdom of iniquity." This seems to be an emendation of the censor, who (correctly) identified to whom the "kingdom of iniquity" was referring. In the language of the Sages, "the kingdom of iniquity" refers to the Roman empire (and its later successors), the embodiment of tyranny and enslavement. The Sages viewed the Roman empire as the "fourth kingdom" of the kingdoms of our exile, the kingdom which continues to our day. Thus, this phrase refers not to individual sinners, nor even to personal gentile enemies, but to the kingdom of evil, the representation of wickedness in the world, the center of enmity to God's rule. This principle is synonymous with the principle of Amalek, which does not refer to a political-national enemy of the Jewish people, but to an enemy and foe of God, the very entity against whom there is "a war of God with Amalek in every single generation" (*Shemot* 17:16).

Hence, this blessing is not a request to save us from an oppressive enemy. The appropriate place for requesting salvation from a particular affliction which is causing us suffering is in the blessing of redemption, in the first six requests. In this section of the *Amida*, however, we are not praying for salvation from timebound problems, whether personal or national, but rather for the fulfillment of the promise of the process of redemption. The blessing relates to evil as an existential reality, as an attack upon God's rule over the world. Immediately after praying for the establishment of a just society under God's rule (the blessing of "Restore our judges"), we turn outward and identify the enemy of God's kingdom: the *kingdom* of iniquity. The militant language of this blessing is now understood. This blessing is not describing the meting out of justice or punishment, a theme included in the far more moderate language of the previous blessing. This blessing is describing victory, the victory of God over the forces of evil, over those who threaten to banish His blessed name from the world. Victory in this war is indeed a basic need of man.

In order to understand this idea, we must once reemphasize for ourselves the fact that Judaism sees evil as a true metaphysical reality. Evil exists as a metaphysical principle that opposes the will of God and His rule. Of course, evil does not exist independent of the will of God, for God is One and everything emanates from Him – as the prophet Yeshayahu states, God "forms light and creates darkness, makes peace and creates evil" (*Yeshayahu* 45:7). But within the created world, evil does not only emanate from the attributes of weak people. There also exists a dimension of evil in its own right, as the antithesis for Divine good. The Sages viewed characters such as Nimrod and Esav as complements to Avraham and Yaakov, all of them characters of great strength. In Kabbalism, this force is called Samael, Sitra Achra, and sometimes it even attains an actual demonic level. This is all summarized in the verse we cited regarding Amalek – "A war of God with Amalek in every single generation." The Sages explain that "His name is not complete nor is His throne complete until the name of Amalek is wiped out entirely."[2]

The world as it is appears to the man of religious faith to be an affront to the kingdom of God, as he envisions it. If, in the previous blessing, we prayed that "You should rule over us, God, alone, in kindness and in mercy," we immediately understand that this kingdom of God, even if based on Jewish society, is impossible as long as the world is in the clutches of forces dedicated to erasing His holy Name.

Having asked of God to "rule over us, You, God, alone, in kindness and in mercy" in the previous blessing, we understand that a Jewish society characterized by righteousness and justice in the Land of Israel is not enough. God's rule cannot exist so long as there are forces at large in the wider world which are dedicated to the erasing of His holy name. Hence, destruction – total destruction, the obliteration of the name of Amalek in its entirety – is a basic need of a person praying for the redemption of the world. We are in the midst of a war, not necessarily a political-national war (although that is an important element in this type of war), but a cosmic war between the forces of good and evil. We are not concerned with revenge here, nor with personal deliverance, but with redemption, redemption of the entire world and redemption of God's presence, politically and spiritually.

4. *MINIM*: HERETICS

This, however, is only the original framework of the blessing. In the wider world there exists a reality of evil and the kingdom of iniquity, and we rouse ourselves to total opposition to its very existence. To this framework, the Sages added a reference to heretics. This clearly refers to Jews, such as the Christian sects in the Land of Israel in the years following the destruction of the Second Temple. By including them together in the blessing of "Who subdues the iniquitous," the Sages are indicating that we are not concerned for their spiritual well-being, but for their destruction. We have reached the point where they are no longer seen

2. And see Rashi, *Shemot* 17:16.

as individual sinners to whom we apply the rule of "Sins shall disappear, and not sinners," but rather as representatives of the kingdom of iniquity, as agents of evil. How does this transition take place, from sinners to forces of evil?

There is no simple answer to this question, but I believe that it is found in understanding the background of the blessing of "Who subdues the iniquitous." On a personal level, the Sages will not pray for the demise of a sinful individual. This is not just a matter of being merciful or loving of all of Israel, but rather it indicates the true target of opposition. As Berurya explained to R. Meir, we are opposed to evil and not evildoers, to sin and not sinners. While it is people who oppress R. Meir, the root cause is sin; and through the power of repentance, today's enemies can be rehabilitated into tomorrow's friends. On the other hand, there exists "the kingdom of iniquity," a reality which unites evildoers together and directs them to an ideological objective. From the perspective of "kingdom," the individual people become secondary. We must fight and oppose these forces of evil and not hide behind the abstraction of "evil." Judaism has never favored pacifism in the face of evil. Passive acceptance of the existence of evil in the world is collaboration and support of it, and this itself is an offense to the kingdom of God and the sanctification of His name in His world. Hence – and this is the difficult part of this blessing – one cannot join the battle against evil, against the kingdom of the iniquitous, without being willing to apply this to specific individuals as well. The notion of opposing evil while still maintaining a loving and warm relationship with every single Jew is naïve, and perhaps even constitutes an internal paradox. A person who knows from the start that he will never condemn any Jew is effectively uprooting his opposition to evil itself. And without total opposition to evil itself, we are not part of the principle of God's rule.

At some point in history, centuries after the original formulation of daily prayer, the Sages decided to attach an explicit prayer against the heretics from within to the request for the destruction of the enemies from without. This could only have been possible if, in one form or another, the heretics had joined the forces of evil, those which oppose the rule of God. This was not an easy decision for the Sages to reach, and in fact they could not find anyone who was able to simply compose this prayer. The reason for this is obvious – no prayer for destruction and demise comes naturally to one who is committed to the realm of the good and seeks its victory. Destruction in its own right can never naturally be part of good. Even Shmuel HaKatan, the author of the blessing, "forgets" it the following year and only after several hours finally succeeds in reciting it. It is difficult to identify with the content of this blessing, because the medium – destruction – opposes the end goal – good. They did not remove Shmuel HaKatan from leading the prayer, because they knew that his hesitation did not arise from his affiliation with heresy, heaven forbid, but the opposite – it arose from his affiliation with good. And despite all of this, the blessing was eventually recited and established.

Shmuel HaKatan is the author of the comment, "Do not rejoice in the fall of your enemies" (*Avot* 4:24). Undoubtedly, that is the characteristic which made him qualified to compose the blessing of the heretics. Shmuel HaKatan was called upon to translate the battle against evil into an offense against individuals, and therefore only he, who does not allow the fall of our enemies to become a personal celebration, is capable of composing this blessing. Only a person such as he can be relied upon to not turn the battle against evil into a personal vendetta. He is not fighting them personally, but only because of their identification with the force of evil. There is no alternative – our opposition to evil obligates us to oppose even those individuals who join the banner of evil. And yet, one year later, he cannot remember the text. The words, even when they are necessary, remain foreign and alien.

In essence, there is indeed a contradiction between the Berurya principle and the principle of opposition to evil. Berurya seeks to differentiate between evil and its actuators, yet our blessing reminds us that, in actuality, the kingdom of evil is made up of evildoers who advocate for it, and one cannot possibly oppose evil without being prepared to actually fight those people. We live with that contradiction, and uncomfortably so – just like Shmuel HaKatan, who authored the blessing which opposes the Berurya approach, had difficulty with the formulation of his own blessing.

Practically speaking, who do we have in mind when reciting this blessing? In the Kabbalistic tradition, there is a tendency to totally skip over individuals within the blessing. In the name of Ari *z"l* it is stated that "*malshinim*," informers, refers to "the *kelippot* (external spiritual impurities), and this is the intention that one should have" (*Yesod VeShoresh HaAvoda* 5:2). In Hasidism, there are several statements which dilute the sharpness of the personal offensive, by demanding identification with the iniquitous. This was brought in the name of R. David of Talna: "Half of the world is contaminated with apostasy and heresy. Do you think this means half of the people? No! Half of every single individual" (*Kovetz Netzach David*). In any event, I do not think that one must have any particular Jew in mind when reciting this blessing. But one must be ready in principle to do so, or else he is inherently undermining his own opposition to evil and his commitment to the forces of good and to the kingdom of God.[3] The blessing exists in the chasmic tension between these two poles.

We continue to hope and pray for the day when all wickedness will vanish like smoke, and then "You, God, alone, will rule over all your creations, on Mount Zion the abode of Your honor, and Jerusalem Your holy city, as is written in Your holy scripture, 'HaShem shall rule forever, your God, Zion, for generation upon generation, praise God.'"

In the next chapter we shall address the mirror image of our blessing; from the demise of the wicked we shall move on to the great reward of the righteous.

3. R. Yaakov Emden writes in his commentary to the *siddur* that this blessing is directed at the uprooting of the evil inclination for idolatry, "and even if that time has not yet come, to not eliminate freedom of choice, we must nonetheless yearn for such a time."

Chapter 18

Mivtach Tzaddikim: Trust of the Righteous

עַל הַצַּדִּיקִים וְעַל הַחֲסִידִים
וְעַל זִקְנֵי עַמְּךָ בֵּית יִשְׂרָאֵל
וְעַל פְּלֵיטַת סוֹפְרֵיהֶם
וְעַל גֵּרֵי הַצֶּדֶק, וְעָלֵינוּ
יֶהֱמוּ רַחֲמֶיךָ יהוה אֱלֹהֵינוּ
וְתֵן שָׂכָר טוֹב לְכָל הַבּוֹטְחִים בְּשִׁמְךָ בֶּאֱמֶת
וְשִׂים חֶלְקֵנוּ עִמָּהֶם, וּלְעוֹלָם לֹא נֵבוֹשׁ כִּי בְךָ בָטָחְנוּ.
בָּרוּךְ אַתָּה יהוה, מִשְׁעָן וּמִבְטָח לַצַּדִּיקִים.

To the righteous, the pious,
the elders of Your people the house of Israel,
the remnant of their sages, the righteous converts, and to us,
May Your compassion be aroused, Lord our God.
Grant a good reward to all who truly trust in Your name.
Set our lot among them, and let us never be shamed,
for in You we trust.
Blessed are You, Lord, the support and trust of the righteous.

After the blessing of the heretics, in which we pray for God to act against His enemies, comes a blessing which asks God to reward His allies. At first glance, the blessings seem parallel to one another, punishment for the wicked versus reward for the righteous. In light of our explanation regarding the previous blessing, however, we will have to carefully check this assumption. In the previous chapter, I claimed that the blessing of the heretics is not a prayer for punishment or revenge, but for the repair of the world through the eradication of the forces of evil and the victory of the forces of good. If so, why is there a need to add a separate blessing which requests reward for the righteous? More broadly speaking, why are we praying specifically for the righteous? Every desirable individual benefit – knowledge, forgiveness, healing, redemption, sustenance – is requested in general terms for all the Jewish people.[1] What additional benefit do we want for the righteous, precisely, and why?

This blessing provides a list of those deserving reward: the righteous (*hatzaddikim*), the pious (*hachasidim*), the elders of the Jewish people (*ziknei amekhu Beit Yisrael*), the remnant of the sages (*peleitat sofereihem*), the righteous converts (*gerei hatzedek*), and us (*aleinu*). We ask for an arousal of compassion for all of them.[2] Following this, we ask for a "good reward" for a different group – "all who truly trust in Your name" (*kol habotechim beshimkha be'emet*). There seems to be special reference to the subject of *bitachon*, trust, in this blessing. In the *chatima*, God is described as "*Mishan uMivtach*," Support and Trust, and in the *me'ein chatima* we emphasize "For in You we trust." We could ostensibly describe this blessing as the blessing of trust and, as a matter of fact, the name of this blessing in the *Yerushalmi* (*Berakhot* 4:3) is "*Mivtach LaTzaddikim*," trust of the righteous. We must clarify this fundamental concept before proceeding to explain the blessing itself.

1. *BITACHON*: TRUST

For centuries, Jewish thought has debated the relationship between the obligation to trust in God and the necessity to act on one's own to solve human and general problems. In the *Musar* literature, this topic is called

1. Even in this blessing, we add "and place our lot among them," although the formulation of the blessing is primarily directed toward the righteous as a separate group. The very separation between the righteous as the primary group and the rest of the Jewish people as an addendum highlights the different and unique emphasis of this blessing, in contrast to all the other blessings.
2. "May your compassion be aroused (*yehemu na rachamekha*), HaShem our God."

the question of *bitachon* and *hishtadelut*, trust and endeavor. Conventional religious wisdom has at times elevated the virtue of trust in God above all else, and this has created a natural tendency to equate religiosity with a certain measure of practical noninvolvement and passive detachment. However, Judaism has never come close to the pacifist and quietist strains found in parts of the Christian world. The notion that this world is not an arena for religious action, and that one must adopt an attitude of acceptance vis-à-vis evil in the world, is foreign to Jewish ethos. A prime example is the attitude to medicine. There are certain Christian sects which view disease as a test of faith. Since it is so easy to see disease as the hand of God, opposition to it is viewed as a lack of acceptance of God's will and a lack of faith in Him. In contrast, the Sages utilized an explicit verse, "And he will surely heal" (*Shemot* 21:19), to derive the principle that "permission was given to the physician to heal." The contemporary position views the field of medicine as sacred work, and even those who fundamentally preferred religious action over reliance on medicine never made peace with the existence of disease. Even Ramban, who claimed that in the era of the First Temple those of perfect faith would consult a prophet rather than a physician, permitted one to go to a physician, and in fact engaged in medical practice himself.

Nevertheless, there is sometimes heard the idea that we are really supposed to rely only on God, and our obligation to act and make an effort is a sort of required *pro forma* exercise, a Divine mandatory decree, based on a prohibition to overtly rely on miracles, but in fact everything is directly taken care of by God alone. In the yeshiva world, the tale is told about one of the great *Musar* masters of the previous generation, who would purchase a lottery ticket every week, explaining: "My financial well-being is dependent solely upon God, but we are commanded to make a human effort (*hishtadelut*). I am fulfilling my obligation of *hishtadelut* by purchasing a lottery ticket, and God will financially support me as He wills." One could adduce many verses which ostensibly teach this doctrine: "Many are the thoughts in the heart of a man, but God's plan – that is what will be" (*Mishlei* 19:21).

Contrarily, R. Yitzchak Arama, the author of *Akedat Yitzchak*, was one of the first to point out that a belief in both the ability and the necessity of man to take responsibility for his surroundings is religiously mandated. Without the ability to efficiently change the course of events there is no meaning to free will, which is of course one of the foundations of religious life. In his commentary to *Parashat Vayishlach*, R. Yitzchak Arama discusses our father Yaakov's measures in preparation for his meeting with Esav. He explains that the basis of man's religious destiny is his freedom, which is predicated on the assumption that he is able to actually perform moral actions. If evildoers cannot actually perform evil deeds with consequences, if they cannot effect evil, then they are not truly free to choose evil. If the righteous cannot make a difference for the better, then their choice to do good is meaningless. Hence, God's charge to man to do good requires that He also hand over to man the practical means to do good and be responsible for what occurs in the world. This reality requires a system of laws, laws of nature, which is granted to man to use in order to achieve his goals. If physical health is a desirable outcome, then health and healing must be achievable through human endeavor, in order that there be a chance for an individual to choose to help another by healing him. Thus, the system of mitzvot itself requires that God not be totally and actively involved, that He limit His presence in the world, in order to place upon man the responsibility for his actions and his surroundings. If God is totally responsible for all outcomes, then man is not responsible for anything, and thus he cannot be a being of moral stature.

This actually results in the conclusion that in order for man to act as God wishes, in order for man to act in accordance with the image of God in which he was created, man has to act as though God did not exist. To give an example: If I pass a lake and see someone drowning, excessive belief in Divine providence will lead me to the conclusion that there is no reason to jump into the water. God will save him without my help, or conversely, will drown him despite my efforts. On the contrary, I am commanded to "not stand on the blood of my fellow," meaning that if I stand by and do not act, his blood is on my hands, for I, and I alone, am responsible for his death. I have total responsibility for my evil deeds. Faith may still declare that God killed him; morality – Torah morality – says that I killed him by my inaction. I once heard a hasidic saying that is based on this idea. The rabbi asked – I cannot remember who the actual author of the saying was – that since it is clear that everything which God created and gave to man is meant to be used to serve God and has a purpose, then what is the point of the inclination of atheism, for that is also part of man? He answered that atheism is a necessary ingredient in moral behavior, because at the moment of moral decision man must choose as though the entire matter weighs only on his shoulders, without God's interference. With this atheistic ingredient, man serves God.

If so, what is the place of the virtue of trust? The standard answer is that trust appears after one has come to a decision how to act. First one makes the decision to go to a doctor, as this is the correct decision, and afterward one goes to the doctor trusting in God that He will grant the doctor the ability to heal. That, explains R. Yitzchak Arama, is what Yaakov our father did. First he devised a plan how to escape from the wicked Esav, afterward he prepared his camp for all eventualities, and only then he prayed to God for success on the path which he had chosen.

2. THE RELATIONSHIP BETWEEN *BITACHON* AND *HISHTADELUT*: TRUST AND HUMAN EFFORT

This solution for the problem of trust in God and human effort does not actually treat the basic problem of who is responsible for what happens to us, but rather only provides practical guidelines on how to act. It instructs us to take responsibility for our surroundings while continuing to believe that everything is in God's hands. The question is, of course, how our actions intermesh with God's ultimate power over everything.

In my opinion, the only conclusion one can each from the premises I outlined above is that the nature of trust in God is somewhat different than is usually assumed. Usually, the bottom line regarding this question is presented as follows: Decide what you want, take actions to achieve it, and trust in God that He will grant whatever you have decided you want. I contend that there are two problems here:

Such trust is misplaced: Why do we believe that God will give us whatever we want?

Such trust is not particularly praiseworthy: It is closer to pride and self-confidence than genuine faith and trust in God.

I would suggest the following contrary formulation:

First one should consider what the desired end is, namely, what is desirable in terms of objective value and not just what he himself wants. It is easy to know what one's heart desires; it is much more difficult to know what God desires, that is, the proper course of action in a given, complicated, real-life situation. We have been granted certain tools to aid us in this complicated endeavor: human intelligence, a sense of justice and a moral compass, the guidance of the mitzvot, the examples of our forefathers, and the advice of the Sages and our teachers.

Secondly, having decided what the goal is, determine a course of action to achieve it, taking into account the morally acceptable means that are available. Then, upon beginning to act, we trust in God that He will make sure that our choices will indeed result in the best possible outcome. Just as the first step was different, since one must choose not based on his desires but based on his moral decision-making ability, so too this step is different: we do not trust that God will necessarily agree to what we have chosen, but rather trust that He will fulfill the goal that has guided us – doing good. The difference is entrenched in the simple fact that even though man has been granted wonderful tools to help us choose correctly, nonetheless the possibility that we have chosen wrongly, especially with moral choice, is a common phenomenon that looms large. Given the complexity of a real human situation, the uniqueness of each situation and its mere partial association to halakhic models and preexisting precedence, given the intricacy of the human soul and the difficulty in unveiling God's will in the world, the risk of error will always be there. If, however, I have done my honest best to choose how to act, having taken responsibility for my actions and the world about me, then I trust in God that, if I have chosen correctly, He will fulfill my plan, and if I have erred, He will undo my counsel. If we are committed to the ultimate goal of good, we can rely on Him to ensure that that end goal is achieved, whether or not our decision was correct. In other words, we trust in God that He will save us from our mistakes and fulfill our ultimate goals.

This trust is based not only on God's benevolence, but on the nature of the partnership described in the *Akedat Yitzchak* above. God wants us to take responsibility for the world, for that is the necessary basis for the exercise of free will and moral development. God's providence, on the other hand, is committed to doing good. The result is a partnership – we take responsibility, and He promises to ensure a good result. If – and I emphasize, only if – we accept upon ourselves that Divine responsibility, making the decisions that to the best of our abilities we believe that God would make, then God fulfills His ultimate responsibility to the world to manage it for the best possible moral result. Since the development of man's free will and human freedom is itself the acme of "best possible moral result," God agrees first of all to fulfill our decisions – by preserving the laws of nature. Afterward, He protects those who trust in Him, as they accept upon themselves the responsibility to act without Him, and saves them from their own mistakes.

3. *BIRKAT MIVTACH LATZADDIKIM*: THE BLESSING OF TRUST OF THE RIGHTEOUS

We can now understand our blessing. This is not a general blessing asking that God be good to good people, but rather one requesting that God fulfill the trust of those who take moral responsibility for the world. We are not asking for prosperity, or health, or redemption, which have their own blessings. Here we are asking for a "good reward" – not a reward for good deeds but a reward of good, of the fulfillment of the goal of good, namely, the actualization of the attribute of trust. This good reward is promised to those who truly trust in God, meaning in the manner I have described, exhibiting not mere religiously tinted optimism, but commitment to an advancement of good in the world. A good reward is not merely prosperity or health, but the realization of the desired objective to which the person who is trying to make a considered moral decision should have been aiming. Just as the previous blessing is recited over a military backdrop to some extent – the battle of light and dark – so too is this blessing directed at those who are active in the fight against evil, those who advance the goal of sanctifying God's name in the world and establishing God's rule.

In this manner we can understand the names which appear in the list of righteous people in our blessing. Firstly, the list is aimed at public functionaries, the "elders of Your people the house of Israel," as well as the "remnant of their sages," people who bear public responsibility, leaders and rabbis. This, I feel, indicated that the "righteous" and the "pious" are also, if on a more private level, people who are exercising responsibility for their surroundings. If the blessing were merely a request that God reward good people, there would not have been a need to formulate such a long list. It would have sufficed to ask for reward for "the righteous" alone. The aim of this list is to emphasize that we are referring to those who are responsible – each person in his own realm – for advancing the good in God's world.

Furthermore, it is hard to avoid the sense of melancholy that characterizes this blessing. This is most evident in the term "the remnant of their sages" (*peleitat sofereihem*). "*Peleita*" means not only "remnant" but also suggests that which has managed to be saved from destruction. When one finishes eating, the food left over on the plate is not "*peleita*" but "*she'eirit*." "*Peleita*" is something that has managed to find refuge, someone who has fled from war or catastrophe. In this blessing the righteous are a miserable remnant, a pale shadow of former glory. Even if this were the true reality at the time that the blessing was composed, it would be irrelevant if the blessing were only asking for reward in the general sense. But since we are asking for "good reward," the realization of trust in God, for those who trust in Him truly, then the blessing is understood. There exists a group of people whose lives are dedicated to a purpose, to the realization of good, but it appears to be at times unattainable. The struggle for perfecting the world with God's kingship may lead them, if but rarely, to the brink of giving up. It is for them that we pray that the object of their trust does not disappoint them – that they not be shamed by the scorn of the cynics, for in You they trust.

The same holds true for another group, one that is rather rare in our prayers. The final group in the list (before we include ourselves) is the "righteous converts." It is rare to find explicit distinction for converts in Judaism, for the simple reason that, once having converted, there is no special distinction. A righteous convert belongs to the righteous, and conversely, a wicked convert belongs to the wicked. The convert's reward for Torah observance is the reward of the righteous. Here, however, where we are not speaking of reward for Torah observance but of the reward for trust, there is a special distinct category for those who have made a further step, taken a moral decision beyond that expected of born Jews, casting their burden and their entire world onto God. The trust implicit in such a decision deserves a special request for a "good reward."[3]

With this we reach the closing lines: "Set our lot among them, and let us never be shamed, for in You we trust." The condition for the trust I have described is that one has truly and honestly tried to make a moral-faithful decision for the good, uninfluenced by extraneous considerations or the desires of the heart. Only then can one trust in God to support the decision for good, since only then is our decision based only on the good. Yet, who can say that he is sure that that is the case? Can we be certain that no selfish influence has tainted our decision, no improper self-interest? Hence, we pray for that as well – place our lot among the groups mentioned above, and let us not be shamed. Help us honestly make the right decisions, so that we can be counted among those who truly trust in Your name, who trust in the "Support and the Trust of the righteous."

The connection to the previous blessing is now understood. It is obvious that these two blessings are a pair. As we have seen, the previous blessing is not referring to punishing evildoers, but to God's kingship and the elimination of rebellion and negation of God's rule in the world. Our blessing refers to the mirror image – the fulfillment of God's kingship. However, God's kingship in the world is not left in the hands of God, but rather depends on the actions of man. We are meant to repair the world. The blessing asks God to integrate Himself, behind the scenes, in our attempts and efforts to bring about the victory of good. His role in our effort to repair the world is the attribute of trust, in which we are sure and certain.

---

3. Similarly, R. Yehuda b. R. Yakar claims that the "pious" in this blessing are *baalei teshuva*, repentant Jews, in contrast to the "righteous" who are wholly righteous. Repentant Jews make a decision which includes a vast change in their personal lives and exhibits an enormous investment in trust in God. Therefore, in our blessing which focuses on matters of trust, repentant Jews receive a special mention.

Chapter 19

Jerusalem and David

וְלִירוּשָׁלַיִם עִירְךָ בְּרַחֲמִים תָּשׁוּב
וְתִשְׁכֹּן בְּתוֹכָהּ כַּאֲשֶׁר דִּבַּרְתָּ
וּבְנֵה אוֹתָהּ בְּקָרוֹב בְּיָמֵינוּ בִּנְיַן עוֹלָם
וְכִסֵּא דָוִד מְהֵרָה לְתוֹכָהּ תָּכִין.
בָּרוּךְ אַתָּה יהוה, בּוֹנֵה יְרוּשָׁלָיִם.

To Jerusalem, Your city, return with mercy,
And dwell in it as You promised.
May You build it rapidly in our days as an everlasting structure,
And establish within it quickly
the throne of David Your servant.
Blessed are You, Lord, who builds Jerusalem.

1. JERUSALEM AND DAVID

"To Jerusalem, Your city, return with mercy" Longing for the redemption is focused on Jerusalem, the location of God's earthly throne, in its two primary manifestations: the rebuilding of the Temple and the establishment of the Davidic monarchy. We hope for the building of a sanctuary for the Divine presence and for the foundation of ideal political rule. At first glance, the first goal is the theme of our blessing, which commences by referring to the Divine presence and addresses the rebuilding of Jerusalem, whereas the second aim seems to be the theme of the next blessing, the blessing of the "plant of David."

In our analysis of the blessing of the heretics, I quoted the words of the *Yerushalmi*: "One includes [the blessing] of heretics and of sinners in [the blessing of] 'subdues the iniquitous.'" The *Yerushalmi*'s statement continues, "And [one includes the blessing] of David in 'Who builds Jerusalem'" (*Yerushalmi Berakhot* 4:3). In other words, the *Yerushalmi* combines the two blessings, that of Jerusalem and that of the kingdom of David, into one blessing.[1] This combination is clearly reflected in the combined *chatima* of this blessing in the *Yerushalmi*: "Blessed are You, HaShem, the God of David and the Builder of Jerusalem."

We do not follow the practice of the *Yerushalmi*. We recite a separate blessing called "the plant of David." The *Midrash Tanchuma* (*Parashat Korach*, 12) states:

> "Bear [our] sin and accept good (*tov*)" (*Hoshea* 14:3). Israel stated: Master of the universe, when the Temple was in existence, we would bring a sacrifice and achieve atonement, and now we have only prayer. "*Tov*" has the numerical value of seventeen. But there are nineteen [blessings] in prayer? Do not count the blessing of the iniquitous which was instituted in Yavneh, nor the blessing of the plant of David which was instituted because of "Test me, God, and try me" (*Tehillim* 26:2).

The midrash strengthens the position of the *Yerushalmi* that the blessing of David is fundamentally not an independent blessing, but rather at some point it was decided to extract David from the blessing of Jerusalem and grant him his own blessing;[2] and thus, together with the addition of the blessing of the heretics, the *Amida* grew from seventeen blessings to nineteen blessings. The question is: Why should these two blessings be together in the first place? The difference between them seems clear – the former deals with spiritual redemption, the latter with political redemption; and given what we have repeatedly established, that the blessings are based on the needs of man, it is clear that these are two

1. And thus, the number of blessings is maintained: eighteen, not nineteen.
2. The reason for this, and the connection to the verse "Test me, God, and try me," will be discussed in the following chapter.

distinct needs. And yet, the tradition of Jewish prayer had a strong inclination to combine them. In fact, even though the themes were eventually separated into two blessings, David continues to appear in the blessing of Jerusalem – at the end of blessing, we add "And establish within it quickly the throne of David Your servant." The situation today, in which there exists a distinct blessing for the plant of David, and despite this a request for the throne of David is inserted into the blessing of Jerusalem as well, clearly indicates a deliberate halakhic reluctance to accept the divorce of David from Jerusalem.[3]

The necessary conclusion is that there cannot be a rebuilding of Jerusalem and the manifestation of God's presence therein without the house of David. In the blessing of the plant of David, there is no mention of Jerusalem, and it follows that one could envision the end goal in that blessing, "Who causes the horn of salvation to grow," without Jerusalem. Conversely, however, one cannot envision the rebuilding of Jerusalem without David. This shall be our starting point in understanding the blessing of Jerusalem.

2. SPIRITUAL JERUSALEM AND POLITICAL JERUSALEM

Our blessing opens with an appeal to God to return to Jerusalem and to have His presence dwell within. If not for the request for the establishment of the throne of David which appears at the very end, we would have undoubtedly concluded that this request is for God's closeness and for the manifestation of His presence in our midst. Jerusalem is the seat of God's presence, which is a spiritual phenomenon, experienced mostly internally, resonating in the depths of the soul that seeks its Beloved.

> Like a hind crying for water, so my soul cries for You, God.
> My soul thirsts for God, for the living God,

3. In Rambam's version of the prayers, the request for the household of David does not appear in the blessing of Jerusalem. In the book *Peri Etz Chayim* it is recorded that "one time a sage came before my master [i.e., Ari] *z"l*, who looked at his forehead and told him that he has never prayed properly. The sage asked him why. He answered that [the sage] did not recite 'And establish within it quickly the throne of David Your servant' in the blessing of dwelling" (i.e., in the blessing of Jerusalem, in accordance with the opening in the Sephardic tradition).

When shall I come and appear before God? (*Tehillim* 42:2–3)

The lone, thirsty soul yearns to come to the Temple of God, to Jerusalem, the place where man meets God, the abode of the Divine presence.

In contrast to this spiritual request, we expect there to be a separate blessing dedicated to the political needs of the Jewish people. The restoration of the Davidic monarchy, political independence, emancipation from the subjugation of the other nations, and national success are all important matters which have a spiritual dimension, but they are inherently distinct from the need of the thirsting soul to cleave to God's presence. This should have led to two distinct blessings, one – Jerusalem – concerning the spiritual element, and another blessing – David – concerning the political element; the former is about the exile of God's presence, and the latter is about our subjugation by the other nations.

What, then, does the instruction of the *Yerushalmi* to include "David" in "Jerusalem" mean, a ruling which we partially follow today even though there is an independent blessing for the plant of David? The implied answer is that the distinction between spiritual redemption and political redemption is essentially false and misleading. The idea of restoring God's presence to Jerusalem is incomplete without political expression, without the throne of David. The complete, ultimate expression of God's return to Jerusalem, of the dwelling of His presence therein, is "And establish within it quickly the throne of David." The proper plane in which God's presence is manifested is not just the internal, experiential sphere of the soul, but specifically in society, in government, on the national level of the Jewish people. God is "present" among us not when we have a particular religious experience, but when Jewish political and social experience is fulfilled according to His will. The absence of Jewish sovereignty is, itself, the absence of the Divine presence. Hence, one cannot divorce the Temple from Jerusalem as the capital of the Jewish kingdom. Historically – and also halakhically – the Temple was built in Jerusalem only after David had made it the capital of Israel. The Sages stress that while God did not appoint David to build the Temple, David was the one who acquired the land, laid out the plans, and even built an altar on the spot.

This point, that the manifestation of God's presence in the world is bound up with the political success of the Jewish kingdom, has often served as a source of confusion for those trying to understand Judaism, and even, for some Jews, as a point of embarrassment. The separation of the spiritual from the temporal is a deeply rooted idea in Christianity, which has influenced and has become the accepted way of thinking in the Western world. Political power and political aspirations were seen as too base to be part of the eschatological hope. Judaism, however, not only unabashedly avows the political hopes of the Jewish people but sees them as part and parcel of the spiritual redemption and the elevation of the Divine presence. We are not ashamed that we yearn and hope for the blossoming of the "plant of David" and its salvation, and we openly affirm that this will be the fulfillment of God's kingdom as well. To put it bluntly, God's kingdom is dependent on David's throne being established, and the kingdom of Israel is the kingdom of God.

3. *BIRKAT YERUSHALAYIM*: THE BLESSING OF JERUSALEM

This blessing is comprised of four requests of God:

1. to return to Jerusalem,
2. to dwell within it,
3. to build it as an eternal building,
4. to establish the throne of David within it.

These four stages reveal to us the depth of the absence of God from the world. The root cause is, first and foremost, absence. God has left, exiled Himself from Jerusalem. Based on a series of visions by the prophet Yechezkel, the Sages (*Rosh HaShana* 31a) state that God's presence was exiled from Jerusalem in ten stages. The exile of God's presence is not perceived in Jewish thought as a lack of God's knowledge or a minimization of Divine providence. The exile of God's presence means something more spiritual – that the world does not reflect the kingdom of God. It is hard to explain the difference between God's providence from afar and His providence from nearby, from being within our midst. It seems that this difference is not expressed in His ability to act, but in how His actions resonate within us. In other words, do we feel God's closeness to us through His actions, with cleaving and love, or do we merely accept the results in the practical sense? The distinction lies in the personal expression and bonding between us and God, and not in providence itself.

Second, we add a request that Jerusalem, an earthly city where we live, should be God's home – not merely a place where He would feel like a guest, so to speak, but a residence, a home. The day that King Shlomo finished the construction of the Temple, he asked, in wonder and amazement, the obvious question:

> I have built for You a house to dwell in, a settled place for You to reside forever. Can it be, that God shall dwell on the earth? Behold, the heavens and the heaven's heavens cannot contain You, How much less this house that I have built! (*Melakhim Alef* 8:13, 27)

If King Shlomo, the wisest of all men, was baffled by the possibility of building a house of God, then I shall not presume to even try to explain it. Yet, despite this, the conclusion is clear. Despite the philosophical and theological difficulties, in some sense this world and man's construction, a house and a city, constitute the dwelling place of God's glory. The King of kings dwells *among us*, and we, our efforts, and the building of our handiwork, are the home in which He dwells.

I believe that this is what lies behind the phrase "as You have spoken" in our blessing. With minimal effort we were able to find a source in the Tanakh for each of our requests in the *Shemoneh Esrei*. Why, then, do we add specifically to our request of "dwell within it" the phrase "as You have spoken"? The answer is now obvious. Everything else that I pray for, I ask for because I myself know that it is a necessity of mine. Man needs financial support, knowledge, and health, and he also knows that he needs Divine closeness. But who has the audacity to claim that he needs God to dwell within him? Surely, we do not even understand how such a phenomenon is possible. Hence, specifically this blessing must be explicitly based on the word of God. Our entire request is based on the fact that God said, "They shall make Me a Sanctuary, and I shall dwell in their midst." I am truly asking for this, but only because You said so.

Third, the building of the city. For if the above is true, then we do not mean this as a mere poetic metaphor. "And I shall dwell in their midst" is not *only* in their hearts and souls. If the world serves as a house for God, then it must look different, even in earthly terms. If God is to dwell in Jerusalem, then it shall be built and established. The whole point of the mysterious union of God and the world is that the world in its physicality and materiality can be the abode of God's presence. Of course, God's majesty is not dependent on bricks and mortar, or on gold, silver, and copper. But we reject the theological insistence that the kingdom of God must be a wholly spiritual concept, detached from the world of physicality and materiality. In many instances, this false insistence is designed to convince us to not try and establish God's kingdom in this world, but to wait for it passively, to anticipate that it fall from heaven. Perhaps it is true that the angelic neighborhood is more beautiful and fitting for the royal capital, but God has chosen to dwell among us; the city of man, of bricks and mortar, is the city of God.

Fourth, the throne of David. If God dwells in the city of man, then He also rules the city of man. God's presence within the world is true sociopolitical sovereignty. At the end of the day, we know that it is not the physical architecture of the city that serves as the abode for God's presence, but rather the social structure, the actions of man, society and its institutions, and all the various ways in which man transcends his egocentric solitude to create a better world. Society is a product of man transcending his lone self, and it is therefore worthy of supporting the supreme and transcendent God. When the first man met his mate, the Sages said, "If there be peace between man and woman, the Divine presence is between them." Jewish society, the fellowship of individuals and their union in following God's law, is, aside from the mutual benefits it confers, the ultimate abode for God's presence. Establishing the throne of David, refining society and its institutions, is the final stage in the foundation of God's kingship within the world.

4. *ME'EIN CHATIMA*

The final line before the *chatima* of the blessing must be a *me'ein chatima,* a summation of the blessing. In the Ashkenazic tradition, the final line is "And establish within it quickly the throne of David," while the *chatima* is "Who builds Jerusalem." Although we have explained the strong connection between the kingship of David and the building of Jerusalem, we must ask: Can the "throne of David" really count as a *me'ein chatima* here? In the *Yerushalmi*'s version there is no issue – we recite, "Build it rapidly in our days as an everlasting structure, and establish within it quickly the throne of David," and then conclude with a double *chatima,* "The God of David who builds Jerusalem." In our version, however, where David appears in the *me'ein chatima* but not in the *chatima,* we seem to be transgressing the rule that a *me'ein chatima* summation must appear immediately before the *chatima.* Indeed, in the Sephardic version the order of the last two requests is reversed, so that the "throne of David" appears first, followed by "And build it rapidly in our days as an everlasting structure" which serves as the *me'ein chatima* immediately before the *chatima.* We can presume that this order reversal is precisely in order to solve the halakhic issue that the *me'ein chatima* must appear immediately before the *chatima.*

The *Bach* (118) argues that the "throne of David" truly is the *me'ein chatima.* The purpose of building Jerusalem, he writes, is to be the seat of the throne of David's kingship. It seems that this is exactly the point which I have expressed above.

R. Avraham b. HaGra explains that we conclude in the present tense – "Who builds Jerusalem" – because God builds His city at every given point in time. May it be God's will that He show us its construction and gladden us with its restoration.[4]

4. R. Shmelke of Nikolsburg, may his merit protect us, explains that "whatever man perfects, it always impacts the building of the Jerusalem on high, stone by stone, and therefore we recite 'Who builds Jerusalem,' because it is built bit by bit every single day. And the explanation of 'Show us its construction and gladden us in its restoration' is that He should show us in our mind what we are accomplishing in its restoration, and in this manner we will be gladdened through this restoration" (*Sefer Divrei Shmuel, Bechukotai* 132:1).

Chapter 20

Tzemach David: The Plant of David

אֶת צֶמַח דָּוִד עַבְדְּךָ מְהֵרָה תַצְמִיחַ,
וְקַרְנוֹ תָּרוּם בִּישׁוּעָתֶךָ
כִּי לִישׁוּעָתְךָ קִוִּינוּ כָּל הַיּוֹם.
בָּרוּךְ אַתָּה יהוה, מַצְמִיחַ קֶרֶן יְשׁוּעָה.

Quickly grow the plant of Your servant David,
And may his horn be raised high by Your salvation,
For we hope for Your salvation all day.
Blessed are You, Lord,
who causes the horn of salvation to grow.

In our analysis of the blessing of Jerusalem, we noted that we mention the "throne of David" in context of "Who builds Jerusalem," even though the "plant of David" merits a distinct blessing. I assumed that the throne of David symbolizes the political-sovereign role of Jerusalem, joining with its spiritual role into one blessing. Most commentators on the *Yerushalmi* assume that the *Yerushalmi*'s position is that there is no blessing of "the plant of David," and that the political redemption is included within the previous blessing. On the other hand, according to our version of the *Amida* it transpires that David appears in the blessing of Jerusalem as well as meriting a separate blessing, and this surely requires explanation.

What are we actually praying for in this additional blessing, and which of man's needs does it come to address?

This blessing is characterized by the repeated use of creative and metaphoric language. The theme of the first line is "*tzemach David*," literally "the plant of David," and the verb used is "*tatzmiach*," to grow. The second line refers to the exaltation of the "horn (*keren*) of David," and these two metaphors are joined together in the *chatima* – "Who causes the horn of salvation to grow." The commentators on the book of *Yirmeyahu*[1] explain that the "plant of David" refers to a future descendant of King David, a child who grows from the ancient stalk. The common explanation for the "horn of David" interprets it as a reference to a ram's horn, a horn rising proudly and mightily before it. We shall examine the Biblical sources for these phrases in order to better understand their significance in the *Amida*. Why does this blessing use such metaphoric language to express the theme of salvation? Why is the coming of the Messiah described as a growing plant?

1. *TZEMACH*: PLANT

Tehillim 132 depicts the building of the Temple by David. Afterward, God says to him:

> God has sworn to David, in truth from which He will not turn,
> From the fruit of your body will I place upon your throne...
> For God has chosen Zion, desired it as His habitation.
> This is My resting place forever, here will I dwell for I have desired it...
> *There will I grow (atzmiach) a horn for David,*
> I have arranged a lamp for My anointed.

We have here, as in our blessing, both the growing metaphor and the horn metaphor. This is not the only place where the salvation of Israel is described as a growing. For example:

1. On the verse, "I will grow for David a plant of righteousness" (*Yirmeyahu* 33:15).

> On that day I will *grow a horn* for the house of Israel. (*Yechezkel* 29:21)

> Behold, the days are coming, says God, and I will raise up for David a *righteous plant.* (*Yirmeyahu* 23:5)

> In those days, and in that time, I will *grow for David a plant of righteousness.* (Ibid. 33:15)

Examining the appearances of the word "*tzemach*" in the Tanakh reveals that almost every mention of growing in the metaphorical sense (rather than vegetation) refers to the salvation of God and the coming of the Messiah, the scion of David. It will therefore not surprise us to learn that "*tzemach*" is a proper name of the Messiah:

> Hear now, Yehoshua the High Priest, you and your friends who sit before you, though they be amazing men, for behold I will bring My servant Tzemach. (*Zekharya* 3:8)

> And you shall say to him thus: So says God of hosts: Behold a man, his name is Tzemach, and from him will grow, and he will build the Temple of God. (Ibid. 6:12)[2]

2. VALUE AND PROCESS

The human mind is wired to judge states. When we evaluate something, or compare two things, we do so by assigning an absolute value to each unit, according to an appropriate scale. This state is worth ten points, another state twenty, and therefore we know that the second is worth more than the first. This is how we reach the conclusion that we should

2. According to the simple understanding of the verses, and as most commentators interpret them, these verses refer to Zerubavel and the construction of the Second Temple. Nonetheless, it is clear that the connotation "*tzemach*" refers to a redeemer from the house of David. The Sages use these verses and the proper name "Tzemach" to refer to the Messiah.

value the second over the first, that it is "dearer," and that it is worth more and preferred. A clear, familiar example is school. How much is a student worth, is he a "good" student or not? The teacher gives him a grade which measures his accomplishments.

The problem that I wish to address is not the fact that the tools for assessment are not accurate enough. That is a well-known problem, a practical problem which stems from failure in the implementation rather than a fundamental flaw in the whole evaluative approach. That problem can be ameliorated by giving more accurate assessments. A good teacher is aware that his testing method is not accurate enough, but that does not undermine the fundamental goal of the test, which is to evaluate the achievements of the student. In an ideal situation, the test is perfect, giving precise results. Let us take, for example, a perfect tester – God – and an ultimate test day – the day of judgment. The accepted picture depicts God, Judge of the entire earth, weighing man, his merits and his transgressions, and reaching a final score. Indeed, the image of scales weighing man is used frequently by the Sages to express the attribute of judgment.[3]

However, there is a different problem with the absolute value approach, and this is a fundamental problem with the whole approach rather than in its practical implementation. Let us take a simple example: I have two students. One is bright, sharp, and industrious, and consistently gets marks in the high nineties. The other is slow, dull, easily distracted, and rather lazy, and hovers at the edge of failing. At some point in the year, through determined effort, he manages to show some real improvement and pulls a 75 on a test. The first student, as usual, has achieved a 95.

According to the regular measure, the first is still a "better" student – better by twenty points. He knows more. But we know that there is a special value in the other one's studies and his achievements, and these are not measured by the test itself, nor are they reflected in his grade. This value is not the absolute value of his knowledge, but in the progress that he has made from 65 to 75, a value completely absent from the student maintaining a consistent 95. This is a value that exists not

3. For example, *Rosh HaShana* 17a.

on any absolute scale but only on a scale that measures process, movement, and progress.

Note that we are dealing with two entirely different measures; there is no way to compare between the scales or to convert them from one to the other. What was present in the second student was totally absent in the first student, and the two evaluations are incommensurate. There are two types of value here. Appreciating progress is appreciating the value of a process, of movement, and that is a different type of appreciation than that found in evaluating absolute value.

The Zohar (*Va'etchanan*, 260a) expresses this distinction in a comparison between the angels, who are called "*omedim*," standers, and humans, who are "*mehallekhim*," walkers. God says to Yehoshua the High Priest, "And I will give you walkers among these standers."[4] Obviously, the angels are on a higher level than humans – they are "worth" more. This is an absolute evaluation. But people have a value which even the highest angel wholly lacks, the value of "moving." The very fact that man is moving toward a higher level (even though this target level will also be lower than that of the angels) gives him a value, a type of value, that is unattainable by the angels. Jewish history begins with the command to go – "Go for yourself, from your land, and from your birthplace, and from your father's house to the land that I will show you" (*Bereshit* 12:1). All the Torah portions which speak about Avraham our father describe him as "*holekh*" (walking) and as "*mithallekh*" (walking about), "*halokh venasoa*" (continuous movement), until God commands him, "Walk before Me and be perfect" (17:1). Avraham's perfection does not lie in an absolute level of perfection; such a level belongs to God alone. *Temimut*, Avraham's state of perfection, lies in the fact that he "walks before Me." For Avraham, perfection is found in the *process of perfecting*, in walking before God.

This relationship between man and God necessitates the recognition of the value of process. If man is measured on an absolute scale, he will always be found wanting, for the absolute scale is measured against God, absolute perfection. A perfect absolute score is not one hundred, nor is it one hundred thousand, but infinity. To be perfect on

4. *Zekharya* 3:7.

this scale is to be "like God, knowing good and evil." To be created in God's image, as we have explained in previous chapters, means not to be perfect like God, but to always be moving toward God, to go after Him (or before Him), and to yearn toward Him. Divine *perfection* is reflected in the man who is in the *process of perfecting* himself. The gulf is infinite, and therefore absolute achievement is necessarily meaningless in its own right; however, the value is not in the achievement but in the movement toward it. Closing the gap, even if that measure of closing is infinitesimal relative to the goal, constitutes a value of perfection on the process scale. In the words of the Sages, "Where repentant people stand, even completely righteous people cannot stand."

It must once more be stressed (as we emphasized in the chapter about holiness) that there is an indissoluble bond between the two types of value, a bond which is expressed in the term "image of God." Movement has value only because it is directed toward the absolute. Wandering aimlessly is not the process of perfection. Avraham was "continuously moving southward," and although "continuously moving" hints at several obstacles along the way, "southward" indicates a clear destination, and hence the Sages established that "southward" refers to the Temple. To strive for the unreachable stars is perfection; to move for the sake of movement is a neurosis. The destination of movement, the destination of repentance, is the infinite God. The Sages stated, "Repentance is great, for it reaches the Divine throne, as it says, 'Return, Israel, *unto* HaShem your God.'" Man is not merely man, but he is also not God. Man is the image of God, namely, man who seeks out God, man on the move toward God, toward the absolute value. Because we value the absolute, we value the process of progression toward it. Man's process of perfection emanates from God's absolute perfection.

"*Tzemach*," I believe, refers to this value of process. When we ask for salvation in this blessing, we are not asking for a particular state, as we do when we ask for wealth, health, and the ingathering of the exiles. These are values that can be quantified on an absolute scale and given an absolute score. There is a particular amount that we require, and we want that and no more. But when we ask for salvation, we are not asking for a particular quantity of something. We are asking for "*tzemach*" – growth. We pray that God will cause the plant of salvation to grow, to reach upward, to rise like the horns of a ram. We are asking to become part of the process, to become part of the infinite walk toward God, to become partners in the perfection of Avraham who walked before God.

3. *YESHUA*: SALVATION

Why was this specific blessing chosen to stress this value?

The answer is found in the blessing itself. There is a unique phenomenon in this blessing. We have seen from the other blessings how the *me'ein chatima* can appear in one of two forms. It is either itself a request, concluding the series of requests in that blessing, as in the blessings of Jerusalem, the ingathering of the exiles, and subduing the iniquitous; or it is a praise which justifies the request, in the form of "*For* You are able to perform that which I am asking for," as in the blessings of forgiveness, healing, and redemption.

Our blessing outwardly has the latter form – "*For* we hope for Your salvation all day" – yet its meaning is different. Are we are asking God to save us, because we hope for His salvation? The conventional template would require a *me'ein chatima* here in the form of "For You are a Savior and Shield," or "For You cause salvation to grow." What is the meaning of this praise, "For we hope for Your salvation all day"?

The answer is that this phrase is specifically explaining the "causing to grow" of the *chatima*. The reason that we pray for growth, rather than a given measure of salvation, is because *it is for His salvation that we hope all day*. The real aim of this blessing is not the solution, the measure of salvation granted by God, but rather God Himself – for we hope for Your salvation – *Yours* – all day. We are not asking for a particular element of political independence, or for an improved economy. We are asking for God's absolute perfection itself, for the infinite. There is no upper limit to this request, for if there were a cap then it would not be the salvation of *God*. We ask for the *growth* of salvation, for the infinite movement toward God. The psychological bed from which this request emanates is *hope* – "For we hope" – which is constant every single day. Our definition as the image of God means that we are defined as hopers, as aspirers, for God's salvation. The form in which God's salvation is granted to man is in growth, in process, rather than in absolute quantity.

Typically, a *me'ein chatima* of this form defines God – "For You..." In this blessing, it defines the person praying – "For we hope for Your salvation all day." The idea is the same – we are dependent on You for this matter, and on You alone.

This is the difference between the earlier blessing of redemption and our blessing. Redemption can be quantified. That blessing refers to a specific problem, similar to sickness and starvation, and the solution is redemption. Salvation does not refer to a specific problem but rather is about the human condition, about existential mortality. To be human is to require salvation, for we wish to be as God, we are created to be as God, knowing good and evil. That yearning for the infinite, for the impossible, is the prayer for the growth of salvation.

4. DAVID AND JERUSALEM

If this is true, the relationship between the blessing of Jerusalem and the blessing of David is the reverse of how we described the relationship at the beginning of the previous chapter. The blessing of Jerusalem is not specifically a "spiritual" blessing – on the contrary, it proclaims the "realization" in the material world of our spiritual aspirations for the redemption process by forging a bond between the manifestation of God's presence in Jerusalem and the establishment of David's throne within. It is a "political" – or spiritual-political – blessing. The contents of that blessing, like all the previous blessings, are quantifiable, defined. We want the building of the Temple, the establishment of the Davidic monarchy, the manifestation of God's presence. In contrast, the separate blessing of David, the blessing of the plant of David, is a request that relates to the suprahuman realm, to the realm of the infinite itself. Jerusalem is the manifestation of God's presence here, within the world. Our blessing refers to the plant of David – and that is something which is found in heaven, or, more accurately, which grows up to heaven. In the previous blessing, we prayed for the Temple; in this blessing, we yearn and hope for the salvation of God.

In the previous chapter, I cited the *Tanchuma* which explained that the blessing of the plant of David exists (in addition to the seventeen "proper" blessings, like the numerical value of "*tov*") because of the verse "Test me, God, and try me" (*Tehillim* 26:2), without explaining the connection between the blessing and this verse. Now everything is clear. The Gemara in *Sanhedrin* (107b) explains that this verse lay at the root of David's failure.

> R. Yehuda said in the name of Rav: A person should never bring himself to undergo a trial, as David, king of Israel, brought himself to undergo a trial and failed.
>
> He said before Him: Master of the universe, for what reason do we say, "God of Avraham, God of Yitzchak, and God of Yaakov," and we do not say, "God of David"?
>
> He said: They have undergone trials before Me, and you have not undergone a trial before Me.
>
> He said before Him: Test me and try me, as it is stated, "Test me, God, and try me..."
>
> Immediately, "And it came to pass one evening that David rose from his bed" etc. (the sin with Batsheva).

The forefathers, God explains, withstood the test, whereas David did not. David asks to be tested, to undergo an ordeal like those of the forefathers. Indeed, the Gemara learns from this incident that one should not ask to be tested, for he knows not whether he will withstand it, just as David did not withstand his test. Yet ultimately, in response to this request of "Test me, God, and try me," David, despite his failure at that junction, does indeed merit to have a blessing named after him in the *Shemoneh Esrei*, like the forefathers. In his request to be tested, David is seeking growth, for it is only through ordeals that a person truly grows and flourishes. David yearned to ascend to greater heights, and this is only possible through being tested. This request, "Test me, God, and try me," is synonymous with the "hope" of "For we hope for Your salvation all day," and it constitutes the foundation of our prayer, "Quickly grow the plant of Your servant David." The two requests are one and the same, a prayer for growth and flourishing.

5. MESSIAH

The dialectical relationship between perfection and perfecting, the perfection of God and the perfecting of man moving toward Him, is inherent in the concept of the Messiah and the Messianic Era. The belief that history moves forward toward an ultimate goal is an inherent belief in Judaism. That goal must be perfection. Just as each individual was created in the image of God, so too was mankind as a whole created in His image. On the one hand, we believe in the coming of the Messiah and in a certain reality which will prevail in his era. On the other hand, this is not merely an intellectual belief in a future state. That yearning, that hope, for the future is translated into a reality in the present, into movement and growth. Messianism is the difference between stagnancy – regardless of one's level, exalted as it may be – and progress and perfecting; in other words, the difference between death, and life and aspiration. Yearning for tomorrow defines who we are today – "For we hope for Your salvation *all day*." With God's help, and with His response to our prayers, we are now moving in that direction. This is the acme of the blessings of requests, and the final one. After we ask for everything that we lack, all the specific things that we wish to add to our lives, we ask for God to put us on the *path* of infinite progress toward His salvation. In other words – having prayed for all the conditions of life, we now ask for life itself, true and invaluable life.

Chapter 21

Shome'a Tefilla: Hearer of Prayer

שְׁמַע קוֹלֵנוּ יהוה אֱלֹהֵינוּ
חוּס וְרַחֵם עָלֵינוּ, וְקַבֵּל בְּרַחֲמִים וּבְרָצוֹן אֶת תְּפִלָּתֵנוּ
כִּי אֵל שׁוֹמֵעַ תְּפִלּוֹת וְתַחֲנוּנִים אָתָּה
וּמִלְּפָנֶיךָ מַלְכֵּנוּ רֵיקָם אַל תְּשִׁיבֵנוּ*
כִּי אַתָּה שׁוֹמֵעַ תְּפִלַּת עַמְּךָ יִשְׂרָאֵל בְּרַחֲמִים.
בָּרוּךְ אַתָּה יהוה, שׁוֹמֵעַ תְּפִלָּה.

Hear our voice, Lord our God.
Spare us and have mercy on us,
And accept our prayer in mercy and favor.
For You are a God who hears prayers and pleas.
Do not dismiss us empty-handed from before You, our King,
For You hear the prayers of Your people Israel with mercy.
Blessed are You, Lord, who hears prayer.

1. THE REQUEST TO HEAR OUR PRAYER

The final blessing in the series of "requests" in the *Shemoneh Esrei* is the blessing of *Shome'a Tefilla,* Hearer of prayer.

This time our task does indeed appear to be simple. This blessing has no inexplicable phrases or metaphors demanding elucidation. The theme of the blessing is straightforward – we are asking God to hear our prayers. Everything is clear, and this surely will be a very short chapter.

Maybe so – but there is one small question that remains. The theme of this blessing is undoubtedly a request that God hear our prayers. But the question is: Why? Why do we need to ask God to hear the prayers we have already offered? What additional request does this blessing present?

Let us compare two cases of prayer:

> Case A: I ask God to grant me a full recovery.
> Case B: I ask God to grant me a full recovery and to hear my prayer for a full recovery.

Is there a difference between the two cases? Or, more accurately, have I asked for anything additional in the second case? And if you will claim that a prayer is not acceptable unless we ask God to accept it, then we would also need a further request – to accept this last request of *Shome'a Tefilla* as well!

> Case C: I ask God to grant me a full recovery, to hear my prayer for a full recovery, and to hear my prayer that He hear my prayer...

Thus, we have returned to the familiar question: What are we really asking for in this request?

2. PRAYER AS A NECESSITY OF MAN

When we were at the very beginning of our discussions, I defined the middle blessings, the requests, as requests for the needs of man. The Sages identified the basic necessities of man. Each request identifies a different basic need of man. These thirteen middle blessings represent the permanent, basic needs of anyone who stands before God, before Him who satisfies the desires of all living things. By applying that definition to our blessing, we come to the astonishing conclusion that prayer is a need of man, no less than food, health, knowledge, and redemption. If, as I claimed in the first chapter, we serve God by presenting our needs to Him, then in this case we serve Him by presenting to Him our need to pray to Him.

Simple examination of the blessing immediately discloses that we are not praying that we be *able* to pray, but that our prayers be accepted. This makes sense in light of the preceding paragraph. We serve God by presenting our need to pray *to Him*, to draw close to Him in prayer. It is not that we have a particular need to say certain words in a synagogue. We have an urgent, crucial need, an existential need, to be able to come before God and speak with Him, worship Him, and serve Him. This need is not the necessity to fulfill all the needs expressed in the preceding blessings. At this moment, I do not need to pray before God because He is the Granter of health, or the Master of forgiveness. Even if we were not to have all these other needs expressed in the preceding twelve requests, we would still have a need to pray before God. In other words, this need is a religious one. Man has an existential need not only for prosperity, forgiveness, knowledge, and redemption, but also for communication and companionship with God.

The difference between asking for our other needs and the essential need to have a communicative bond with God is beautifully exemplified in the Gemara in Tractate *Taanit*.

> Shmuel HaKatan decreed a fast, and rain fell for them before sunrise (i.e., before the fast even began). The people were of the opinion that this was an indication of the praiseworthiness of the community. He said to them: I will tell you a parable. To what is this matter comparable? To a slave who requests a reward from his master, and [the master] says to [his ministers]: Give him what he asks for and let me not hear his voice. (*Taanit* 25b)

This, I believe, is what "acceptance" of our prayer means. If we were to merit the fulfillment of all our needs, but without having to request them from the King, then this would not be a privilege but a missed opportunity. We would be satiated but ostracized. In the blessing of "Hearer of prayer," we are not asking for a favorable answer to the previous requests – each blessing includes its own request for a favorable response. We are asking for literal acceptance, in the sense that the paper on which we have presented our requests be registered, accepted, into the Divine registry. We are asking that God not only provide for us, but that He hear our voice as well.

This is clearly indicated in the continuation of this blessing, by what would otherwise be an excessively modest request – "Do not dismiss us empty-handed from before You, our King." Are we now asking and praying that our previous requests be answered only partially, symbolically? We are certainly grateful for any measure of goodness that God grants us, but are we, in the request itself, asking for a partial response? When I asked for health, was I asking for a little health, that I should not leave empty-handed? Of course not! I was asking for a *full recovery* for all our wounds. When I asked for sustenance, did I state that I would settle for half a meal a day? When we asked for the building of Jerusalem, did we suggest that even a few renovations in the Jewish Quarter would suffice? Absolutely not! In each blessing, I asked for the maximum Divine good, the fulfillment of all my needs. It is true that after the fact, if God gives me a small fraction of what I asked for, I will thank Him wholeheartedly for what I know is a free gift that is more than I deserve. But in the prayer itself, we do not lower our sights. We present God with the whole list, precisely because these are essential needs and we know that there is no other source which can provide them, and in this manner, we fulfill the obligation of serving God. To aspire for less than the maximum would be neither human nor a reflection of our absolute dependency on our Creator and King, Master of everything.

So why, after having asked for everything, do we pray that God not send us away "empty-handed"? Is this some sort of fallback blessing, a backup position? Are we conducting negotiations on the "requests" market – that if not everything, at least give us something? I think not. This blessing is about communication and connection, about cleaving unto God. We have spoken, asked, and prayed – and we now ask that this prayer be a real communication, that a true measure of contact with God exist. We ask that God give us something and not leave us empty-handed, not because that will be a partial fulfillment of our requests in the previous blessings, but because that will be a fulfillment of our need to have a meaningful bond with God. "*Reikam*," empty-handed, does not mean here "failure to receive anything," but rather the sense of emptiness itself. Do not turn us away from praying to You feeling empty, meaningless, lonely, and lost. We do not say "empty-handed," but "empty-handed *from before You.*" When a king sends away someone from before him, this can imply dismissal, the severing of a link.[1] We are praying to not be *dismissed* from His presence, and instead to receive from Him something that demonstrates a real, live bond between us. To "dismiss us empty-handed" means to cast us out. To not dismiss us empty-handed means to accept our prayers – and us – before Him.

3. *RACHAMIM*: MERCY

The word "*rachamim,*" mercy, appears three times in this blessing (four in the Sephardic tradition). There appears to be a special connection between the acceptance of prayer and mercy.

It is worthwhile to compare this blessing to one we recite when are in urgent need of help. At a time of great trouble, we institute a fast day, and recite the *Aneinu* prayer. "Answer us, God, answer us, on the fast day of our affliction, for we are in great trouble." In this entire blessing, the attribute of mercy is not mentioned even once! In general (and this is not an absolute rule), references to God's mercy will be found in the context of prayers of forgiveness for one's sins and in requests for repentance. This rule is not absolute, and I am sure you can find plenty of exceptions. Nonetheless, finding "*rachamim*" as so central a theme of our *berakha,* where all we are asking is that God answer our prayers, is extraordinary. The explanation, I believe, is based on what we have asserted above. Mercy in our blessing is not a means to obtain something else, but the main content of the request itself. We are not requesting that something or other be granted to us *with* mercy; we are asking for mercy itself. Mercy is not the way to increase our chances of receiving

---

1. Compare: "But to the sons of the concubines which Avraham had, Avraham gave presents, and *sent them away* from his son Yitzchak while he yet lived, eastward, to the east country" (Gen. 24:6). What was Avraham doing? He was severing any link, any sense of obligation, between Yitzchak and the other children. He was "dismissing" them. We are praying not that we receive presents from God, but that we be not dismissed from His presence. As the case of Avraham makes clear, it is possible to receive presents even while being finally and completely dismissed.

sustenance or salvation, but rather is the sought-after object itself. The personal relationship with God, which we are seeking out, is expressed by prayer on our side, and by mercy on His.

The commentators point out that the root of "*rachamim*," mercy, is "*rechem*," womb. The feelings of a mother for her child, who has stirred and grown within her, are the root meaning of mercy. This not the same as the pity which we feel when we see poverty on the streets, a feeling based on moral imperative.[2] Mercy does not emanate from a moral imperative, but from the feeling that we are one with the other, just as a mother is one with her fetus. In Aramaic, "*racham*" means love, and is not connected whatsoever to the recipient's pitiable state. Even in Hebrew, "*rachamim*" does not always denote the strong helping the weak. "Can a mother forget her child, or not '*rachem*' the fruit of her belly? Though they may forget, I will never forget you" (*Yeshayahu* 49:15). "*Rachamim*" here is the opposite of forgetting. A pregnant woman is constantly aware of the life in her womb, it is forever in her consciousness. Mercy emanates from the internal sense of unity, from a mutual connectedness, and this feeling of togetherness is mingled with a concomitant responsibility and care.

In other words, mercy is not induced by being on our knees, but by our being in need, dependent on God, by our being recipients of His kindness and grace. Accordingly, in contrast to all other blessings, this blessing commences (in the Sephardic tradition) with the call of "*Av HaRachaman*," "Merciful Father." A Father who loves as a father loves mercifully. Thus, we conclude the blessing, "For You hear the prayers of Your people Israel *with mercy*."

4. WHOSE PRAYERS?

Generally speaking, I have not emphasized the differences, minor in nature, between the Ashkenazic and Sephardic traditions. In this case, there is a small but highly significant difference between the two traditions in the final line. In the Ashkenazic tradition, the line reads, "For

2. "*Rachmonus*," as the Hebrew word "*rachmanut*" is pronounced in Yiddish, denotes such pity.

You hear the prayers of Your people Israel with mercy." In the Sephardic tradition, we recite, "For You hear the prayers of every mouth."

The difference is obvious. The Ashkenazic version refers to the prayers of Jews alone. We are familiar with this sort of conclusion in the blessing for health, and the reference to Jews is somewhat implicit in most of the other blessings as well. The Sephardic version explicitly widens the focus of this blessing, appealing to God as the Hearer of prayer from every mouth, from all the inhabitants of the world. The Scriptural basis for this phrase, as noted by the medieval commentators, is the verse: "Hearer of prayer, all flesh will come to You" (*Tehillim* 65:3).

Based on what I explained above, the basis for the Ashkenazic version is understood. The blessing is not suggesting that God does not hear the prayers of non-Jews. Rather, there is a special connection established between the Jew who prays, who comes before his King and engages with Him in an intimate relationship through service and prayer. This does not mean that God will grant more requests to Jews than to non-Jews. As we have seen, this blessing is not dealing with the fulfillment of the other requests, but with establishing a relationship and connection with God. The acceptance of our prayers *with mercy*, the fond reception of one who prays to God and stands in His presence, an intimate discourse – these are all part of the covenant between the Jewish nation and their God, between the King of Israel and His people who cause His name to dwell in their midst – "They shall make Me a Sanctuary, and I shall dwell in their midst."

When King Shlomo completed building the Temple, he explicitly prayed that God hear prayers and grant requests. First, he spoke specifically of the prayers of the Jews, who had built the Temple:

> And You shall hear the prayer of Your servant and Your people Israel, who shall pray at this place,
> And You shall hear from Your dwelling place, from the heavens, and You shall hear and forgive...
> If Your people Israel shall be smitten before the enemy...
> If the heavens be shut up and there be no rain...

> And You shall hear from the heavens and forgive the sin of Your servant and Your people Israel…
> If there be famine on the earth, if there be pestilence…
> Every prayer, every supplication of any man of Your people Israel, where a man knows the affliction of his heart and he lifts his hands to this house.
> And You shall hear from the heavens, Your dwelling place, and forgive and act, and give to every man according to his ways, as You know his heart, for You alone know the heart of every person. (*Melakhim Alef* 8:30–39)

But immediately after, Shlomo prayed for the prayers of others.

> And also the stranger, who is not of Your people Israel, who will come from a far land for the sake of Your name.
> For they shall hear of Your great name and of Your mighty hand and outstretched arm, and he shall come and pray at this house.
> You shall hear from the heavens, Your dwelling place, and do all that the stranger called out to You,
> In order that all the peoples of the earth know Your name, to fear You like Your people Israel,
> And to know that Your name is called over this house which I have built. (41–43)

Both prayers will be answered, for it is clear that God hears them both. There is, however, a noticeable difference. God responds to the prayers of His people, Israel, because He "knows his heart," namely, His response derives from the attribute of mercy as I explained above. With non-Jews, this rationale is missing, and with it the attribute of mercy. Therefore, this blessing, the blessing of mercy, is rooted in the special relationship of God to His people.

In the Sephardic tradition, this final line deliberately widens the scope, looking forward to the day when "all flesh will come to You." The verse in *Tehillim* does not actually state that God will hear the prayers of all who come to Him, but rather the converse. God hears prayer, and *therefore* all flesh will come to Him. "Hearer of prayer, all flesh will come to You." Prayer is the cause of something greater, of coming close and cleaving unto God. Prayer causes such a situation to be created, that all flesh shall seek out God, coming close from a faraway land to the house of God in Jerusalem. This is a goal and a dream. In this version of Jewish prayer, the supplicant cannot conclude prayer without hinting at this goal.

Chapter 22

Avoda: Service

רְצֵה יהוה אֱלֹהֵינוּ בְּעַמְּךָ יִשְׂרָאֵל, וּבִתְפִלָּתָם
וְהָשֵׁב אֶת הָעֲבוֹדָה לִדְבִיר בֵּיתֶךָ
וְאִשֵּׁי יִשְׂרָאֵל וּתְפִלָּתָם בְּאַהֲבָה תְקַבֵּל בְּרָצוֹן
וּתְהִי לְרָצוֹן תָּמִיד עֲבוֹדַת יִשְׂרָאֵל עַמֶּךָ.
וְתֶחֱזֶינָה עֵינֵינוּ בְּשׁוּבְךָ לְצִיּוֹן בְּרַחֲמִים.
בָּרוּךְ אַתָּה יהוה הַמַּחֲזִיר שְׁכִינָתוֹ לְצִיּוֹן.

Find favor, Lord our God,
in Your people Israel and their prayer.
Return the service to the Sanctuary of Your house,
And the fire offerings of Israel
and their prayers with love accept with favor.
May the service of Your people Israel always find favor.
And may our eyes witness Your return to Zion in compassion.
Blessed are You, Lord, who returns His Presence to Zion.

1. *RETZEI*: FAVOR

Rambam defines the last three blessings of the *Shemoneh Esrei* as "*hodaa*," thanks.[1] In his *Laws of Prayer*, Rambam establishes that the *Shemoneh Esrei* is comprised of a three-part structure:

1. Although "*hodaa*," thanks, is actually the name given to the second of these three blessings – the blessing of *Modim*.

> The obligation of this commandment is thus: A person should plead and pray every day, reciting the praise of the Holy One, blessed be He; then afterward he asks for his needs which he requires by request and petition; *then afterward he gives praise and thanks to God* for the good which He has granted him – each person according to his ability. (Rambam, *Hilkhot Tefilla* 1:2)

This division carries halakhic ramifications. For instance, one is permitted to add personal requests in the middle blessings, but not in the opening or the concluding blessings.[2] Similarly, one who makes a mistake in one of the middle blessings goes back to the place where he made the mistake, whereas one who makes a mistake in the last three blessings goes back to the beginning of that unit, to the blessing of *Retzei*.[3]

This division raises a new fundamental question regarding the blessing of *Retzei*. What is the difference between the blessing of *Retzei* and the preceding blessing of *Shema Kolenu*? They both request that our prayers be accepted. This question arises, firstly, because it seems unnecessary to recite the same request twice; but the defining of the first blessing as "request" and the second as "thanks" leaves us even more perplexed. How can it be that what seems to be more or less the same blessing is defined once as a request for man's needs and once as "praise and thanks"?

2. DEFINING THE INNER DIVISION OF THE *SHEMONEH ESREI*

The Gemara in *Berakhot* (34a) explains the three-part division of the *Shemoneh Esrei* in different terms than the Rambam:

> R. Yehuda said: A person should never ask for his needs in the first three or last three [blessings], but only in the middle ones, as R. Chanina said: The first [three] are like a servant who presents praise before his master; the middle ones are like a servant who asks for a portion from his master; the last ones are like a

2. See *Shulchan Arukh O.C.* 112:1.
3. Ibid. 113, in accordance with the Gemara in *Berakhot* 34a.

> servant who has received a portion from his master, and takes his leave and departs.

R. Chanina's parable is foreign to the ears of the anyone in the modern era. Someone who comes to pray may very well feel a need for a religious experience, wishes to come close to God, or to request something important. In contrast, this Talmudic passage places prayer in a framework of service to the master, a framework which is nearly incomprehensible to us, who live in a world that is devoid of real lords and masters, and imbued with the principles of equality and freedom.

However, it is not merely a question of lack of familiarity with royal protocols and our incomprehension of servitude. We have been educated – and not only in school – in a manner that deprecates the relationship that a servant has toward his master and king. Until about 150 years ago, a positive attitude to the value of "service" was dominant in Western society. The values of democracy, the egalitarian value of human dignity, and the ever-growing emphasis on the universal rights of man have all come together to discredit this value. We despise the self-abnegation inherent in service. On the one hand, service is based on the recognition that one is attending to one's betters, to superiors, and the first thing we learn, both as democratic Westerners and as Jews, is that all men are created equal. On the other hand, we are used to seeing self-fulfillment as a superior value, and hence serving the goals of another person does not accord with "service" of ourselves. Our beliefs tell us that the King of the world, Creator of heaven and earth, is of course not included in that general egalitarian principle; however, we have lost the natural understanding of the significance of a servant's relationship with his king, due to lack of such a model in our own civil lives. The use of social metaphors regarding God is based on the assumption that they are naturally understandable. When we appeal to God with the title "our Father," this immediately resonates with the relationship of a human father,[4] whereas when we appeal to "our King," we lack any

4. Of course, it is not necessarily true that we understand our relationship with our fathers as the Sages did. C. S. Lewis once pointed out that when moderns appeal to God as "our father who art in heaven," they are really thinking of a doting grandfather.

appreciation of or sympathy for the societal framework from which the metaphor draws meaning.

It is not only real kings who have been dethroned. *All* authoritative figures, whether political or social, have been divested of the marks of royalty – respect and awe. Our political leaders are not more than our neighbors, fathers are no longer patriarchs, and teachers today are not sages or elders. This is why the halakhic expressions of *kavod* and *yira* (respect and awe) with respect to them (such as not sitting in their seat, standing up when they enter, not contradicting them) do not seem natural, and have become ceremonial acts at best, religious dictates rather than genuine expressions. The great principles of freedom and equality have leveled all positions in society, and therefore the whole concept of servitude and service regarding a king exalted over his people has been emptied of all meaning. A real effort is required to understand and internalize the Talmudic parable and to apply it to God, and specifically to prayer.

3. TAKING HIS LEAVE AND DEPARTING

For the first two sections of the *Shemoneh Esrei,* the Talmudic parable does change things, but does not fundamentally transform their meaning. The praise which comes at the start of the *Shemoneh Esrei* is still praise, rescued from being sycophancy addressed to someone from whom we hope to achieve benefit by being redefined as praise before someone whom we revere. The requests are still requests, appeals for our needs, offered not only because we hope to gain something, but out of a recognition that God is the Master of everything. It is in the third section, however, that the full force of adopting R. Chanina's parable becomes evident. "Taking leave" is barely relatable to any experience in the modern world, and it takes a major effort of imagination to comprehend it – and even more so to begin to feel it as an existential experience within.

"Taking leave" has a formal, almost feudal ring to it. I dare say, no one "takes leave" of anyone anymore. It is an act that one does when permission is needed to leave – for instance, when a servant takes leave of his master, or a medieval knight of his lord. A person who stands before God (and prayer is indeed defined as "standing before the King") cannot simply get up and leave whenever he wants. To leave a lord, one "takes leave," by blessing him and thanking him for his graciousness in conducting an audience with us. In Hebrew, in every framework, the blessing of departure is the blessing of *Shalom*, peace – as is the last blessing of the *Shemoneh Esrei*. In a more general sense, taking leave of God means expressing those ideas which form part of what it means to leave His presence in order to go out into the wider world, the world which He has created. The last two blessings in this section fit easily into this scheme. First, we thank Him (*Modim*) for everything that we have in our world, and next, we bless and pray for peace (*Shalom*), not as a need of man, but because this is the realization of God's will regarding the world. We shall return to these two themes in the following chapters. Now we have to understand the first blessing in this section, as part of the framework of "taking leave" – the blessing of service, the blessing of *Retzei*.

4. *AVODA*: SERVICE

This blessing is referred to by the Sages as *Birkat Avoda*, the blessing of service. "*Avoda*" refers, naturally and in its primary sense, to the service in the Temple. In fact, not only is the Temple service mentioned twice in the blessing, it is also highlighted in the *chatima* – "Who restores His Presence to Zion." Were this blessing a request to accept our prayers, this *chatima* would not fit. The *chatima* would have to be something like "Who wants prayer," similar to the *chatima* of the blessing "Who hears prayer." On the contrary, it is clear that the framework of this blessing seamlessly blends the request to accept "the fire offerings of Israel and their prayers" into the wider framework of returning the Temple service, the sacrifices, the incense, the bread arrangements, the libations, and the flour offerings.

At first glance, one can discern a small but highly significant difference between the previous blessing and this one. Previously we were referring to the acceptance of prayer, but here we are referring to the acceptance of sacrifice. My teacher Rabbi Joseph B. Soloveitchik would often point out the crucial significance of the word "*retzei*," favor – a word taken from the world of sacrifices. The prophet foresees that "their offerings and their sacrifices shall find favor (*leratzon*) on My altar" (*Yeshayahu* 56:7). The purpose of the sacrifices is to be "*leratzon*," to find favor in God's eyes, to fulfill His will. The word "*ratzon*," in its different forms, is found repeatedly in all the Torah portions about sacrifices. The Torah commands that sacrifices are to be offered "*lirtzonekhem*" (*Vayikra* 19:5; 22:19; 23:11). A person whose sacrifice is successful in its mission is "*nirtza lo*" (*Vayikra* 1:4), atoned for and favored. This blessing, then, asks that our prayers be acceptable and pleasing in God's eyes, like an offering or a sacrifice atop the altar, just as He promised regarding the Temple service.

Once we place this blessing in the context of "taking leave from one's master," the difference between it and the previous blessing – and the entire previous section – becomes clear. The blessing of *Shema Kolenu*, as I explained in the previous chapter, addressed a *need* of man. We asked that our prayers be accepted, that a personal communication be established between ourselves and God. The blessing was about our relationship with God, and this relationship is a need of ours. The blessing of *Retzei* is not about something we need. With all the importance that the Sages ascribed to the Temple, they saw prayer nowadays as a fulfillment and substitute for that need which the Temple fulfills. At the very least, at the very moment we are standing in prayer, engaged in "worship of the heart," we do not experience a further existential need to stand and serve in the Temple. We do of course feel a need to feel the closeness of God and the Divine presence that dwells in God's Sanctuary – but for that there was another blessing instituted, the blessing of Jerusalem. We are not, at least in these moments, feeling a basic inability to serve God – for we are indeed doing that, through the medium of prayer.

The prayer of *Retzei* addresses the opposite – not a need of ours, but our "taking leave" of our Master. In what may certainly appear to be a daring move, perhaps even "chutzpa" on our part, we ask that our prayers be accepted favorably, that they be pleasing in God's eyes. We are not praying for our own needs, but for Him. After having prayed, after having taken up several minutes of God's time, so to speak, we pray and wish Him that it should have been an acceptable experience, a "pleasant" experience for Him as well. The aim of these "wishes" is not to make God respond positively to our requests; these wishes are themselves part of our service of the Master. Just as God has stated that He desires and is satisfied by the pleasant fragrance of the sacrifices, which would rise and be favorable (*leratzon*), so too we hope that the words of our mouth should be favorable. Is this possible? Is this not flagrant audacity, "chutzpa"? Can one presume to think that his prayers could be a pleasant experience for God? I do not know why, but the answer is yes, it is certainly possible, for that is what the Torah has stated regarding the sacrificial service. Hasidic literature has turned this notion into a basic principle of all human life – man's aim is to give gratification (*nachat ruach*) to his Creator.[5] "*Nachat*," for those fooled by the Sefardi pronunciation, is the same as the Yiddish word "*nachas*," the feeling a child gives a parent when he does something well, the desired end of parenting. The desire to give "*nachat*" to God is an essential part of the religious personality. Since we are serving God in order to serve Him, and not serve ourselves, we hope and pray that our service finds pleasure in His eyes and was not a burden or an imposition. We cannot actually provide any service to God, for He lacks nothing, but we can give Him "*nachat*," as a child does to his parents, for that is what God desires from His children.[6]

5. *ISHEI YISRAEL*: THE SACRIFICES OF ISRAEL

"And the fire offerings of Israel and their prayers with love accept with favor." The phrase "*ishei Yisrael*," literally "fires of Israel," which seemingly refers to the sacrifices, posed a difficulty for the commentators. Surely there are no sacrifices nowadays, and if so, then why are we asking for them to be accepted with favor? The *Tur* (120) cites three explanations. One of them suggests connecting "the sacrifices of Israel" to the

---

5. The source is in *Berakhot* 17a: "Fortunate is one who grows in Torah, and whose toil is in Torah, gives *nachat ruach* to his Creator, grows with a good name, and departs the world with a good name." In terms of an obligation upon man, we have found a statement in the *Tanchuma, Bereshit* 4: "So our Rabbis *z"l* taught: One who builds a new house recites the blessing of *Shehecheyanu*, in order to give *nachat ruach* to his Creator." In hasidic literature, this notion has been established as the primary function of the servant of God, for instance in the following statement of the "*Or HaMe'ir*": "The Jewish people, the primary aim of their souls in Torah, prayer, and commandment observance is simply to give *nachat ruach* to their Creator" (*Vayikra, Parashat Emor*).
6. Rashi (*Tehillim* 5:13) explains the word "*ratzon*," favor, as "*nachat ruach*."

preceding phrase, so that it is part of the request of "return" rather than the request of "accept" – namely:

> And return the service to the Sanctuary of Your house – and the sacrifices of Israel;
> And their prayers, with love, accept with favor.

A second explanation sees "the sacrifices of Israel" as a synonym of "their prayers," since prayers were instituted in place of the sacrifices.[7]

The third explanation is based on a midrash:

> And in the Midrash, it says: Mikhael the great minister[ing angel] offers up the souls of the righteous on the heavenly altar, and it is for this that they instituted [the phrase] "and the sacrifices of Israel."[8]

The souls of the righteous are sacrifices, and the archangel Mikhael, the great minister, is the priest who offers them up. It is obvious to all that this is not a prayer to accept our previous requests. For what connection is there between the souls of the righteous and our hope to receive what we asked for in our own prayer? Never have we found a request to accept something "in exchange" for the offering of the righteous souls of Israel. Such a notion is wholly foreign to Judaism. According to our explanation, that we are talking about a request that the Jewish people's service should be favorable, a pleasant fragrance, and a source of "*nachas*" for God, the explanation is clear.[9] This is the great sacrifice, which exists in every generation throughout history, and we are asking that it should

7. The *Beit Yosef* explains that "the sacrifices of Israel and their prayers" are one entity, namely, the prayers of Israel are essentially sacrifices. The *Bach* explains that "the sacrifices of Israel" are the fixed prayers, Shacharit, Mincha, and Arvit, which are in place of the sacrifices, and "their prayers" refer to other prayers of the individual which one prays voluntarily.
8. *Tur* 120, based on *Tosafot Menachot* 110a.
9. The very notion of a sacrifice comprised of the souls of the righteous requires a separate discussion, not for now; however, within the context of departing from before the King and "taking leave of one's Master," the idea, I hope, is clear.

rise favorably before Him, that He should have "*nachas*" from His world. The perfected souls of the righteous, who in this world strove to reflect the perfection of God, is the desire of God in creation.

6. *MACHAZIR SHEKHINATO LETZIYON*: WHO RETURNS HIS PRESENCE TO ZION

Given that the theme of the blessing is a request that our prayers should be favorable, we immediately turn to the Temple, the ideal model of the "*leratzon*" experience in our world. Since it is our desire that God have "*nachas*" from His world and His service, we pray that He return the service to the Sanctuary of His house. And to whom do we appeal with the request that our service should be "*leratzon*"? To the One who returns His presence to Zion, of course, a promise which is testament to the fact that God truly does favor our service, our prayers, our deeds, and our souls. Given that God has promised to return His presence to Zion, we know that, for some reason beyond our comprehension, He desires our service, and that it can be favorable and a source of gratification to Him. We appeal, even today, to the One who is still planning His house in Zion, and pray that our meager service be accepted by Him favorably.

There are two aspects to Divine service. The first, which I have tried to explain in each of the previous chapters, starting from the introduction to the first chapter, is our recognition that everything is from God and that everything is dependent on Him. The second, which appears in the "blessing of service," is our desire to give to Him, to Him who needs nothing from us, something of ourselves. This is done by offering a sacrifice, or by a substitute – prayer. The requests include both aspects of Divine service; for the very request and recognition that everything comes from Him provide a source of "*nachas*" to God and constitute an offering which *finds favor*. This is what we are specifying in the blessing of *Retzei*.

Chapter 23

Hodaa: Thanks

מוֹדִים אֲנַחְנוּ לָךְ.
שָׁאַתָּה הוּא יהוה אֱלֹהֵינוּ
וֵאלֹהֵי אֲבוֹתֵינוּ לְעוֹלָם וָעֶד.
צוּר חַיֵּינוּ, מָגֵן יִשְׁעֵנוּ
אַתָּה הוּא לְדוֹר וָדוֹר.
נוֹדֶה לְּךָ וּנְסַפֵּר תְּהִלָּתֶךָ
עַל חַיֵּינוּ הַמְּסוּרִים בְּיָדֶךָ
וְעַל נִשְׁמוֹתֵינוּ הַפְּקוּדוֹת לָךְ.
וְעַל נִסֶּיךָ שֶׁבְּכָל יוֹם עִמָּנוּ
וְעַל נִפְלְאוֹתֶיךָ וְטוֹבוֹתֶיךָ
שֶׁבְּכָל עֵת עֶרֶב וָבֹקֶר וְצָהֳרָיִם.
הַטּוֹב, כִּי לֹא כָלוּ רַחֲמֶיךָ וְהַמְרַחֵם, כִּי לֹא תַמּוּ חֲסָדֶיךָ
מֵעוֹלָם קִוִּינוּ לָךְ.
וְעַל כֻּלָּם יִתְבָּרַךְ וְיִתְרוֹמַם שִׁמְךָ מַלְכֵּנוּ תָּמִיד לְעוֹלָם וָעֶד.
וְכֹל הַחַיִּים יוֹדוּךָ סֶּלָה, וִיהַלְלוּ אֶת שִׁמְךָ בֶּאֱמֶת
הָאֵל יְשׁוּעָתֵנוּ וְעֶזְרָתֵנוּ סֶלָה.
בָּרוּךְ אַתָּה יהוה, הַטּוֹב שִׁמְךָ וּלְךָ נָאֶה לְהוֹדוֹת.

We give thanks to You,
for You are HaShem our God and the God of our fathers
For ever and all time. You are the Rock of our lives,
Shield of our salvation from generation to generation.

We will thank You and declare Your praise for our lives,
Which are entrusted into Your hand;
For our souls, which are placed in Your charge;
For Your miracles which are with us every day;
And for Your wonders and favors at all times,
evening, morning, and afternoon.
The Good – for Your compassion never fails,
The Merciful – for Your kindnesses never cease.
We have always placed our hope in You.
For all these things may Your name be blessed and exalted,
our King, continually, for ever and all time.
May all the living thank You, *sela*!
and may they praise Your name in truth,
God, our Savior and Help, *sela*!
Blessed are You, Lord,
whose name is good and it is fitting to give thanks to You.

The seventeenth blessing is the longest blessing in the entire *Shemoneh Esrei*. Because of its length, printers of the *siddur* have become accustomed to splitting it into multiple paragraphs, such that one often loses sight that it is in fact one blessing. Despite its length, there is no doubt about its central theme. The verb "*lehodot/hodaa*" is repeated – in one form or another – four times in the blessing, twice at the beginning and twice at the end. It is only natural, therefore, that the name of the blessing should be "*Hodaa*." Our first task is to understand this word. What does "*hodaa*" really mean?

1. GIVING THANKS

The first and simplest meaning of this word is to give thanks, to show gratitude in response to receiving a gift from another person. The obligation to thank a person who gives you something is one of the first lessons in education. Already from around the age of two, we stop the infant who receives a candy from his aunt and instruct him to "say thank you." In this sense, "*hodaa*," giving thanks, is a verbal expression of emotion, a positive and warm feeling toward someone who chooses to give you something good. Reading our blessing in this way produces a lucid and plausible reading, based on the logical and moral truth that we are obligated to give thanks to God, who grants us an infinite number of kindnesses, evening, morning, and afternoon.

There is only place where this reading does not flow smoothly, and that is at the opening of the blessing. "We give thanks to You, for You are HaShem our God and the God of our fathers." The emotion of thanks comes adjacent to the situation which engenders it. For what, for which kindnesses, are we giving thanks in this opening statement? Is it for "our lives which are entrusted into Your hand, and our souls which are placed in Your charge, and Your miracles which are with us every day"? Seemingly not, for before this list we will repeat the verb – "We will thank You and declare Your praise." One might attempt to claim that we are thanking God for being "HaShem our God," but this explanation is forced. If we were referring to the fact that He has agreed to be our King and to care for us, it would have been simpler to spell that out, as indeed the continuation of the blessing does regarding the miracles and wonders which occur every day.

2. ACKNOWLEDGMENT

In Hebrew there is another meaning of the word "*hodaa*," and that is confession and acknowledgment of facts. This can mean confession of guilt or sin, as in the verse, "And Aharon shall put his two hands on the head of the live goat, and he shall confess on it all the transgressions of Israel and all their iniquities for all their sins."[1] In Rabbinic Hebrew, this can mean confession of a monetary debt, as in the halakhic principle, "The confession of the litigant is equivalent to one hundred witnesses." In the wider sense, it can mean acknowledgment of a specific truth, usually an obligating truth. According to this meaning, one does not give thanks *for* something, but rather acknowledges *that* something is true – for example, "We acknowledge to You, *that* You are HaShem our God." We are not giving thanks to God and expressing gratitude for the fact that He is God; rather we are acknowledging that He is God and are accepting this fact upon ourselves. *Hodaa* here means "confession of faith."

1. *Vayikra* 16:21.

According to this, the term "*hodaa*" will have a different meaning later on in the blessing, as "We shall '*nodeh*' You... for Your miracles which are with us every day" seems to be closer to the former meaning, of thanks.

3. PRAISE

If we look at the verb "*lehodot* in the Tanakh, particularly in the book of *Tehillim*, we discover its frequent use as a synonym of "to praise." The word appears without a cause of thanks, and also without a direct object as the subject of an acknowledgment. A simple and well-known instance appears at the beginning of *Pesukei DeZimra* – "'*Hodu*' to God, call out in His name." Of course, one could claim that this means give thanks, but it is strange that there is no given specific reason for thanking God. There are dozens of such cases in *Tehillim*, and I think we really do understand them instinctively as being praise. Similarly, "*lehodot*" is affixed to the list of verbs of praise at the end of the *Nishmat* prayer – "*lehodot, lehallel, leshabe'ach, lefa'er, leromem, lehadder, le'alleh, ulkalles.*"

An especially striking case is found in the prayer of Shlomo which we cited in our discussion of the blessing of *Shome'a Tefilla*.

> If Your people Israel shall be smitten before the enemy because they have sinned before You, and they return to You and "*hodu*" *Your name,*
>
> And they pray and beseech You in this house.
>
> And You shall hear from the heavens and forgive the sin of Your people Israel,
> And You shall return them to the land which You gave to their fathers. (*Melakhim Alef* 8:33–34)

Here "*lehodot*" comes as part of a process of repentance and before the petition – certainly before the salvation. It seems incongruous, at best, to explain that the people here are "giving thanks" to God for His kindness that arises because of their being smitten before their enemies.

These verses illustrate another feature of applying this meaning of "*hodaa*" – the "*hodaa*" takes as a direct object the *name* of God. In the act of praise, it makes sense to direct the praise to the *name* of God. Firstly, because the act of praise is an action of speech, which practically speaking is directed at the name of God in the sentence; and secondly, because the result of praise is the glorification of the name of God, of the presence of God in people's mouths. In contrast, "*hodaa*" in the sense of giving thanks should be directed to God Himself, and not to His name.

This meaning of "*hodaa*" is reflected in the conclusion of our blessing, before the *chatima*. "And may all the living '*yodukha*,' *sela, and may they praise* Your name in truth."

We have identified three different meanings of "*hodaa*": 1) giving thanks; 2) acknowledgment; 3) praise. The three all differ in their intent, and are discerned by their use of different prepositions in Hebrew: 1) "*lehodot al*," to give thanks *for*; 2) "*lehodot she…*," to acknowledge *that*; 3) "*lehodot et shemo*," to praise His name. All three appear in this blessing, scattered across its entire length. We now need to determine the common basic meaning behind all of these definitions, thereby understanding not only our blessing, but also the true meaning of a basic attitude which is central to religious and moral life.

4. FEALTY

Although gratitude is an accepted value that is common to all cultures, it is a puzzling and mysterious concept. It is obvious that by saying thank you to someone who has given me something I am not saying that I promise to pay him back. On the contrary, the essence of that which engendered gratitude was that something was done for free, without a request or an expectation of payment. If so, precisely what am I trying to express?

In order to understand the meaning of this verb, as well as the concept itself and the moral obligation, I suggest that we look once again at the Talmudic parable which we discussed in the previous chapter. The Gemara established that the final blessings are like a servant who has received a prize from his master and is taking his leave and departing. As I pointed out there, this parable is to be understood from a non-modern perspective, as taken from the experience of the ancient world or the

Middle Ages, and describing the interaction between a subject and his lord. What does a subject feel when he takes leave of his lord? In place of the word "gratitude," I would like to suggest a different notion – fealty. In the feudal system, the subject pledges his fealty to the lord, meaning he *recognizes* and accepts that the lord has sovereignty over him and deserves his loyalty. In more modern terms, "*hodaa*" is a pledge of allegiance and an acceptance of obligation – not obligation to pay a particular price, but obligation to be loyal, to serve as need be. A gift places one in a state of obligation, not to repay (though sometimes that is what we would like to do, in order to rid ourselves of the obligation of gratitude!), but rather a far more existential obligation. The act of giving turns the giver into the lord, and the receiver into a subject. This sense is, I believe, what we are meant to express in showing gratitude. By saying "thank you," I am saying that I pledge myself to be at your service, just as in the formal sense a medieval knight would pledge his right arm to the service of his lord. The gift forges a relationship – an unequal relationship – between the giver and the receiver, and the "*hodaa*" is recognition of this relationship.

I think that the reason that I continually find myself returning to medieval terminology and relationships is because the commercialization of modern capitalist society has indeed reduced gratitude to a commodity, to a form of payment. Thanks is expressed in payment or a gratuity. This process has desiccated the true meaning of gratitude, and of course, would be totally inappropriate if expressed toward God.

This meaning – fealty – includes giving thanks in the usual sense, as well as acknowledgment, in the sense that it requires an *acceptance* of a truth and a *commitment* to abide by it. We acknowledge *that* You are HaShem our God and give thanks to You *for* all the good that You have done for us. It is also, when addressed to God, a form of praise, as praise itself is a form of what is required from the subjects of the lord, and the fact that we pledge fealty to him constitutes praise. Praise is recognition of the superior value of the object of praise. To proclaim and declare that God is King and Master is praise in itself. It is also understandable why it is addressed to the *name* of God, for we are pledging allegiance to God's name, in the sense that we are entering our own names on the roll of God's loyal subjects. "'*Hodu*' to God" means pledge yourself to Him and commit yourself to being His loyal subject.[2]

The connection between "*hodaa*" and pledging fealty is illustrated explicitly in *Tehillim.*

> *Lamenatze'ach,* a psalm of David:
> Deliver me, HaShem, from an evil man,
> save me from the violent person,
> Who think evil in their hearts, every day they gather for war...
> *I said to HaShem, You are my God,*
> hear, HaShem, the voice of my supplication.

King David continues to pray that God save him, and then concludes:

> I know that HaShem will fight the cause of the poor
> and the right of the destitute.
> Surely the righteous *will "yodu" to Your name,*
> the upright shall sit in Your presence. (*Tehillim* 140)

This is no simple expression of thanks. The *hodaa* in the first half of the last verse is parallel to the upright sitting in the presence of God in the second half, namely standing to attention before Him like a servant before his king. The expression of *hodaa* was already given in the pre-

2. Maharal (*Netivot Olam, Netiv HaAvoda,* ch. 8) understood that, in the sentence "We shall '*node*' to You...for our lives which are entrusted into Your hands," the second part is not the cause of gratitude, but its content. We are being "*modim*" and entrusting ourselves to God. Although such a reading seems difficult to me, his understanding of "*nodeh*" as entrusting ourselves to God seems accurate, as he summarizes: "When one mentions '*hodaa*' every day, he is entrusting himself to God, blessed be He, for the good that He has done for him, for this is the essence of *hodaa*...that with every *hodaa* he entrusts himself to God, blessed be He...and for this reason, mankind and the earth all belong to God, and nothing has left His possession, blessed be He." Maharal explains the connection between receiving good from God and the obligation of *hodaa.* When we accept something from Him, we immediately declare that everything still belongs to Him.

vious verse – "I said to HaShem, You are my God." This verse is pure *hodaa* – a declaration of allegiance.

It is clear why in the prayer for the inauguration of the Temple, King Shlomo saw *hodaa* as an essential element of the repentance of the nation, after the trouble and before the salvation. When the people were being smitten, it was a direct result of their alienation from God. When as a result of this punishment the people come to ask for forgiveness and redemption, they first have to declare their loyalty and accept His kingship upon themselves, for it is only by the right of being God's loyal subjects that they can approach Him. The *hodaa* here is not a response to an abundance of goodness, but a preparation for repentance, yet this too is called "*hodaa*," because it is expressed by subjugation and recognition of God's kingship, and the acceptance of what this necessarily means – our being His servants.

5. THE BLESSING

The blessing begins with an acknowledgment ("*hodaa*") that HaShem is our God – "Our God, and the God of our fathers, for ever and all time, the Rock of our lives, the Shield of our salvation, You are Him from generation to generation." Note the emphasis on the permanency and eternalness of the relationship. It is not the specific gifts that we have received recently that are important, such that we should give thanks for them, but rather the permanent relationship between us which defines our position in relation to Him – our being receivers, and therefore subjects.

Second, we continue to enumerate all the good which we receive, on a regular basis, "at all times, evening, morning, and afternoon." Here too the emphasis is on the present and the future. The blessing is not "payment" for what God has given us in the past day, but a declaration of fealty as a response to the permanent relationship between us. In fact, this fealty is inexhaustible and unlimited, for the dependency between us is unlimited – "The Good, for your compassion never fails, and the Merciful, for your kindnesses never cease."

If the theme were gratitude in the usual sense, we would have expected an emphasis of "Our lives which are entrusted into Your hands *and which You return to us*," and "Our souls which are placed with You *and which You give back to us*." However, since gratitude here means loyalty, our souls are always in His hands, and He is responsible for them and takes care of them, in His benevolence. We praise, acknowledge, and declare our loyalty to Him in whose hands our lives and souls are entrusted.

At the end of the first paragraph, we state, "We placed our hope in You." What does "hope" have to do with this blessing? Our relationship with God is one of dependence. Our hope and trust in God are the other side of the coin of our loyalty to Him. We are His subjects not because He has enslaved us, but because He has freed us from the bondage of Egypt, because He is our Overlord and grants us His protection. The relationship of lord to subjects is a two-way street, after all, and is based on the protection accorded by the lord. Our loyalty and our faith go hand in hand.

6. *VEKHOL HACHAYIM*: AND ALL THE LIVING – PRIVATE *HODAA* AND PUBLIC *HODAA*

The first part of the blessing enumerates the causes that engender *hodaa*: "For our lives which are entrusted into Your hands, and for our souls which are placed in Your charge, and for Your miracles which are with us every day, and for Your wonders and favors at all times." The blessing reaches a certain climax, with the declaration of "We have always placed our hope in You." Next, the blessing proceeds to expand the arena of individuals giving *hodaa*:

> For all these things,
> may Your name be blessed and exalted, our King,
> Continually, for ever and all time.
> May all the living "*yodu*" You, *sela*,
> and may they praise Your name in truth,
> God, our Savior and Help, *sela*.

After having given personal *hodaa* to my Creator and King, I widen the scope to include all mankind, and perhaps even all living things. Why?

In light of our explanation, that "*hodaa*" means a declaration of fealty and entrusting ourselves into God's hands, this is quite clear. Were "*hodaa*" to mean only gratitude in the usual sense, there would be no place in our blessing for the desire that the entire world express thanks to God's name. Of course, the hope that everyone would act properly is natural and itself an expression of moral sensitivity, but it would not follow that it is an essential part of our obligation to give *hodaa*. Were *hodaa* to mean gratitude, another person's *hodaa* would add nothing to my own. But once we have defined *hodaa* as a declaration of fealty, as an entrusting of our lives to the King of kings and Creator of the world, then there is tremendous importance in the *hodaa* of the rest of the world. The fact that many subjects of the King do not express their fealty toward Him and do not serve Him is an unacceptable situation for a true subject. Our desire to see His kingship be complete is part of our loyalty to the King of kings. We recognize His absolute rule, but the very fact that not everyone shares this recognition detracts from His rule.

The belief and the hope that all mankind will one day turn to God are always expressed in the context of God's kingdom. A classic example is the second paragraph of the *Aleinu* prayer – "Therefore we hope":

> Therefore we hope to You, HaShem our God,
> To see speedily the beauty of Your might,
> To rid the earth of idols,
> And the gods shall be exterminated,
> To complete the world in the kingdom of God,
> And all flesh shall call on Your name,
> To make all the wicked of the earth turn to You…
> And all shall accept the yoke of *Your kingdom,*
> *And You shall reign over them* speedily for all eternity.
> For kingship is Yours,
> And forever shall You rule in glory,
> As is written in Your Torah, "God shall rule for all eternity."

But I think there is an even deeper idea here.

7. *KOL HACHAYIM*: ALL THE LIVING

In his commentary to the *siddur*, on the expression "May all the living '*yodu*' You *sela*," R. Yehuda b. R. Yakar, Ramban's teacher, cites the verse in *Yeshayahu*: "The living, the living, he shall '*yodeh*' You, as I do this day" (*Yeshayahu* 38:19). In order to understand his intention, let us take a look at the context of this verse.

Chapter 38 of *Yeshayahu* describes King Chizkiyahu's illness. Chizkiyahu is "deathly ill," and Yeshayahu comes to him and tells him to set his house in order, "for you are dying and will not live" (38:1). Chizkiyahu turns to God in prayer, and is granted an additional fifteen years of life. Chizkiyahu then writes the following:

> I said: in the noontide of my days shall I go to the gates of the grave,
> I am deprived of the remainder of my years.
> I said: I shall not see God, God in the land of the living,
> I shall not behold man again with the inhabitants of the world...
> *For the grave cannot "todeh" You,* death cannot exult You,
> They who go down to the pit cannot hope for Your truth.
> The living, the living, he shall "*yodeh*" You, as I do this day,
> The father to the children shall make known Your truth. (*Yeshayahu* 38:10, 18–19)

In this poem, Chizkiyahu explains the value of life. Echoing the theme of our blessing, Chizkiyahu writes that there is no *hodaa* other than in life – "For the grave cannot '*todeh*' You." It is not only the act of *hodaa* that is lacking in death, but also – surprisingly – truth! "They who go down to the pit cannot hope for Your truth." How are we, who accept the doctrine of the immortality of the soul and the World to Come, meant to understand these words?

Before we analyze Chizkiyahu's words, it is important to stress that the belief in the World to Come never leads in Judaism to a denigration of the value of life in this world. In Judaism it is obvious that death is an expression of evil, and even the ultimate evil. The immediate and halakhically mandating consequences of this principle are that one is obligated to oppose death, both his own death and the death of others. Pacifism, in the philosophical sense of the acceptance of evil in the world, is totally foreign to Jewish belief. At every funeral, we repeat the verse that, one day, "He will destroy death forever, and HaShem God will wipe away tears from all faces" (*Yeshayahu* 25:8). Life is the ultimate halakhic value. Death is the source of impurity, and impurity undermines sanctity.

I would like to suggest the following: Life, in Jewish thought, means the ability to act and create, to grow and progress. Building and creating are the essence of life in this world. The material world is the arena for creation. The Sages contrasted the life of the angels, who do not reproduce and do not die, with the life of humans, who reproduce but die.[3] In Chizkiyahu's poem, the value of life is summarized in the words "*The father to the children* shall make known Your truth." Life is the ability to teach the next generation and shape it, to advance knowledge of God's truth and spread it further.

This is God's "truth" – the source and cause of growth and creativity in the world. The living receive this source and are able to grow; the dead "cannot hope for Your truth," because they, at least as far as appears to us, are not engaged in growth and creativity. Only "the living, the living, he shall praise You."

How does this notion of life apply to our blessing of *hodaa*? Why did Chizkiyahu stress that the living will give God *hodaa* and not the dead? I explained that *hodaa* means not mere gratitude, but a declaration of fealty, enlisting as a servant of God. This is not just recognition of a truth, but obligation, commitment, and enrollment, entrusting one's soul into His service. Therefore, only the living can engage in *hodaa*. Only in the world of action and creativity is there significance to man's dedication to the service of God. Only one who can act, who can sanctify the name of God by increasing His name in the world – a "father to the children" – is truly able to give *hodaa,* namely, to give over oneself to service of God and to be enrolled as His servant. This is the *hodaa* of Chizkiyahu, who received fifteen years of life from God. He is not merely expressing gratitude to God for a precious gift. He is expressing that life is precious specifically because it allows the possibility of giving *hodaa* to God. In those fifteen years, Chizkiyahu can continue to increase God's glory and build God's kingdom, and he is "*modeh,*" he commits himself, to continue to do so. In a world which is wholly good, a world free of confrontation with evil and without a struggle to

3. *Pesikta Rabbati* 43.

perfect the world with God's kingship, there is no meaning in obligating oneself to serve in God's army. If he dies, Chizkiyahu will cease to be a loyal subject and obedient servant in this sense, in which case "in the grave who can praise you?" The living, the living, he shall praise You!

8. THE LIVING KING AND GOD

R. Yehuda b. R. Yakar adds to the verse "the living, the living, he shall *yodeh* You, as I do this day" the following comment of the Midrash: "And who gives You *hodaa*? He who is living and bows before the Living, as it says: The living, the living, he shall '*yodeh*' You." We give *hodaa* to God because we are living, and He is living.[4] What is meant by this is that God is not just a source of good. A river is a source of water, but we do not give it *hodaa*, neither in the normal sense nor certainly in the sense that I have suggested for understanding *hodaa* in our blessing. What we receive from God is a grant from Him, a gift from His hand and expression of His benevolence. Since we are alive, and He is alive, the relationship between us is personal. As receivers, we are bound to the Giver. God has decided that He needs our service in order to achieve His aims in the world. It is His truth which animates the world and us, and so we enroll in His service in order to achieve the same goals.

9. *AVODA*: SERVICE

We emphasized from the very beginning of our analysis of the *Shemoneh Esrei* that prayer is defined as *avoda*, service. In this blessing, we commit to becoming servants, not in a particular way or through specific actions, but through our very existence. We are entrusted and committed to His service; we recognize and give *hodaa* that He is HaShem our God, the Rock of our lives and the Shield of our salvation. There are *Rishonim* who awarded the blessing of *Modim* a special status, regarding the halakha that intention in prayer is a necessary condition in at least one blessing. Our version of the Gemara establishes that the blessing in which intention is crucial is the blessing of the fathers; there is, however,

4. R. Yehuda b. R. Yakar adds further: "And the dead will praise immediately when they come to life, as we say in *Pirkei Nechamot*, God turns His head and casts it toward the dead, and they come to life, stand on their feet, and praise His name."

a version which adds the blessing of *Modim*. Both blessings describe our relationship with God and proclaim Him as our God. The former is the ticket of entry to His presence – the person praying identifies himself as a child of Avraham our father. The latter is the granting of permission to leave His presence and go out into the world of action – the person praying identifies himself as a faithful servant in whatever he does, and commits to God's service and His will. A person who gives *hodaa* to God is saying something about himself as well – that he is a servant of God. Hence, the *chatima* reflects this duality – "Your name is good," and on our part, "it is fitting to give *hodaa* to You." You truly are our Master, and it is a privilege for us to serve in the ranks of Your servants. In this way we continue our identity as servants of God even as we depart from the act of service of the heart.

Chapter 24

Shalom: Peace

שִׂים שָׁלוֹם טוֹבָה וּבְרָכָה
חֵן וָחֶסֶד וְרַחֲמִים עָלֵינוּ וְעַל כָּל יִשְׂרָאֵל עַמֶּךָ.
בָּרְכֵנוּ אָבִינוּ כֻּלָּנוּ כְּאֶחָד בְּאוֹר פָּנֶיךָ
כִּי בְאוֹר פָּנֶיךָ נָתַתָּ לָּנוּ יהוה אֱלֹהֵינוּ
תּוֹרַת חַיִּים וְאַהֲבַת חֶסֶד
וּצְדָקָה וּבְרָכָה וְרַחֲמִים וְחַיִּים וְשָׁלוֹם.
וְטוֹב בְּעֵינֶיךָ לְבָרֵךְ אֶת עַמְּךָ יִשְׂרָאֵל
בְּכָל עֵת וּבְכָל שָׁעָה בִּשְׁלוֹמֶךָ.
נִזָּכֵר וְנִכָּתֵב לְפָנֶיךָ, אֲנַחְנוּ וְכָל עַמְּךָ בֵּית יִשְׂרָאֵל
לְחַיִּים טוֹבִים וּלְשָׁלוֹם.
בָּרוּךְ אַתָּה יהוה, הַמְבָרֵךְ אֶת עַמּוֹ יִשְׂרָאֵל בַּשָּׁלוֹם.

Grant peace, goodness, and blessing,
Grace, kindness, and mercy to us and all Israel Your people.
Bless us, our Father, all of us as one,
in the light of Your countenance.
For by the light of Your countenance You have given us,
Lord our God, the Torah of life and love of kindness,
Righteousness, blessing, mercy, life, and peace.
And it is good in Your eyes to bless Your people Israel
at every time, in every hour, with Your peace.
Blessed are You, Lord, who blesses His people Israel with peace.

1. *SHALOM*: PEACE

The theme of the final blessing is peace. That is how the blessing commences – "Grant peace" – and that is how it concludes – "Who blesses His people Israel with peace."

The definition of the word "*shalom*," peace, is obvious. There is no doubt that peace is the opposite of war. This contrast is evinced by numerous Biblical verses, the most incontestable of them being in *Kohelet* – "A time for war and a time for peace."[1] Our problem here is not the definition of the word, but the significance of the concept, and especially when the request is directed toward God. Just what do we want Him to do for us when we ask Him to "grant peace, goodness, and blessing"?

As I have just noted, this blessing is clearly phrased as a request. We commence with a request – place peace – and continue with requests for goodness, blessing, grace, kindness, and mercy, and then again blessing and peace. We know that the place for requests is in the thirteen middle blessings. Peace is certainly a need of man – so why do we not ask for it in the middle blessings, the requests? Why is this one at the end of the *Shemoneh Esrei*, in the section commonly called "*Hodaa*," which we defined a few chapters ago, in light of the Gemara, as "taking leave and departing?"

Upon examining the other themes in this request – goodness, blessing, grace, kindness, and mercy – we immediately perceive that they are not goods desired for their own sake. We do not want kindness for its own sake, nor do we want mercy or grace. These are attributes of God. We hope, by way of these attributes, to achieve other things, which we presumably already requested in the middle blessings. Peace seems different, something desired for its own sake, but then how does it fit in with the other themes in the blessing?

2. *BIRKAT KOHANIM*: THE PRIESTLY BLESSING

At the beginning of the blessing of peace we find the priestly blessing. The connection to our blessing is, of course, peace. The priestly blessing concludes with peace, and the blessing of peace commences with it. However, the comparison does not end there. Like the blessing of peace,

1. *Kohelet* 3:8.

the priestly blessing is also characterized by its lack of specific objects, without real specific content. Apart from peace, the priests bless the Jewish people with blessing and protection, with the shining of countenance and grace, and with the lifting of countenance. The opening of the last two verses in particular stand out, both involving the "countenance" of God: "May God shine His countenance toward you" and "May God raise His countenance toward you." What do these terms mean?

It is clear that we are not asking God for something concrete, like the content of the middle blessings. In other words, we are not dealing here with the fulfillment of needs. The realization of the priestly blessing will undoubtedly be expressed in material gain for the Jewish people, but the main theme of the blessing is not that gain.[2] The shining and

2. The Midrash (*Bemidbar Rabba, Naso, Parasha* 11) provides a multitude of explanations as to the content of the various parts of the priestly blessing:

> *May God shine His countenance toward you*: May He give you light in your eyes; alternatively... may He look upon you brightly and not angrily; alternatively, "shine" is the light of the Torah, that He may make your eyes and heart shine with Torah, and give to you children of Torah, as is said, "For commandments are a candle, and the Torah light"; alternatively... may He bring forth from you priests who brighten the altar, as is said, "And you shall not brighten my altar for nothing," and it says (*Vayikra* 6), "And the fire on the altar shall be burning upon it, it shall not be extinguished."
>
> *And may He be gracious to you*: Behold they are blessed and protected, and God's presence is among them, but from where do we know that they are graced with knowledge and understanding, therefore the Torah says, "And may He be gracious to you," just as we pray, "You grant man knowledge, and teach mortals understanding"; alternatively... may He grant you knowledge so that you may be gracious to one another and merciful to one another, as it says, "And He shall grant you mercy" etc.; alternatively... may He grace you with children, as is said (*Bereshit* 33), "The children with whom God graced your servant," and it says (*Bereshit* 43), "May God be gracious to you, my son"; alternatively... as is said (*Tehillim* 67), "May God grace us and bless us, may He shine His countenance with us, *sela*"; alternatively... may He grace you with your wishes, and so it says (*Yeshayahu* 30), "He will surely be gracious to you at the sound of your voice, when He hears He will answer you"; alternatively... R. Chiyya HaGadol taught, "May God encamp in you midst"; alternatively... may He bring forth from you prophets, as is said (*Zekharya* 12), "And I shall pour upon the house of David spirit, grace, and supplications"; alternatively... may He grant His grace upon you wherever you go, as is said (*Bereshit* 39), "And He granted him grace in the eyes of" etc., "And Esther bore grace" etc. (*Esther* 2), "And God granted Daniel

raising of countenance do not refer to receiving something from God, but to God's *attitude* toward us. In simple terms, the priests bless us that God should relate to us favorably. The raising of countenance is a kind of smile. Somewhat deeper, we are asking for the light of His face to shine on us, namely, to have a close, personal, and loving relationship with God. At the start of our analysis, when we dealt with the blessing of knowledge, I pointed out that "*viychuneka*" (be gracious toward us) means to give us of Himself, so to speak, and to share His holiness with us. That is how the priestly blessing concludes in *Parashat Naso* – "And they shall place My name on the children of Israel." If we are "*chanunim*" (graced), it means that His name has been placed upon us. In Biblical Hebrew, and more so in the language of the Sages, one's name is one's personality. In other words, we are no longer asking for specific things

---

> grace," "And he finds grace and good wit" etc. (*Mishlei* 3); alternatively, and may He grace you with Torah study, and so it says (*Mishlei* 4), "Grant your head an accompaniment of grace" etc., "For they are an accompaniment of grace for your head" etc. (*Mishlei* 1); alternatively...with a free (*chinnam*) gift, and so it says (*Tehillim* 123), "Grace us, God, grace us" etc., "For our eyes are to HaShem our God until He is gracious to us" (*Tehillim* 123); alternatively...to take you out of subjugation to the kingdoms, as is said (*Tehillim* 123), "Grace us, God, grace us, for we have been overly sated with scorn"; alternatively... to redeem you, as is said, "God, grace us, for You" etc.

The sheer multitude of suggestions shows that these are not literal explanations for the content of the verbs of "shine" and "grace," but an overview of the practical outcomes of shining countenance and grace. For our purposes, the suggestions for the final verse are especially interesting, as is the connection between the priestly blessing and peace:

> *May God raise His countenance* etc.: May He turn His face toward you; there is no comparison between one who greets his friend head on and one who greets his friend facing away, rather may God raise His countenance toward you, may He turn His face toward you, as is said (*Vayikra* 26), "And I shall turn to you and make you fruitful." *And may He grant you peace*: Peace when you enter and peace when you exit, peace with every person; R. Natan says, "And may He grant you peace" – this peace is the peace of the Davidic monarchy (*Yeshayahu* 9), "For abundant authority and for peace without end"; Rebbi says, this is the peace of Torah, as it says (*Tehillim* 29), "God shall give strength to His people" etc.... And so are Israel blessed with peace every day, as it says, "And may He grant you peace."

from God; rather we are asking for *peace* – for a relationship, to be noticed, to share in His "light" and His goodness.

This request is not an attempt at receiving blessings in order to fulfill our needs, but an attempt at continuing into the world of action the essence of the connection implicit in the world of prayer itself. The *Shemoneh Esrei* is first of all, as we have noted several times, an experience of service of God, the quintessence of the relationship between a servant and his master. At the time of prayer, we stand in the presence of God – standing before the King. Now we are about to leave His presence, exiting into the wide world. In the Sages' terminology, at the end of the service the servant "takes leave and departs." The servant's receiving of permission includes the request to continue the relationship, to continue to be a loyal servant, even after taking three steps back. We are praying that the deep prayer experience continues to resonate in us by God shining His countenance toward us and imbuing us with peace, goodness, and blessing.

3. PEACE AND WAR

This still leaves the question of what the notion of "peace" actually means, and why peace was specifically chosen as the ultimate framework for expressing the concept of God's continuous presence in our midst beyond the world of prayer. In other words, what is the connection between God's blessing and peace?

In his work *Akedat Yitzchak*, R. Yitzchak Arama discusses the concept of peace in his homily on the priestly blessing (*Akedat Yitzchak* 74). His main argument is that peace should not only be defined in a negative manner, as the absence of conflict. The Sages state that "*Shalom*" is God's name, and it is seen as the seal and culmination of all blessing. Surely it must mean more than the negation of a deficiency. Among other proofs, he cites the striking question posed by David to Uriya the Hittite when he left the battlefield and came to Jerusalem. "And Uriya came to him, and David asked about the '*shalom*' of Yoav, and the '*shalom*' of the people, *and the 'shalom' of the war*" (*Shmuel Bet* 11:7). Is there indeed such a thing as the "peace of the war"?! In practice, while "*shalom*" clearly means the cessation of war, most instances of "*shalom*" in the Tanakh are not in a context of strife or battle at all.

R. Yitzchak Arama argues that "*shalom*" means the harmonious working together of distinct and individual parts, in such a way as to form a unified and integrated functioning whole. Since in society every man works for his own end, the possibility of strife and conflict is inevitable. Social peace is the existence of a blending of individual ends and aspirations so that the entire society operates harmoniously.[3] The peace of the entire world is God, for only God can provide the framework and the inclusive totality to bind together all private individual creations.

Let us elaborate a little on this idea of the *Akedat Yitzchak*.

Each individual creation has its own purpose and own ends. This is especially true of people, created in the image of God, but on a lesser level it is true for all created things. By their distinctiveness, by the fact that each is different and unique from its very inception, each one has a different destiny when measured only in terms of itself. This is not a defect in creation, but part of the purpose of creation. The Sages emphasized (regarding mankind), "Just as their faces are different, so their personalities are different" (*Berakhot* 58a). The desire for a unity that nullifies all difference, which is commonplace in some of the world's mysticisms, has no real place in Rabbinic Jewish thought. Hence, in the very nature of individual creation lies the seed of conflict. Truth – the true essence and value of an individual – is the enemy of peace. In several sayings of the Sages, we find truth and peace in opposition;[4] one such expression is found in the halakhic leniency that "it is permitted to lie for the sake of peace" (*Yevamot* 68a). For that reason, true peace in the sense of the *Akedat Yitzchak*, rather than just the laying down of arms, exists only in heaven, where all individual conflicted values are reconciled within the unity of God. My teacher Rabbi Joseph B. Soloveitchik explained that God, in His very unity, is the reconciliation between mercy and justice, between peace and truth, and between all the Divine attributes which appear to us to be contradictory. God is

3. This aim is accomplished, according to the *Akedat Yitzchak*, by having a leader and a law – king and Torah – but this is not relevant to our topic right now.
4. For example: "R. Yehoshua b. Korcha says: It is a mitzva to mediate, as it says, 'Truth and the judgment of peace' – wherever there is truth there is no judgment of peace, wherever there is peace there is no judgment of truth" (*Yerushalmi Sanhedrin* 1:1).

the reconciliation of contradictions, the *coincidentia oppositorum* (to quote the medieval thinker Nicholas of Cusa). That is the peace of God, the peace of the heavens. We pray that something of that peace can be reflected in our mortal world as well.

As the *Akedat Yitzchak* explains, this harmony is not achieved by annulling the differences, but rather by coordinating them together in a way that combines them into a larger organic unity. The assets and deficits of every creature are combined together, so that the whole is greater than the sum of its parts. This is the way that the Ran (*Derashot*, 1) explains the value and merit of community and the Jewish people – each individual brings his own unique virtue, and each of them balances out the others' shortcomings within the organic whole. This is the true meaning of the unity of creation – not a bland blending of all into a featureless oneness, but the rich panoply of a many-hued iridescent unity, where all the parts contribute to the whole and in their individuality complement each other. In Havdala, we recite "Who creates the lights of fire" and not "the light of fire," and the Gemara explains that "there are many lights in a fire" (*Berakhot* 52a). Fire, which commences the week of action after Shabbat, is made up of many fires, many colors, and that is what lights up the darkness.

Since God is one, His creation is also one. This fact remains true even though creation brings with it difference and individual uniqueness. Overall unity is preserved in the unity of the Creator, and its echo remains in our souls, which were created in the image of God. This is the meaning of peace – a harmonious unity of the different parts. This of course necessitates the absence of strife – any attempt to explain a positive notion of peace which is not antithetical to the very notion of war is ridiculous and inherently inconsistent. But it is far more than that. If we all live for ourselves and our personal aims alone, even if we somehow manage to avoid active conflict and strife (which is unlikely, if not impossible), we are still not experiencing peace in the true sense. As long as we do not see the contradictory aspects of creation, the beliefs, values, and virtues of each individual, reconciled into a greater harmonious whole and a mutual fruitfulness, we are not truly experiencing the fullness of the peace of God. Peace is the wholeness that exists beyond the individualism of each creation.

That is the reason that this blessing seems to hover on the border of the unrealizable ideal. On the one hand, peace is the true state of creation. On the other hand, it exists in reality only in God. It is the true culmination only when seen as a whole and is graspable only when seen from the vantage of God. Therefore, peace, in contrast to all the themes of the other blessings in the *Shemoneh Esrei*, is called here "*Your* peace," God's peace. Hence, peace comes only "by the light of Your countenance": "For by the light of Your countenance, You have given us the Torah of life and love of kindness, righteousness, blessing, mercy, life, and peace." We know that we need it, and, at the same time, this is not something that can be requested in the usual order of requests. We are not asking for a particular gift, but something of a higher order, the harmony of all the other gifts. Not a present or gratuity, but the harmony of all of them. When we take leave of our Creator, as we depart from the state of communion which characterized our standing before Him, we try and take some of this higher state of existence with us back to the particularized and somewhat fragmented world in which we live.

4. THE FORMULATION OF THE BLESSING

1. "Bless us, our Father, all of us as one." We emphasize, in an explicit manner, the nature of peace. On the one hand, the blessing of peace must include *all of us*. This is not just the regular formulation in prayer for the plural form, but an emphasis that the content of the blessing should apply to all of us. On the other hand, it is for "all of us *as one*." It is a blessing of harmony in diversity, of distinct individuals uniting in an organic whole, that does not annul differences of the individuals but reconciles them all in a superior wholeness.
2. "As one, in the light of Your countenance." Peace is neither created by God nor handed to us as a gift from above. It flows from the fact we exist not in our own light but in the light of God's countenance. In the look of His eyes, in His gaze, exist unity and peace. Standing in the light of His countenance means transcending individual particularity to exist as an aspect of the Divine will for creation, where all is unified in the unity of God.

Chapter 25

Supplications After Prayer

1. THE FORMULATION FOR PRIVATE PRAYER

Seemingly, we have finished the *Shemoneh Esrei*. But in every *siddur*, after the blessing of peace, comes a supplication which begins with the words, "My God, guard my tongue from evil." This supplication does not take the form of a *blessing* – it neither commences nor concludes with "*Barukh*." The number of blessings in the *Shemoneh Esrei* is also clear – eighteen, or nineteen, and we have already finished reciting them. The halakhic definition of this additional paragraph is "supplications after prayer" (*Berakhot* 29b).[1]

It is clear from the text of the Gemara that reciting this supplication is not an obligation, for the Gemara referred to one "who *usually* recites supplications." Similarly, from the Gemara's words it transpires that there is no fixed formulation for this supplication at all. The text of the Gemara indicates that there is a specific place at the end of the *Amida* where one can add supplications, without instituting a fixed formulation for them. This is in contrast to the *Amida* prayer itself, which

1. The Gemara states that one "who usually recites supplications after his prayer" may go back and recite *Yaaleh VeYavo* if he forgot to say it in its proper place, as long as he has not yet finished his supplications. Rashi (s.v. *tachanunim*) explains: "Namely '*Elokai netzor leshoni mera*' which we recite in the *Amida* after the [main] prayer."

was composed by the Men of the Great Assembly, and then reestablished by Rabban Gamliel in Yavneh. The fixed text in all the *siddurim,* and which is recited today in every tradition, is simply the formulation for the "prayer of the individual" recited by Mar son of Ravina. The Gemara on 16b presents eleven different prayers, each by a different Sage at the conclusion of prayer. Jewish custom chose to enter one of them into the *siddur,* but it is clear from the Gemara itself that there is no mandatory text, nor is there an obligation to recite any formulation at all. On the contrary, the very existence of a list of eleven prayers recited by eleven individuals indicates that fundamentally each individual worshipper can – and perhaps should – formulate his own personal prayer. Therefore – in contrast to our discussions in the other chapters of this book – this time we will not analyze the language of the prayer, but rather the framework of "supplications after prayer."

The very classification, "supplications after prayer," requires explanation. If there is room to add supplications, then why wait until the conclusion of the *Amida* prayer? Surely every prayer is supplication.[2] If a person has a particular need or request, he can add it to any of the blessings of the *Shemoneh Esrei* according to the theme of that blessing, and also add anything that is on his mind in the blessing of *Shome'a Tefilla.* Why is there a need for a framework beyond the framework, a deliberate postponement of supplications until after the completion of the fixed section of mandatory prayer? Note that, despite the title "supplications *after* the prayer," the Gemara declares that one who adds supplications after his prayer extends the prayer service itself, and thus he is not considered as having already finished his prayer.[3] Why, then, are there two intertwined frameworks, the prayer of blessings and the

2. "When you pray, let your prayer not be conversation, but rather supplication before the Holy One" (*Avot DeRabbi Natan* A, ch.17).
3. If a person forgot to recite *Yaaleh VeYavo,* and has already finished praying, he must return to the beginning of the *Shemoneh Esrei* and pray again. But if one remembers before the end, he only goes back to the blessing of *Retzei.* The Gemara adds to this that if one usually recites supplications after his prayers and has not yet finished these supplications, he may go back to *Retzei* and recite *Yaaleh VeYavo,* and does need to repeat the whole *Shemoneh Esrei.*

prayer of supplications? In order to understand this point, I wish to return to a fundamental idea in our discussions.

Throughout all our discussions, from the very beginning, it has been repeatedly clear that Jewish prayer is a formal and ceremonial exercise. There are fixed times for prayer, rules of how to stand, and most importantly, a fixed and mandatory text. The text itself is based mostly on Biblical verses, and hence the formal, dignified language of the prophetic sources is preserved in prayer. Similarly, there is a requirement that prayer be recited in the plural form. "Abaye said: One should always include oneself together with the community" (*Berakhot* 23b). This entire series of analyses is based on the premise that the phrasing of the prayers encapsulates basic ideas of Jewish philosophy, chosen with enormous care by the Sages.

Historically, thinkers of every generation have struggled at times with this aspect of prayer. If our prayer was bequeathed to us by the Men of the Great Assembly, and it is forbidden to deviate from the fixed text that was coined by the Sages, if we are instructed to repeat it three times daily, evening, morning, and afternoon, all one's life – does this not contradict the soul of prayer, the meaning of prayer as a heartfelt outpouring of one's inner emotions, its role as a spontaneous, genuine meditation, as a deepening of the meaning of one's life, and a chance to connect from within the core of one's being with the Creator of the world, our Father and our King? Has not the legal and halakhic nature of the prayer ritual dessiccated the living inner soul of prayer?

The answer to this question is, to a large extent, what has been beneath all of our discussions. From the very first chapter, which served as an introduction to the study of the text itself and discussed the meaning of service, I emphasized that prayer is defined as *service*, the service of God – based on obligation, on dedication, and on servitude, and not on an internal personal need to express the feelings of the heart or to reach the Infinite. Halakhic prayer is not the lonely cry in the night of the soul, lost in darkness. One is not expected to pray thrice daily with deep inner longing, with the feeling that "my father and mother have abandoned me, and God takes me in." Man *serves* God by praying, by declaring that he is dependent on Him, by turning to God and asking that He provide his needs.

Halakha distinguishes between *tefilla*, prayer, and *ze'aka*, crying out. Ramban argues with Rambam's assertion that prayer is a Biblical precept and ruled that the obligation of prayer is a Rabbinic commandment. Yet even Ramban counted *ze'aka*, crying out to God in times of distress, as a Biblical obligation. Rambam discusses crying out in times of distress, although not in the *Laws of Prayer* but in the *Laws of Fasting*. It is not that Judaism does not believe that one can cry out and plead before God, but rather that one who comes to cry out from a place of heartbreak is not bound by all the laws which circumscribe fixed prayer. Prayers on a fast day, in times of distress, take place in the streets of the town and not in the synagogue. One who needs to cry out to the king can burst in and disturb him in the middle of his private business, without keeping to the rules of royal protocol, like the cry of one of wives of the disciples of the prophets to Elisha (*Melakhim Bet* 4:1) or like the Shunamite woman (ibid. 4:27). Regular prayer bears a different character. In daily prayer, one cannot burst in before the King and cry out in distress. One enters before the King, according to the rules of royal protocol, and stands and recites the fixed prayers. One who prays recites the words that the Sages deemed worthy to utter. The prayer which the Sages composed includes the true needs of the ideal man and expresses the genuine nature of man's relationship with his Creator. The *Amida* includes phrases which are so far above our usual state that the Sages said of them that had they not been uttered by the prophets we could not have thought of saying them ourselves. Prayer is not spontaneous self-expression, but service and dedication; not man as he is, but as he should be and as whom he strives to become.

Notwithstanding this, the individual, in his own personal current state, has a need to speak to God as well. This need cannot be mandated, as part of the commandment and ritual. Therefore, at the end of prayer – in its halakhic sense as service – we find that individual Sages said that which they needed to say, each in his own personal style. The Gemara never states that there is a requirement to recite supplications after prayer. Rather we learn from the example of individual Sages. The Gemara presents us with life examples rather than halakhic regulations. Supplication after prayer is the place for the individual soul, not for defined halakhic rulings. It is not a clause in the *Shulchan Arukh*, rather a chapter in the lives of R. Elazar, R. Yochanan, R. Zeira, R. Chiyya, R. Yehuda the Prince, R. Safra, R. Alexandri, R. Hamnuna, Rava, and Mar son of Ravina (*Berakhot* 16b). Looking at the supplications cited in the Gemara, we are immediately struck by the absence of the usual grandeur of the prayer text. These prayers lack Biblical imagery and extravagant metaphors of grand national themes. The prayers are characterized by an unmistakable simplicity, by the murmur of the still soul, one small voice alone with its Creator. The formal prayer is over, we have taken leave of the King with the blessing of peace, the décor people have begun to pack up their equipment, the band has already left, but right before leaving the palace, the individual adds a few words from the bottom of his heart and from the depths of his soul. One touches the corner of God's garment and expresses, in a simple outpouring of the inner heart, what his soul needs. It is as though, as one is about to leave the presence of the King, God asks, what does your soul truly yearn for, my son? Each person answers differently.

There is a certain irony in the fact that Jewish tradition has formalized for us even the text of the spontaneous prayer. Our *siddurim* have a fixed, standard text telling us how to pray a non-fixed prayer. The Jewish people, it seems, fell in love with Mar son of Ravina's prayer, "My God, guard my tongue from evil, and my lips from speaking deceit." Perhaps this reflects human failing, the poverty of our inner lives. The inarticulate needed someone else to express for them that which is personal and unique. But this should not obscure the fundamental definition and true nature of this prayer. Even if the words are borrowed from one Talmudic Sage or another, the prayer is not a fixed, public, and eternal prayer, but a personal prayer. And of course, this is indeed the place to add, even with one's own lame tongue, whatever one needs to add, before he takes three steps backward and departs.

It is worthwhile and recommended to open up the Gemara in *Berakhot* (16b) and read all the prayers that are cited there. This is what the *Yaavetz*, R. Yaakov Emden, did in his *siddur*. After the *Shemoneh Esrei*, he cited all the prayers ("The precious jewels of the Divine Sages") without placing "*Elokai netzor*" first. At the end, he added the following words:

> Now I have presented individually each prayer and each supplication of the Talmudic Sages as the spirit of God appeared on them. Every man may innovate for himself a prayer according to his needs, and as he knows his pain and affliction, so he can explicate the pain in his heart accordingly, even if this will not be phrased eloquently. It is the primary service of prayer in the heart of the pure and ready – one who knows to innovate words from the depths of the pure and clean heart. He should place God before him and pour out his soul in words, before God when he wraps himself in His spirit – not as a fixed prayer, out of habit, like a burden or a bother. Hence, how good and how beautiful is one who innovates words of prayer and request of his own volition, according to his mind he shall be lauded, and this is his praise. And he should not bind himself to one particular formulation…

2. THE PLACE OF PERSONAL PRAYER WITHIN THE FRAMEWORK OF THE *SHEMONEH ESREI*

The Gemara in *Berakhot* (28b) inquires about the number eighteen, which was chosen for the number of blessings in daily prayer.

> To what do these eighteen [blessings] correspond?
>
> R. Hillel, son of R. Shmuel b. Nachmani, said: Corresponding to the eighteen mentions [of God's name] that David said in [the psalm], "Give to HaShem, O sons of might."
>
> R. Yosef said: Corresponding to the eighteen mentions in the recital of *Shema*.
>
> R. Tanchum said in the name of R Yehoshua b. Levi: Corresponding to the eighteen vertebrae in the spine.
>
> [And] R. Tanchum said in the name of R Yehoshua b. Levi: One who prays must bow until all the vertebrae in the spine protrude.

Three sources are presented here for the number eighteen. The first is based on the chapter in Psalms, "Give to HaShem, O sons of might" (*Tehillim* 29). We shall return to this opinion shortly, but first let us analyze the two other opinions. R. Yosef said that it corresponds to the number of times that God's name appears in the paragraphs of *Keriat Shema*. The paragraphs of *Keriat Shema* are the essence of accepting the yoke of heavenly kingship. Each name in the text is an expression of accepting the yoke of heavenly kingship. Therefore, R. Yosef expresses the opinion that the acceptance of the yoke of heavenly kingship is split into eighteen paths, and this is expressed in reciting the eighteen blessings of the *Shemoneh Esrei*. In other words, the *Amida* prayer is a specific act of accepting God's kingship. This opinion fits well with the model that we have presented – that prayer and request express service and servitude, for they present our dependency on God, and this dependency defines our relationship with God – He is the Master and His kingship reigns over us. Furthermore, *Keriat Shema* is not just a notification of God's kingship, but a practical acceptance of God's kingship. Its recital is not merely an expression of an established fact, but a performative act, a declaration of loyalty which obligates the declarer. Similarly, prayer, despite – and perhaps because of – its recital as a request for man's needs, is itself an act of declaring and establishing kingship. By way of our prayers, we establish His kingship over us, and this is the very principle of kingship.[4]

The question of "to what do these eighteen [blessings] correspond" is essentially a question of why we need to particularize and specify in prayer. Why were the Sages not content with one general blessing and prayer, "May it be Your will that You fulfill all the desires of our heart for good" (*Berakhot* 17b), or "Hear the cry of Your people Israel and grant their request speedily" (*Berakhot* 29b)? One could claim that it would be far more appropriate this way – for can one truly be so audacious as to tell God exactly what he wants, like a person presenting a shopping list at a store? Is this not total "chutzpa" toward God, toward Him who knows better than I what I want and what I need? The answer is, precisely so, if prayer were only a medium to achieve our needs, it would have been preferable to shorten it and just express our hope that God fulfill all our desires. Precisely because it is about the service of God and the acceptance of the yoke of heavenly kingship, there is a need to express servitude in every realm of man's life, for each of them con-

4. For, as we know, there is no King without a people.

tains a different aspect of the servant-Master relationship. The kingship itself in magnified by the fact that it is reflected not only in general, but in each and every aspect of man's life, in his knowledge, his atonement, his health, his redemption, his wealth, his national desires, and in the inner thoughts of his heart.

The third explanation in the Gemara for the number eighteen is given by R. Yehoshua b. Levi – corresponding to the eighteen vertebrae in the spine. The intent is clear – prayer expresses submission. The idea is similar to the previous one, for submission and "the protruding of all the vertebrae in the spine" constitute man's position before the King. Here the multiplicity in the number eighteen directly expresses the multiplicity in man's personality – man must submit all the vertebrae in his spine, every aspect of his personality. A general and vague recitation could have expressed an attitude of accepting kingship, but without totally negating all aspects of resistance. The kingship of God requires that "all my bones shall say, God, who is like You," and this mandates the submission of each vertebra separately, one after the other.

There is a difference – small but significant – between the two opinions. The count of eighteen names in *Keriat Shema* emphasizes the multitude aspects of the kingship, the grandeur, and consequently, the obligation of man. The count of eighteen vertebrae in the spine emphasizes the necessity of man's self-submission before the King. *Keriat Shema* is performed with one's mouth – and one's heart – whereas prostration of one's stature is performed with the body itself. The former act is intellectual, the latter existential. The former is primarily about obligation and acceptance, the latter primarily about negation – the negation of the upright stature of the spine, man's natural upright stature. And yet, the similarities between both opinions are greater than the differences. Both emphasize that the eighteen blessings are a framework of service of the King, of submission and acceptance of His kingship. The length of the blessings and their large number are not to be understood as an attempt to enrich man's speech and to improve the eloquence of the murmurs of his heart, but as a full expression of the relationship between servant and King.

The first opinion in the Gemara, corresponding to the eighteen names of God which David recited, is somewhat different. Simply put, the book of *Tehillim* in general, and chapter 29 specifically, is an expression of praise.[5] Can we conclude that, according to this opinion, prayer is primarily praise? Rashi (*Berakhot* 28b) explains the connection between the chapter of "Give to HaShem, O sons of might" and prayer as follows:

> For it is an allusion to [the blessings of] the fathers, mighty deeds, and the holiness of God's name (the first three blessings of the *Shemoneh Esrei*), as we say in *Rosh HaShana* (32a), "From where do we know that we recite [the blessing of] the fathers? From what is written, 'Give to HaShem, O sons of might' etc."

Rashi explains that, from a technical perspective, the connection between prayer and this chapter is limited to the first three blessings, blessings which are defined as praise. The number eighteen is taken from the chapter, even though the chapter parallels only the first part of the *Shemoneh Esrei*.

I believe that we should understand the matter as follows. It is clear that prayer is not a state whose primary function is praise. This chapter in *Tehillim* constitutes a basis and source only for the first blessings, in which one fulfills the precept to precede request with praise. The main part of prayer is request. Therefore, why did the Sages particularize the requests and why do they require that we specify the requests rather than relying on God to do what is best for us, according to His wisdom and kindness? According to this opinion in the Gemara, the answer is that, from the perspective of service, it is indeed unnecessary (and perhaps unfitting) to appear before Him with a detailed list. The extended specification comes to express praise in a more complete way. Regarding praise, it can be said that whoever recites much is praiseworthy. The praise is intensified by the quantitative multitude. Hence, since we have found eighteen expressions of praise in the aforementioned chapter in the book of *Tehillim*, the Sages stated that we should elaborate in prayer corresponding to them, and through the requests there

5. Maharal (*Netiv HaAvoda*, ch. 9) explained that the names of God in this psalm represent the eighteen "levels of *mercy*," although, as we shall see, this is not the simple explanation of the psalm. Rashi, as we shall see, explained differently.

will be a proper fulfillment of praise as well. The content of the middle blessings is not praise, but it is clear that by directing our requests to the King we are increasing praise. It is necessary to elaborate and particularize in prayer in order to intensify the praise whose source is in the first blessings.

Hence, the Gemara suggests that the structure of eighteen blessings in prayer expresses its character as the service of the King. The two poles of prayer are God-King on the one side, lauded and transcendent, and man-servant on the other side, lowly, needy, and insignificant. Yet precisely this point strengthens the need to offer supplications after prayer – not as a servant serving his Master, but as someone pouring forth his plea, as a poor man enwrapped in distress. Supplications are located specifically *after* prayer, after completing the framework of service and servitude, when the formal barrier has been lowered, and man can lay out what is in his heart. In the words of the Gemara: "When he has finished his prayer." You have finished the section of obligations – you now have the opportunity to express what is in your heart, even if it does not fulfill the service of the King.

However, one should note that the place for reciting supplications, after the conclusion of prayer, is nonetheless attached to the framework of prayer. The Gemara emphasizes that the supplications are before one takes three steps back. Moreover, as long as one has not yet taken three steps back, he can go back to the place where he made a mistake and does not need to repeat the entire *Amida* in the event of a mistake. How should we define this point, which is on the one hand after prayer and beyond its framework, and on the other hand within prayer and before its conclusion? The answer comes naturally. What is the significance of taking three steps back at the conclusion of prayer? This is clearly an act of leaving, of departing from before the King. At the end of prayer, man withdraws from the King's presence. In other words – prayer is standing before the King. Prayer is not merely delivering words to God, a line of communication between man and He who dwells on high. When man stands to pray, he enters and stands before the King. Rambam writes similarly (*Hilkhot Tefilla* 4:16): "What is intention? That one should clear his heart of all thoughts and view himself as if he is standing before God's presence."

This point is even more prominent in the laws that Rambam compiled in chapter 5: "There are eight things which one should be careful to do when praying, but if it is difficult or impractical, or if one transgressed and did not perform them, they do not withhold [one's prayer]." Rambam enumerates a list of laws, which do not in fact invalidate one's prayer *post facto*, and all of which encompass this point, that one who prays is standing before the King. Some of these things are more explicit, such as the first in the list – standing – and even more so the third – one's body posture. Rambam writes (5:4): "What is the correct posture of the body? When one stands to pray, one must carefully place one's feet side by side; and he should cast his eyes down as though he were looking at the ground, while his heart is cast upward as though he were standing in heaven; and he should place his hands closed over his heart, the right over the left; and he should stand like a servant before his master, with awe and reverence and fear." Some of these things are less explicit, such as the fourth in the list, proper dress – the definition of correct dress for prayer is "in the way that the locals stand before great people" (5:5). Regarding taking steps back, Rambam writes (ibid. 10–11):

> When one finishes prayer, he bows and takes three steps back, and when he bows, he grants peace to his left and then to his right, and then he raises his head from the bow… and why does one grant peace to his left first? Because his left is the right of the person facing him, namely, when he stands before the King, he grants peace to the King's right and then to the King's left, and they instituted that one should take leave of prayer in the same way that one takes leave of a king.

Thus, "*Elokai netzor*" is recited after one has concluded his prayer but before he has taken leave of the King. The prayer is over, yet the person praying is still standing before the King. Since prayer is fundamentally not just communication but service, it is understandable that it takes place in the presence of the King when the person praying stands to serve before Him. But, at the conclusion of the prayer-service, we are not driven out from before Him, nor do we rush to take leave and depart. The worshipper is granted an opportunity to pour forth a plea, to lay out what is on his mind, to beg and pray for his life, while he is still standing before God.[6] On the one hand, the prayer-service has finished, yet still, the worshipper can remain standing before God's presence, in the inner chamber, before the Hearer of prayer to whom all flesh will come. It is specifically standing in God's presence that opens the lips and heart of man: "O God, open my lips." Emerging from fixed service, man can go on to offer an additional sacrifice, his lone soul.

And hence, once man has reached service as a result of the sacrifices themselves, and with the aspiration to cleave in *deveikut* to God's presence, how can he not turn to the focus of the fulfillment of *deveikut*, and to the focus of *deveikut*:

That the Temple be built quickly in our days,
and that You grant our portion in Your Torah.
And may the tribute of Yehuda and Jerusalem be sweet to God,
as in the olden days and ancient years.
May the words of my mouth and the thoughts of my heart
find favor before You, God, my Rock and Redeemer. Amen and amen.

6. *Bereshit* 18:22 – Avraham seizes the opportunity, *while he is still standing before God,* in order to pray for the lives of the people of Sedom.

About the Author

RABBI EZRA BICK has taught Talmud and Jewish Thought at Yeshivat Har Etzion since his *aliya* from New York in 1977, and has served as Director of the Israel Koschitzky Virtual Beit Midrash since 1995. Rabbi Bick earned his *semikha* from the Rabbi Isaac Elchanan Theological Seminary, where he studied under both Rabbi Aharon Lichtenstein and Rabbi Joseph B. Soloveitchik. He also holds an M.S. degree in Jewish Philosophy from Yeshiva University and an M. Phil. degree in Philosophy from Columbia University. Rabbi Bick founded and currently teaches in a special program at Yeshivat Har Etzion for sixth-year students and above, who wish to continue high-level Torah study while concurrently attending Hebrew University. Rabbi Bick's previous book, *In His Mercy: Understanding the Thirteen Midot*, has been hailed as one of the most important works of Jewish theology in recent decades.

Maggid Books
The best of contemporary Jewish thought from
Koren Publishers Jerusalem Ltd.